PREPARING FOR BATTLE

PREPARING FOR BATTLE

A SPIRITUAL WARFARE WORKBOOK

Mark I. Bubeck

MOODY PRESS

CHICAGO

ISBN: 0-8024-9082-4
Printed in the United States of America

CONTENTS

EXPANDED CONTENTS

UNDERSTANDING SATAN'S STRATEGY AND PERSON

Scripture Memory Verses:

To the Jews who had believed him, Jesus said, "If you hold to my teaching, you are really my disciples. Then you will know the truth, and the truth will set you free." (John 8:31–32) Jesus answered, "I am the way and the truth and the life. No one comes to the Father except through me." (John 14:6)

Unit Learning Goal:

Knowing the Enemy.

Overview of Unit 1:

Lesson 1: The Biblical Perspective of Warfare

Lesson 2: Where Did Satan Come From?

Lesson 3: The Kingdom of Darkness

Lesson 4: Satan's Kingdom Rising

SUMMARY STATEMENT

In order to defeat our enemy rather than be defeated by him, it is critical that we understand who he is, where he came from, where he gets his power, the means he uses to attack us, and the deceitfulness of his methods.

Unit 1 Thought Focus:

John 10:10 says it all in very plain language: "The thief comes only to steal and kill and destroy." This is the description Jesus applied to Satan. In stark and total contrast, Jesus claimed of Himself, "I have come that they may have life, and have it to the full."

Satan's strategy is to use whoever and whatever, wherever and whenever, however and why ever to destroy our God-given, blood-bought opportunity to live out our eternal, glorified life in the presence of our Lord Jesus Christ.

If you knew someone was planning to break into your home, you would be prepared, on guard, ready to take appropriate action. But what if you knew someone was intent on destroying your marriage, hurting your children, and wreaking havoc in your life? What would you do? Certainly you wouldn't stand by and do nothing.

But too often, when it comes to the spiritual realm that's exactly what we do—nothing. As a result, the forces of hell have a heyday messing with our lives, and we seem to be clueless, stumbling around in the dark, moaning, "Why is this happening to me?"

The reality is just as Jesus said—and Jesus is not a liar, is He?—Satan is intently focused on our destruction. No one is too precious, too young, too sweet, too good, or too anything else to be immune to his attacks. And Satan is quick to take advantage of the person who is unsure, doubtful, skeptical, or cynical about his existence and power. People such as these are easy targets for Satan and his devouring fallen angels.

In 1998 in Greenville, Tennessee, six young people who had been dabbling in the occult were sentenced to life in prison without parole. Why? Because their dabbling had led to death—they kidnapped, terrorized, and murdered a husband, wife, and their six-year-old daughter. A two-year-old son, Peter, survived a bullet in the eye. Perhaps these six young people began giving ground to the devil by playing with tarot cards or reading horoscopes. Maybe they were fascinated by angels or by the darker side of rock music. However it began, their ill-fated spiritual quest led to a deepening involvement with the occult.

It's amazing that there is such a resurgence of interest in the spiritual realm even as many people are insistently cynical when it comes to warning about the danger of dabbling in the occult, witchcraft, New Age thinking, spirit guides, and more. They refuse to believe that not all angels are good angels. They don't want to acknowledge that even Satan and his demons can appear as sweet angels of light.

Many professed Christians don't really believe that the spirit world is real or relevant or needs to be dealt with. They may not often verbalize this, but it is obvious by the way they react. As Timothy Warner, professor emeritus at Trinity Evangelical Divinity School and an advisory board member at the International Center for Biblical Counseling (an agency counseling people suffering from spiritual oppression), says, "People may not always live what they profess, but they will always live what they believe."

We are in a fierce battle with the Enemy of our souls. Spiritual warfare is a biblical reality. It occurs whether we acknowledge it or not. Satan doesn't need our assent to attack us. If we are not on guard, wearing our spiritual armor and equipped with the tools of biblical warfare, he will try to rip our lives apart.

These attacks may be viewed as merely struggles with drug dependency, juvenile delinquency, emotional instability, family dysfunction, mental illness, or a thousand other labels for problems we view as normal. Or perhaps we or our family are plagued with unusual illnesses, injuries from frequent accidents, and other medical maladies. We'll spend thousands of dollars on therapists, doctors, detox therapies, surgeries, enlightenment seminars, books, retreats, and more, but fail to consider spiritual oppression. Some problems seem to get better, but new ones always surface. And many of the old ones come back. It never ends, and we scratch our heads wondering why.

The question is not *whether* we wrestle demonic spirits, but who's winning. Do the spirits have us pinned down in defeat? Have we conceded our souls and our families to the rule of bondage to darkness?

It's not too late to take action. But first we need to understand who and what we're dealing with. Then we need to become equipped with the tools of warfare and begin fighting back. The good news is that even though we may be wounded at times, the battle is guaranteed to be a victory for those who stand in Christ!

Are there areas in your life or members of your family you believe are being attacked by Satan? List below those areas or the names of family members, describe what's happening, and give a brief explanation of why you think Satan is involved. Do not share this information with others at this time. Rather, as you proceed through this study, keep these in prayer before the Lord. As you receive new insight, add or delete from this list as the Holy Spirit directs:

_____

_____

_____

LESSON 1: *The Biblical Perspective of Warfare*

Scripture for Meditation:

For our struggle is not against flesh and blood, but against the rulers, against the authorities, against the powers of this dark world and against the spiritual forces of evil in the heavenly realms. (Ephesians 6:12)

A Beginning Prayer:

Heavenly Father, open the eyes of my heart that I might see the truth of who my true enemy is so that I can avoid the snares and pitfalls he lays before me. Through the quickening of Your Holy Spirit, help my mind to grasp the power of the truth who lives in me. Let the blood of Jesus Christ cover all areas of my being to cleanse, protect, and deliver me from the fear of him who has no authority over or rights to my life or family. In the name of my precious Lord Jesus Christ, seal me with Your salvation and righteous protection and make me be an overcomer in all things. Amen.

Lesson:

SELF-CONTROLLED AND ALERT

A common lament heard when believers sin goes something like this: "The devil made me do it! I couldn't help myself!" Oh, how we love to assign responsibility for our failings on someone other than ourselves. And if we can tack it onto the devil, all the better. However, this is not the scriptural view of why we sin.

A more accurate statement could be: "The devil influenced me to do it, but I made the final choice."

That the Enemy of our souls will use every trick in the book—and then some—to defeat us is reality. We all like to quote the second half of 1 Peter 5:8, which says, "Your enemy the devil prowls around like a roaring lion looking for someone to devour." We too often ignore the first part of that verse that states, "Be self-controlled and alert."

Being in control and alert applies to several aspects of our lives. Below, check the activities where we need to be in control and alert. Discuss your responses.

❑ 1. Driving our children to school
❑ 2. Eating dinner with the family

☐   3.   Operating heavy construction equipment

☐   4.   Preparing our income taxes

☐   5.   Disciplining our children appropriately

☐   6.   Disagreeing with a friend or our spouse

☐   7.   Walking in an unfamiliar neighborhood

☐   8.   Making ethically sensitive business decisions

☐   9.   Choosing whom to marry

☐ 10.   Talking about people and events at our church

If our stumbling was all due to the devil's attacks, why would we need to be self-controlled? Wouldn't being alert be enough? But we are called to be both. Satan sets the snares, and he's clever in his trapping. But the Holy Spirit who lives in us is clear-eyed and quick to alert us to the pitfalls. Once alerted, our responsibility is to avoid the dangers—to *flee* evil desires and *pursue* righteousness (2 Timothy 2:22).

In each of the examples in the exercise above, being in control and alert are critical. For example, around the dinner table we need to be alert to what others are saying, alert to our own responses, and in control of how we react toward and treat each individual. The bottom line for Christians is that there is *never* a time when it's safe not to be in control and alert.

Success in spiritual warfare needs a biblical, doctrinal approach. Subjective emotions, sincere feelings, and fervent desire mean nothing to Satan. He yields no ground to emotion or sincerity. He backs off only when he is confronted with the authority we possess in the Lord Jesus Christ. This authority is grounded in God's Word.

> **Hebrews 4:12:** *For the word of God is living and active. Sharper than any double-edged sword, it penetrates even to dividing soul and spirit, joints and marrow; it judges the thoughts and attitudes of the heart.*

> **Ephesians 6:17:** *Take the helmet of salvation and the sword of the Spirit, which is the word of God.*

> **Revelation 19:15:** *Out of his mouth comes a sharp sword with which to strike down the nations. "He will rule them with an iron scepter." He treads the winepress of the fury of the wrath of God Almighty.*

With what weapon is the Word of God frequently compared? Why?

_____

_____

What is the Word of God?

_____

_____

What are some effects of reading and knowing the Bible?

Ephesians 5:26 _____

_____

(to make holy, cleansing by the washing with water through the word)

Romans 12:2 _____

_____

_____

  (renewing of the mind)

Matthew 4:4 _____

_____

_____

  (life and strength)

List other Scriptures that describe benefits from reading and learning the Word. List the benefits described. (A concordance or Bible dictionary will be useful.)

_____

_____

_____

STANDING FIRM

In Matthew 4 Jesus gives us an example of how to stand against and defeat the devil when he comes against us. Knowing the Word allowed Christ to stand confidently in His position of authority. Using the Word against Satan was the same as wielding a powerful broadsword. Victory in this encounter was not instantaneous, as Satan attacked at least three times that are recorded. So it is with us. The Enemy is persistent and will attack over and over. To be able to stand means knowing all the Scripture we can and being alert to use it.

Read Matthew 4.

What did Satan use in his attempts at tripping up Jesus? Circle the correct answer:

  A. Guile

  B. Cunning

  C. Scripture

  D. All of the above

When did Satan approach Jesus in the desert? Circle the correct answer:

  A. As soon as Jesus entered the desert

  B. After Jesus had prayed and fasted

  C. After forty days

  D. Both B and C

What did Satan offer Jesus? Circle the correct answer:

  A. Power

  B. Wealth

  C. Recognition

  D. All of the above

Under what authority or influence did Satan tempt Jesus? Circle the correct answers:

    A. Satan was just very clever and smart.

    B. Satan was and is the ruler of the air and the earth.

    C. Satan really had no basis for his temptations.

    D. God allowed Satan to approach Jesus.

Review/Conclusion:

Satan is our enemy. He is ruthless and ceaselessly persistent in his attempts to rob us of the promises of God and blind us to our position in Christ. He knows that his efforts are pointless and that in the end he is destined for an eternal damnation that defies imagination in the fires of hell. Satan is a loser who irrationally refuses to acknowledge his defeated, impotent status. He functions from the defeated state of dysfunctional denial.

The evil character of Satan is what drives his destructive behavior. He is the epitome of the human concept that "absolute power corrupts absolutely." Satan's power is not absolute, yet it is fathomless compared to any earthly power, and he seeks constantly to expand his range of power.

Before the beginning of time, Satan was a true angel of light ordained by God to guard the holiness of heaven. He was perfect in goodness, appearance, and motives. There was no other created heavenly host that outshone Satan. He was the "morning star, son of the dawn" (Isaiah 14:12).

So what happened? We'll look at that in the next lesson.

LESSON 2: *Where Did Satan Come From?*

Scripture for Meditation:

No, in all these things we are more than con-querors through him who loved us. For I am convinced that neither death nor life, neither angels nor demons, neither the present nor the future, nor any powers, neither height nor depth, nor anything else in all creation, will be able to separate us from the love of God that is in Christ Jesus our Lord. (Romans 8:37–39)

A Beginning Prayer:

Lord Jesus Christ, let me know and walk in the reality of Your power in me. Clothe me in Your righteousness and protect me with Your holiness. Let Your shed blood cover every area of my life and keep me marked as one bought by Your grace. Amen.

Lesson:

Satan once enjoyed the pleasures of heaven. He was chief among the angels who guarded the throne of God and the choir director of glory. The startling reality is that Satan came from heaven. So what happened? Let's consider some biblical references to Satan, his fall, and his nature.

    Isaiah 14:11–17: *All your pomp has been brought down to the grave, along with the noise of your harps; maggots are spread out beneath you and worms cover you. How you have fallen from heaven, O morning star, son of the dawn! You have been cast down to the earth, you who once laid low the nations! You said in your heart, "I will ascend to heaven; I will raise my throne above the stars of God; I will sit enthroned on the mount of assembly, on the utmost heights of the sacred mountain. I will ascend above the tops of the clouds; I will make myself like the Most High." But you are brought down to the grave, to the depths of the* *pit. Those who see you stare at you, they ponder your fate: "Is this the man who shook the earth and made kingdoms tremble, the man who made the world a desert, who overthrew its cities and would not let his captives go home?"*

What two names are applied to Satan in this passage?

_____

_____

What position did Satan aspire to attain?

_____

_____

Who alone is to rule our lives and sit on the throne of our hearts?

_____

_____

Revelation 12:7–9: *And there was war in heaven. Michael and his angels fought against the dragon, and the dragon and his angels fought back. But he was not strong enough, and they lost their place in heaven. The great dragon was hurled down—that ancient serpent called the devil, or Satan, who leads the whole world astray. He was hurled to the earth, and his angels with him.*

How successful was Satan in his attempt to overthrow God?

_____

_____

Was Satan the only spiritual being cast out of heaven? Who were the others?

_____

_____

Ezekiel 28:11–19: *The word of the Lord came to me: "Son of man, take up a lament concerning the king of Tyre and say to him: 'This is what the Sovereign Lord says: "You were the model of perfection, full of wisdom and perfect in beauty. You were in Eden, the garden of God; every precious stone adorned you: ruby, topaz and emerald, chrysolite, onyx and jasper, sapphire, turquoise and beryl. Your settings and mountings were made of gold; on the day you were created they were prepared. You were anointed as a guardian cherub, for so I ordained you. You were on the holy mount of God; you walked among the fiery stones. You were blameless in your ways from the day you were created till wickedness was found in you. Through your widespread trade you were filled with violence, and you sinned. So I drove you in disgrace from the mount of God, and I expelled you, O guardian cherub, from among the fiery stones. Your heart became proud on account of your beauty, and you corrupted your wisdom because of your splendor. So I threw you to the earth; I made a spectacle of you before kings. By your many sins and dishonest trade you have desecrated your sanctuaries. So I made a fire come out from you, and it consumed you, and I reduced you to ashes on the ground in the sight of all who were watching. All the nations who knew you are appalled at you; you have come to a horrible end and will be no more."'"*

What was the sin that entered into Satan's heart?

_____

_____

Look up and write out this verse: Proverbs 16:18.

_____

_____

Pride entered into Satan's heart and caused him to rebel against God. Pride, which is the love and preservation of the self, is an insidious agent of sin that we must continuously guard against. Christ calls us to die to ourselves daily. This involves denying, or turning away from, our own motives, desires, and wants and yielding to those of our Lord.

What are some of the ways pride exhibits itself in your life?

_____

_____

Ephesians 2:1–3: _As for you, you were dead in your transgressions and sins, in which you used to live when you followed the ways of this world and of the ruler of the kingdom of the air, the spirit who is now at work in those who are disobedient. All of us also lived among them at one time, gratifying the cravings of our sinful nature and following its desires and thoughts. Like the rest, we were by nature objects of wrath._

Who is an active ruler of this world we live in?

_____

What spirit is it that drives the behavior of unbelievers?

_____

What spirit rules in believers?

_____

Have you accepted Jesus Christ as Lord of your life?

_____

John 8:43–45: _"Why is my language not clear to you? Because you are unable to hear what I say. You belong to your father, the devil, and you want to carry out your father's desire. He was a murderer from the beginning, not holding to the truth, for there is no truth in him. When he lies, he speaks his native language, for he is a liar and the father of lies. Yet because I tell the truth, you do not believe me!"_

What is Satan the father of?

_____

_____

Whose desire do people carry out if they are not serving Christ?

_____

_____

Is all truth God's truth? Why or why not?

_____

_____

2 Corinthians 11:13–15: *For such men are false apostles, deceitful workmen, masquerading as apostles of Christ. And no wonder, for Satan himself masquerades as an angel of light. It is not surprising, then, if his servants masquerade as servants of righteousness. Their end will be what their actions deserve.*

Are angels real beings?

_____

_____

Are all angels good angels?

_____

_____

Is it possible for Christians to mistake the activity of Satan for the activity of the Holy Spirit? Why or why not?

_____

_____

John 16:11b: *"The prince of this world now stands condemned."*

Is there any possibility of an ultimate positive outcome for Satan?

_____

_____

Does Satan have any real authority over a Christian's life?

_____

_____

Review/Conclusion:

Satan's origin was heaven. As a heavenly being he has far less power than God. Compared to God, Satan is incredibly handicapped and limited in what he can do. Unlike God, Satan is not omnipotent, omniscient, or omnipresent.

Although Satan is a powerful spiritual being and his goal is our destruction, Jesus Christ has defeated Satan's power to rule our lives. Satan can afflict us and cause us trouble, but in Christ we are "more than conquerors," for "greater is He who is in us" than Satan.

Salvation guarantees us eternal life with Christ. As we walk in Christ's way of righteousness, Satan will have no power to rule our lives. Living out the Word is our way to resist the Enemy, who flees from us as we stand in Christ.

Satan's power has only destined him for eternal destruction.

LESSON 3: *The Kingdom of Darkness*

Scripture for Meditation:

You, dear children, are from God and have overcome them, because the one who is in you is greater than the one who is in the world. (1 John 4:4)

A Beginning Prayer:

Father in heaven, I thank You that You are all-powerful and all-caring. In You I am secure and safe from all harm. Nothing can touch me without Your permission, and I know that You will never allow the Enemy to destroy me. I rejoice and take comfort in Your supreme protection. Amen.

Lesson:

CHRIST THE CREATOR

Satan's kingdom is a structured organization of supernatural evil. Originally it was part of Christ's perfect creation and under His authority. Scripture plainly reveals that the Lord Jesus Christ created those in Satan's kingdom. As the Creator He holds the kingdom of darkness answerable to Him.

> **Colossians 1:15–17:** *He [Jesus Christ] is the image of the invisible God, the firstborn over all creation. For by him all things were created: things in heaven and on earth, visible and invisible, whether thrones or powers or rulers or authorities; all things were created by him and for him. He is before all things, and in him all things hold together.*

Who created all things?

_____

_____

List by category some of these things that God created:

_____

_____

Can Satan create anything that does not already exist?

_____

_____

As a structured kingdom, the throne of darkness is still subservient to Christ. Thus, in Christ's power, we can stand against the devil's schemes.

Read Ephesians 6:11–12.
What do you need to do to be prepared to stand against the schemes of the Enemy?

_____

_____

Against who or what do we really struggle in our spiritual walk?

_____

_____

SATAN'S UNCREATIVITY

Satan is not a creator. The Colossians text makes this very clear. Having been created by the Lord Jesus Christ, the thrones and powers (v. 16; "dominions," NKJV), where Satan and his demons do their work, remain under the full authority of Jesus Christ. Indeed, Jesus has won the final victory over Satan and all the fallen angels. They cannot even "consist" (v. 17 NKJV) and hold together apart from the sustaining power of the Creator. For sovereign purposes known only to God, the kingdom of darkness is allowed to continue to rebel and function until God's perfect time comes to judge Satan and his host. At that moment, God will cast all the fallen spirit beings into the lake of fire prepared for them.

Read Matthew 25:41.
What is the ultimate destination of the devil and his angels?

_____

_____

Will anyone else be assigned to this place? If so, who?

_____

_____

Read Revelation 20:10.
What was the devil's main activity as described in this verse?

_____

_____

How long will the devil remain in the place described in this verse?

_____

_____

SATAN'S COUNTERFEITS

Satan's kingdom has a counterfeit, parallel plan for nearly everything God does in His perfect plan of redemption. Though Satan has only temporary influence, he has a counterfeit plan—a crafty imitation of the real. We must not forget that Satan is exceedingly clever. When he fell in his rebellion, he did not lose the gifts and genius God put into him. He is a master deceiver. When talking of Satan, many adjectives are required: powerful, beautiful, clever, crafty, subtle, deceptive, mighty, ruthless, and sinister are a few. He also is enslaving, manipulating, cruel, brutal, angry, mean, and destroying, as is his kingdom.

Are you surprised to learn that Satan has a plan for your life? What do you believe are some elements of his plan for you?

_____

_____

Here are five ways Satan's dark kingdom counterfeits, or falsely imitates, everything God has done:

(1) *Satan offers those who follow him a counterfeit family.* In explaining the parable of the sower, the Lord Jesus illustrated how clever Satan is to intermingle his family members with the Lord's family (Matthew 13:37–43), comparing them to weeds growing among the wheat. Those following Satan will be so plentiful and deceptive they will even mingle in our churches and be hard to detect. Like family, they will find much in common as they seek pleasure, independence, and their own approaches to life, apart from God.

What kinds of organizations or groups are frequently viewed by adherents and members as families?

_____

_____

(2) *Satan has created a counterfeit gospel* (Galatians 1:6–9; 1 Timothy 4:1–3). Satan has his own "good news," which he uses to pervert the ways of truth and enslave the nondiscerning. This "gospel" is one of greed, legalism, and twisted perversions concerning foods and even marriage, according to the apostle Paul. In our day, the extreme of this gospel has appeared in published form as the so-called Satanic Bible. New Age teaching, the prosperity gospel, Hinduism, Buddhism, and neo-Christian cults like Mormonism, Jehovah's Witnesses, and Christian Science must be placed with Satan's gospel. There are many shapes and shades to the counterfeit gospel Satan uses to pervert and confuse the message of the Gospel of Jesus Christ.

(3) *Satan also has established counterfeit ministers* (2 Corinthians 10–11). A counterfeit gospel must be relayed by counterfeit messengers. The apostle Paul warns of those who pose as ministers of God and His Gospel but in reality are ministers of the devil. Their goal is to exalt Satan's realm and destroy the kingdom of God. Paul climaxed his warning with these forceful words about their end danger: "His ministers also transform themselves into ministers of righteousness, whose end will be according to their works" (11:15 NKJV; cf. vv. 13–14).

Is it possible that well-meaning individuals could contribute to Satan's tactics by preaching an inaccurate gospel? If so, how can this be guarded against? What measures do we need to take as individuals to avoid these errors?

_____

_____

(4) *Satan offers a counterfeit righteousness* (Romans 9–10). Man's most serious problem arises when he goes about to invent his own righteous standards while passing up the righteousness of God. Such deception has its origin in the master deceiver, Satan himself. He continues to mislead people to believe that their own actions done in their own way can please God. In Romans 9 and 10, Paul details the false righteousness people embrace in lieu of God's true righteousness. A key verse is Romans 10:3: "For they being ignorant of God's righteousness, and seeking to establish their own righteousness, have not submitted to the righteousness of God" (NKJV).

What are some of the evidences of self-righteousness? Are there things you do that are really self-righteous acts?

(5) *Satan seeks his own, counterfeit worship* (1 Corinthians 11:14–33). Satan's desire to exalt himself to be as God includes his desire to receive worship, just as God receives worship from those who love Him. It's still surprising to me the number of people who have been tempted to worship the devil. Yet they are in good company, for Jesus Himself was tempted to worship Satan as He fasted in the wilderness, and He understands that temptation (Matthew 4:8–9). We must resist such temptation. The answer Jesus gave is still the best: "Away from me, Satan! For it is written: 'Worship the Lord your God, and serve him only'" (v. 10).

SATAN'S DECEPTIVE RULE

Satan rules by deception, fear, and ignorance. Satan has no reality to present. Everything about him is counterfeit, deceptive, and misleading. Even when he tells the truth, he twists it into a lie. He quoted the truth of Scripture in his temptations of the Lord Jesus, but his purpose in doing so was to tempt and deceive. This is still his chief tactic against God's people. Jesus understood that ignorance of the truth can enslave, whereas knowledge of the truth sets free. So He told His followers:

"If you abide in My word, you are My disciples indeed. And you shall know the truth, and the truth shall make you free. . . . Therefore if the Son makes you free, you shall be free indeed." (John 8:31–32, 36 NKJV)

Jesus also knew that those who follow Satan are often deluded and unable to comprehend spiritual things. Thus Jesus said to the deluded religious leaders of His day:

"Why do you not understand My speech? Because you are not able to listen to My word. You are of your father the devil, and the desires of your father you want to do. He was a murderer from the beginning, and does not stand in the truth, because there is no truth in him. When he speaks a lie, he speaks from his own resources, for he is a liar and the father of it." (John 8:43–44 NKJV)

In our spiritual lives is there any neutrality? Is there any middle ground, spiritual DMZ, or fence to sit on? Explain your answer.

_____

_____

Deception and its fear can only succeed when we are ignorant of the truth. Satan can and does hold his bondage on a believer and his family when they function within the sphere of the devil's deceptive tactics. Ignorance concerning truth is as useful to Satan's purposes as the believing of his blatant lies. That is why good Bible teaching and doctrinal study are so necessary to walk in personal freedom. To protect our children from the rule of darkness in their lives, parents must know the truth of their authority to apply the truth of God to their children's needs.

Satan is an illusionist. He deceives by offering us a pretend life that is not real. He uses the world and its media methods as his theater to spread his illusions. Television, videos, movies, and the world's music offer a menu of pretend. They entice with a false message about what constitutes "the good life." Revenge is presented as a desirable virtue. Enjoying the sensual and finding sexual conquest are touted as bringing ultimate pleasure. Movies and television shows portray those with money or power as achieving maximum success. These entertainment media depict the mysteries of occult power as exciting and worthy of pursuit.

Satan's kingdom is behind this deceptive offering of perverted values. Only godly, Christian parents can stand between their children and Satan's plans for his deceptive control.

Can Satan ever tell you the truth?

_____

_____

What is truth, or rather, *who* is truth?

_____

_____

How can you avoid being deceived by anyone in any situation?

_____

_____

How does fear affect your ability to think clearly and act rationally?

_____

_____

Does fear come from God? Why or why not?

_____

_____

Review/Conclusion:

Satan is a liar, deceiver, and master manipulator. But our heavenly Father is all-powerful. He has given us His Word and placed His Holy Spirit in us that we may have discernment. We can overcome Satan by the blood of Jesus and our spoken resistance (Revelation 12:11). We have nothing to fear as we stand on God's Word against the wiles of our defeated enemy.

LESSON 4: *Satan's Kingdom Rising*

Scripture for Meditation:

"At that time if anyone says to you, 'Look, here is the Christ!' or, 'There he is!' do not believe it. For false Christs and false prophets will appear and perform great signs and miracles to deceive even the elect—if that were possible. See, I have told you ahead of time. So if anyone tells you, 'There he is, out in the desert,' do not go out; or, 'Here he is, in the inner rooms,' do not believe it. For as lightning that comes from the east is visible even in the west, so will be the coming of the Son of Man."
(Matthew 24:23–27)

A Beginning Prayer:

Lord Jesus Christ, I look forward with great anticipation to Your soon return. Through the power of Your Holy Spirit, place within me strong resolve and determination to remain steadfast in You until that time. Strengthen my spirit to resist the Enemy and the darkness he spreads around me. Set a strong hedge of protection around my family, and let us be beacons of light to the lost. Make us ministers of hope that we might draw back those the Enemy seeks to destroy. Maranatha—come quickly! Amen.

Lesson:

As we come closer and closer to the end of time and our Lord's glorious return, Satan will inevitably increase the intensity of his activity. Wickedness unlike anything we've ever seen will abound more and more. In fact, we can see it happening already.

Our culture has embraced and been penetrated by the demonizing power of darkness. The kingdom of Satan is rising in an attempt (1) to enslave and destroy as many lives as possible before the end, and (2) to create the appearance of strength and dominance, confusing "even the elect—if that were possible" (Matthew 24:24).

SIGNS OF SATANIC REVIVAL

(1) *Sexual immorality, including pornography and the free expression of sensuality.* One of the most obvious and prevalent areas Satan has used to destroy the lives of millions is through the perversion of sexuality. From blatant displays of pornographic materials to the use of sexually explicit images in sexual education courses, this God-created gift of sexual expression has been twisted, abused, and contorted into one of the most destructive forces we contend with.

Everywhere we look and everywhere we listen—newspapers, magazines, books, television, movies, advertising, music, radio, commercials, the Internet, computer games—sex pervades and invades our senses. And this invasion is not even close to the beautiful experience God intended for sex between a man and woman united in marriage.

In *The Rise of Fallen Angels* (pages 26, 28), I state:

Human sexuality is one of God's most sacred gifts to the human race. Not only is the gift of sex the means God has chosen for human procreation, but within marriage it also expresses some of God's best gifts to mankind—loving intimacy, oneness, and the giving of ourselves to each other.

God chose this intimacy as the ideal, human-level illustration of the oneness between Christ and His church (see Ephesians 5:22–23). Could this be the reason Satan distorts sexuality—to soil that biblical illustration of oneness?

. . . [The] perverseness of our times, which includes rampant distribution of pornography and many kinds of "free expression" of sensuality, is more than an expression of human sexual freedom. It is more than merely man's fallen nature expressing itself in immoral activity. It is even more than an evolving product of the world system and the attitudes ingrained by our mass media and entertainment industry.

I believe we're seeing a carefully orchestrated conspiracy at work, too sinister and subtle to be entirely of human origin. This conspiracy flows directly out of the realm of evil supernaturalism, from Satan and his corps of fallen angels. Any change will require divine, supernatural intervention. Only God's power, manifested in the hearts of a caring, concerned citizenry, can stop this onslaught of evil.

List all the ways you can think of that sexuality has been perverted in our culture:

_____

_____

For each of the things you have listed above, what would be the God-ordained, biblical alternative?

_____

_____

(2) *A preoccupation with violence and death.* We must not miss this vital insight: Violence in all its expressions carries Satan's fingerprints, for "he was a murderer from the beginning" (John 8:44). Drug-related murders, abortion, suicidal deaths, and every other kind of violence all closely identify with the powers of darkness that work overtime to create havoc among peace-loving peoples.

Whereas God respects all life He has created, Satan and the fallen angels who obey him disrespect life. They want men and women to disrespect their own lives and the lives of others. Through violence and death, Satan and the angelic powers of darkness are able to desensitize them to the value of every person (see *Rise of Fallen Angels,* 29).

Within just the past week, how many news items can you recall that dealt with some form of violence being expressed toward another person or group of people? Violence in our cities, our country, and our world has reached epidemic levels. Kids are killing kids in schools. Wives are killing husbands in homes. Strangers kill strangers over minor traffic mishaps. It happens so frequently that another killing a few blocks over, or another mass slaughter half a world away, barely grabs a minute of our attention.

But beneath these ultimate expressions of violence there are dozens of levels of expression that surround us and of which we may even fall prey. Spousal abuse and the abuse of children is making victims of everyone—husbands, wives, sons, and daughters. This abuse is physical, emotional, verbal, and spiritual—it happens at all levels in all degrees.

What are some expressions of violence you can think of that may not be as obvious as murder or physical abuse? List as many as you can think of.

_____

_____

What are ways we as Christians can respond to these acts of violence?

_____

_____

(3) *Growing involvement in the occult.* "Spiritism pervades American society in many forms. Interest, experimentation, and involvement in the occult seems epidemic. It has entered every level of our culture" (*Rise of Fallen Angels,* 31).

In how many ways you can think of do products and programs aimed at *children* (birth to preteen) incorporate occult themes and images? Be as specific as you can.

_____

_____

In how many ways you can think of do products and programs aimed at *youth* (teens to young adult) incorporate occult themes and images? Be as specific as you can.

_____

_____

In how many ways you can think of do products and programs aimed at *adults* incorporate occult themes and images? Be as specific as you can.

_____

_____

What are some of the evidences you've seen of New Age thinking and expression in your community?

_____

_____

For all the items you've listed in the exercises above, what are tactics and actions we as Christians can and must employ to combat these satanic influences in our lives, our families, our churches, our communities, and our culture? List and discuss.

_____

_____

_____

_____

Review/Conclusion:

Instead of growing fearful and alarmed as we see more and more evidences of Satan parading his power, we as believers should be filled with a sense of anticipation and great impending victory. Christ's return is imminent! He is coming back, and the devil knows it's very soon. The evil that surrounds us is evidence of Satan's final desperate gasp. We know who holds the real power—and our souls are secure in Him!

As blood-bought, God-armored Christians we need to stride into this dying world, defeating the strongholds of darkness everywhere we encounter them. Warfare means knowing where the battles are to be fought. With minds enlightened and eyes opened by the Spirit, we can perceive the ploys of the Enemy and take strategic aim with our all-powerful sword—God's Word. We may not see the damage done to the kingdom of hell, but we know Him who is truth and we know that darkness will always be wounded by light.

ORGANIZATIONAL LEVELS OF SATANIC CULTS

There are a variety of ways of categorizing satanic cult involvement. We present only one here that may prove useful in understanding satanism and recognizing its expressions.

Traditional Satanists: Those who are deeply committed to worshiping Satan are at this highest level. They maintain strict vows of secrecy under pain of death. Individuals from all walks of life, particularly those in positions of power and influence, are often involved at this level. There are strong transgenerational ties in this form of satanism. It is believed by some investigative authorities that there is maintained at this level a global network of satanists implementing a strategy of seeding evil into the world's cultures. It is at this level that human sacrifice occurs.

Organized Satanists: Those at this level generally follow the teachings of Anton LeVey, a former police photographer and circus performer who founded the

Church of Satan in San Francisco in 1966. LeVey died in 1996. Strict vows are adhered to under threat of severe punishment. Using a satanic calendar, groups called covens are headed by a high priest. Adherents frequently engage in sexual perversions and abuse, often directed at children. Witchcraft and conjuring demons are often employed to intimidate participants.

Self-Styled Satanists: People in this group are often caught up in a variety of illegal and antisocial behaviors, which include drugs, pornography, prostitution, and the like. Some serial killers and habitual criminals use their satanic beliefs as justification for their actions. There is no organization among those categorized at this level. They are often loners, sociopaths, and psychopaths. It is speculated that many in this group belonged to organized cults at one time and suffered severe mental breakdown as a result of being demonized.

Dabblers: Those who are at this level, dabbling in the occult out of curiosity, are clear targets for being recruited into the higher levels. This is the level where many children, teens, and young adults are, being drawn in by horror movies, fantasy games, satanic rock, and more. The sensual pull of these is very strong on those going through puberty. Involvement at this level is often revealed through the satanic symbols and images they emblazon on their bodies, clothing, and possessions, as well as defacing public structures. Animal mutilations also occur at this level. The consequences of this dabbling include emotional disturbance, family conflict, criminal activity, and even suicidal and murderous acts.

Our Position in Christ

Scripture Memory Verse:
We know also that the Son of God has come and has given us understanding, so that we may know him who is true. And we are in him who is true—even in his Son Jesus Christ. He is the true God and eternal life. (1 John 5:20)

Unit Learning Goal:
Understanding who we are in Christ.

Overview of Unit 2:

Lesson 1: Your Legal Rights

Lesson 2: When It Hurts Anyway

Lesson 3: Who We Are

Lesson 4: Battling the Flesh, the World, and the Devil

Lesson 5: You Are a Winner

SUMMARY STATEMENT

There is no more secure place to be than in Christ. Hebrews 12:28 states solidly that "since we are receiving a kingdom that cannot be shaken, let us be thankful, and so worship God acceptably with reverence and awe."

Unit 2 Thought Focus:

Despite the fierceness with which Satan will come against a believer, we can still stand. We have the incredibly wonderful advantage of being preordained winners in every spiritual struggle. As long as we stand in faithfulness to Christ, victory in spiritual warfare is our undeniable right and hope. Failing to keep this truth firmly entrenched in our minds and hearts will give the advantage to our enemy.

Hesitation in battle can be costly. Being uncertain of your strength in a struggle will leave you vulnerable. In business, school, and all other areas of life, the indelible mark of a successful person is confidence. Successful people know who they are and understand what they can accomplish. They have learned that even their weaknesses can be leveraged to advantage. And they know the value of being networked with other successful, supportive people. This factor has a biblical model we can use in spiritual warfare.

We are Christ's own chosen. We are united with Christ in His victory. We love Him because He first loved us. By our union with Him we have full authority against our unseen enemies. If any have reason to be confident, we do. And if we are to believe the Word, we know what we can accomplish in Christ—*all things*. All the time.

And our weaknesses? Christ specializes in turning weaknesses into incredible strengths, turning what was meant for harm into good. Not only do we have the power of Christ in us, but we are part of the most powerful network of supportive, like-minded people—the body of Christ. Being His priests, we are all highly placed in the kingdom of God!

LESSON 1: *Your Legal Rights*

Scripture for Meditation:

These, then, are the things you should teach. Encourage and rebuke with all authority. Do not let anyone despise you. (Titus 2:15)

A Beginning Prayer:

Dear Lord Jesus, in You I have all the authority I need to resist and defeat the attacks of the Enemy against my family and me. Thank You for that authority. Help me to stand firmly in You so that I will always have access to Your power and authority. Grant to me the wisdom to discern all factors that may be giving my enemies advantage over me. Amen.

Lesson:

Being the father of lies and the author of confusion, and with the single-minded goal of stealing everything good from us, killing us, and destroying all those around us, Satan is relentless and insidious in his attacks. Seldom obvious, he will magnify our own human weaknesses, whether physical, spiritual, mental, or emotional. Difficult circumstances will be stirred up to impossible-appearing dimensions. Friends who merely disappoint will appear to us as low-blow backstabbers. Tiny events that normally occur in the lives of everyone will feel like total catastrophes in our lives. A small personality quirk virtually invisible to others will look to us like a mountain of death on our souls!

DAILY TROUBLES

Stacie, a single working mother, woke up and began getting ready for work. After dressing, she roused her seven-year-old daughter, Shelby. It was cold outside, the temperatures having dipped into the single digits overnight. Stacie worried if her car would start. Shelby groused at being wakened, not wanting to leave the warmth of her bed. "Leave me alone!" she moaned loudly.

Oh no, thought Stacie, *here we go again,* recounting in her mind other occasions of having to battle her daughter out of bed. She was running late and needed to get outside to get the car warming. Plus, she was beginning a new job. She had to be on time and perform well her first day. "Shelby!" Stacie snapped, "I'm not in the mood for this. Get up right now and get dressed. I'm going out to start the car. When I come back in I expect you up and getting dressed. *Now,* Shelby!"

Shelby winced, moaned, and rolled up more tightly in her blankets. She hated being told what to do. She knew she needed to get up, but her bed was soooo warm and cozy. Stacie threw on her coat and headed out the door.

The sharp cold slapped her in the face, startling her. It was still really cold. The car was covered with frost. She pried the door open, got in, inserted the key in the ignition, pumped the gas once, and turned the key. The engine tried briefly to turn over, but wouldn't. Stacie was near tears.

Her mind and heart reeled. She hadn't slept well the night before, tense with the anticipation of starting a new job. She'd been up late ironing clothes and getting things prepared so she and Shelby would be able to get ready quickly. What was she going to do? She went back to the house to call her brother to see if he could come over and help get her car started. He lived nearby, and she was pretty sure all she needed was a jump start. As she dialed the phone, she became aware of how quiet the house was. There was no sound of stirring, which meant Shelby was still in bed. Stacie's temperature was rising.

She got her brother, who said he'd come over, but it would be about thirty minutes or so. It was the best he could do. It meant she was going to be late for work. Tiredness, frustration, and anger suddenly overwhelmed Stacie. She stormed into Shelby's room, screaming and threatening. The loudness and intensity of her outburst frightened Shelby and tapped into her own anger and insecurities. The situation escalated into a horrific shouting match that left them both dazed, drained, and damaged.

Ultimately, Shelby got to school, but late, along with several other stragglers who had been hampered by the cold weather. In fact, the school had delayed opening due to icy conditions on the road. Stacie was late to her new job, but her boss was understanding of her situation. Others in the office had car problems due to the severe cold. All in all, the situation was no big deal. Yet for Stacie and Shelby, it had been made into a seemingly immovable, crushing obstacle.

DEBRIEFING

What happened? Why was Stacie's reaction so "big"? Was Shelby's behavior unusual for a girl her age? How would this situation impact the relationship between mother and daughter? What could they do to promote forgiveness and healing? Discuss this story with your group and write down the insights shared.

_____

_____

How much of this situation was due to Stacie and Shelby's own expectations, insecurities, and a human, fleshly response to frustration?

_____

_____

How much of this situation was due to the influence of Satan?

_____

_____

How much of this battle was directed at "flesh and blood" instead of the unseen enemies of sin and natural circumstances?

_____

_____

We can all identify with situations like the one described above. What isn't included in the narrative is the incessant self-talk that takes place in our heads when we're upset, those stream-of-consciousness thoughts that add fuel to the fire of our dilemmas. Can't you just hear those nagging voices? Stacie's were probably bringing back to her remembrance every guilt-inducing experience she'd had over the past several years. Telling her she was not being a good mother, that she would lose this job like she'd lost another, that she would not be able to survive without a husband, that she should have gotten up earlier, that she should have known her car wouldn't start, that her daughter was being rebellious just to make her angry, and on and on.

Where do these thoughts—which are all lies—come from? From Satan and our fleshly mind. Suddenly, a small situation becomes a raging inferno of broken trust and an insurmountable dilemma. Once the lies are believed, the sinful behavior begins and escalates. We hurt ourselves, others, and God.

But it doesn't have to be like this! Let's take a look at Romans 6.

THE WAY OF VICTORY

Romans 6:1–7: *What shall we say, then? Shall we go on sinning so that grace may increase? By no means! We died to sin; how can we live in it any longer? Or don't you know that all of us who were baptized into Christ Jesus were baptized into his death? We were therefore buried with him through baptism into death in order that, just as Christ was raised from the dead through the glory of the Father, we too may live a new life. If we have been united with him like this in his death, we will certainly also be united with him in his resurrection. For we know that our old self was crucified with him so that the body of sin might be done away with, that we should no longer be slaves to sin—because anyone who has died has been freed from sin.*

Circle **T** for True or **F** for False and then discuss your answers:

T   F   When you accepted Christ you died to sin.

T   F   Someone physically dead can continue sinning.

T   F   Our sinful self-man died with Christ on the cross.

T   F   Either Christ owns us or sin owns us.

T   F   Thinking mean thoughts is not sinful.

T   F   In Christ all parts of our life are new and different.

Romans 6:8–11: *Now if we died with Christ, we believe that we will also live with him. For we know that since Christ was raised from the dead, he cannot die again; death no longer has mastery over him. The death he died, he died to sin once for all; but the life he lives, he lives to God. In the same way, count yourselves dead to sin but alive to God in Christ Jesus.*

Explain in your own words what "dead to sin but alive to God in Christ Jesus" means to you:

_____

_____

Romans 6:12–13: *Therefore do not let sin reign in your mortal body so that you obey its evil desires. Do not offer the parts of your body to sin, as instruments of wickedness, but rather offer yourselves to God, as those who have been brought from death to life; and offer the parts of your body to him as instruments of righteousness.*

Circle **T** for True or **F** for False and then discuss your answers:

T F Satan can make you sin.

T F You can choose to not sin.

T F Sin just happens.

T F Other people can make you sin.

T F When you sin you are an instrument of wickedness for Satan.

Give examples of how you can "offer the parts of your body to sin, as instruments of wickedness":

_____

_____

Give examples of how you can "offer the parts of your body to God, as instruments of righteousness":

_____

_____

What else besides "parts of our body" do you think Paul is implying we can offer to God as "instruments of righteousness"?

_____

_____

Romans 6:14–16: *For sin shall not be your master, because you are not under law, but under grace. What then? Shall we sin because we are not under law but under grace? By no means! Don't you know that when you offer yourselves to someone to obey him as slaves, you are slaves to the one whom you obey—whether you are slaves to sin, which leads to death, or to obedience, which leads to righteousness?*

Circle **T** for True or **F** for False and then discuss your answers:

T F Sin doesn't matter to me since I'm under grace.

T F In grace I don't have to observe God's law.

T F Obedience to God and His law leads to righteousness.

T F Slavery can be a choice.

T F Christians are not slaves to anything.

T F Slaves don't have choices.

Romans 6:17–19: *But thanks be to God that, though you used to be slaves to sin, you wholeheartedly obeyed the form of teaching to which you were entrusted. You have been set free from sin and have become slaves to righteousness. I put this in human terms because you are weak in your natural selves. Just as you used to offer the parts of your body in slavery to* *impurity and to ever-increasing wickedness, so now offer them in slavery to righteousness leading to holiness.*

Paul states that Christians are "slaves to righteousness." Why do you think we are so uncomfortable with the idea of being a slave?

_____

_____

Paul implies that following a path of impurity leads to "ever-increasing wickedness" (see also Ephesians 4:17–18), meaning that sin is never satisfied. Sin always demands more, always needs more, always takes more. Give examples from your experience and the experiences of those you know that illustrate how insatiable sin is:

_____

_____

_____

Compare and contrast the insatiable appetite of sin against the pursuit of holiness and righteousness. Does "hungering and thirsting" after righteousness feel the same as seeking after sinful pleasure? Why or why not?

_____

_____

Romans 6:20–21: *When you were slaves to sin, you were free from the control of righteousness. What benefit did you reap at that time from the things you are now ashamed of? Those things result in death!*

Refusing to invite the Holy Spirit to control you yields what kinds of results?

_____

_____

Romans 6:22–23: *But now that you have been set free from sin and have become slaves to God, the benefit you reap leads to holiness, and the result is eternal life. For the wages of sin is death, but the gift of God is eternal life in Christ Jesus our Lord.*

What are the costs and wages of sin?

_____

_____

What are the costs and wages of being in Christ?

_____

_____

Review/Conclusion:

Either we are slaves to sin and Satan by default, or we can choose to be slaves of righteousness and Christ. There's no middle ground. If we do not choose Christ, Satan's kingdom is ready to choose us. As slaves of righteousness we willfully choose to give up further choices in that we accept joyfully all our direction from Christ as ministered through the Holy Spirit. All our choices are made for us by God. Freed from the burden of choosing, we are to invite our Lord to walk the path He places us on and head in the direction He points out.

Our flesh hates this truth and demands the "right to choose" how we live, what we do, who we become, where we go, who we partner with. Choice is touted as the ultimate freedom, so we always seek to expand the array of choices from which to choose. From ice cream flavors to ethics and morality, our sinful flesh-man cries out for and demands more and more choice.

But infinite choice is not freedom. It is bondage. It requires ceaseless sifting, examining, debating, weighing, and guessing. It yields confusion and error. It weighs on us and slows us down, diverting our energies and distracting our minds. In the end, we usually choose wrong solutions.

There is only one choice that yields peace—choosing Christ. Then, in Him we can rest and trust and follow. Who better than God to determine all the aspects of our lives?

If we remain firmly planted in Christ (dead with Him to sin), our lives and sin will be like oil and water—nothing will make them mix! But if we resurrect our crucified life and place it in sin's territory, we make ourselves vulnerable. In Christ, we are free of any legal right or authority Satan tries to exercise over us. Where we place ourselves and live out our lives is our choice and our responsibility.

LESSON 2: *When It Hurts Anyway*

Scripture for Meditation:

In this you greatly rejoice, though now for a little while you may have had to suffer grief in all kinds of trials. These have come so that your faith—of greater worth than gold, which perishes even though refined by fire—may be proved genuine and may result in praise, glory and honor when Jesus Christ is revealed.
(1 Peter 1:6–7)

A Beginning Prayer:

Majestic heavenly Father, all things hold together in Your hands, and nothing comes into my life except it comes through Your hands first. All that comes to me through You is for my good and Your glory. Your desire for me is that I will be refined and purified, even through fire. And at Christ's return, I will be part of His bride, without spot or wrinkle, ready to reign with Him in glory forever. In all things teach me to rejoice and trust in You always. Amen.

Lesson:

We know that Satan has no legal right to harass Christians. Yet we know he does, sometimes with severe intensity over time. Two prime biblical examples are Job and Paul.

JOB

In Job's case, God allowed the trial for two reasons. One was to demonstrate to the devil that he was not omnipotent or omniscient. Satan believed that if God were to withdraw certain protections from Job then Job would surely "curse God and die." God knew Job's character better and had no doubt about the results—which is an incredible testimony to Job!

But Job was not perfect. He had a dangerous flaw that, if not refined away, could have yielded far greater damage than Satan inflicted. This is the second reason God allowed the trial—to surface Job's most significant character flaw: Job harbored self-righteous pride.

One of the most quoted verses from Job is nearly always quoted for the wrong reason. The first half of Job 13:15 states in the King James, "Though he slay me, yet will I trust in him." What a testimony, right? But let's take a look at the entire verse in the *New Living Translation:* "God might kill me, but I cannot wait. I am going to argue my case with him." In fact, even the King James is revealing: "But I will maintain mine own ways before him."

What Job is really saying is, "Yes, I trust God. But I know I'm right, and I'm going to argue my case to His face. He can kill me if He wants, but I'm still going to have my say!" If your teenager or a worker you supervised were to speak to you like this, how would you react? If Job really trusted God, wouldn't he have just shut up? How many times have you ever said something like, "I know God loves me, but I just hate the way He shows it." We say things like this with a chuckle, but I don't think God is laughing.

By the time Job comes to the end of his ordeal, his tune and tone have changed: "I know that you can do all things; no plan of yours can be thwarted. You asked, 'Who is this that obscures my counsel without knowledge?' Surely I spoke of things I did not understand, things too wonderful for me to know. You said, 'Listen now, and I will speak; I will question you, and you shall answer me.' My ears had heard of you but now my eyes have seen you. Therefore I despise myself and repent in dust and ashes" (Job 42:2–6).

What Satan intended as harm for Job, God allowed for Job's good. Job suffered, and in the process the quality of true humility and reverence before God was refined into his character. What a wonderfully ironic defeat of Satan's intentions!

Circle **T** for True or **F** for False and then discuss your answers:

T   F   Satan can't touch my life without God's permission.

T   F   If I'm under attack it's because I'm being punished by God.

T   F   When Satan attacks me it means God doesn't love me anymore.

T   F   God is faithful to protect me even when I sin.

PAUL

In 2 Corinthians 12:6–9 there is a record of Paul's buffeting by Satan.

Second Corinthians 12:6–9: *Even if I should choose to boast, I would not be a fool, because I would be speaking the truth. But I refrain, so no one will think more of me than is warranted by what I do or say. To keep me from becoming conceited because of these surpassingly great revelations, there was given me a thorn in my flesh, a messenger of Satan, to torment me. Three times I pleaded with the Lord to take it away from me. But he said to me, "My grace is sufficient for you, for my power is made perfect in weakness." Therefore I will boast all the more gladly about my weaknesses, so that Christ's power may rest on me.*

Paul recognized and stood on his biblical legal rights to be free of the devil's influence in his life.

What did Paul do when he recognized that this torment was from Satan?

_____

_____

How many times did Paul pray, and what did he pray for?

_____

_____

After praying, Paul realized that the specific answer he sought was not forthcoming. However, God did answer Paul's prayer and Paul accepted the answer he received.

What was the response God gave Paul to his request?

_____

_____

What was Paul's response to God's answer?

_____

_____

Circle **T** for True or **F** for False and then discuss your answers:

T   F   If I pray for deliverance and don't receive it, it's because I'm unworthy.

T   F   Satan never attacks spiritual giants like pastors and evangelists.

T   F   If I remain spiritually strong all the time Satan will leave me alone.

T   F   Being a Christian doesn't exempt me from suffering or problems.

BELIEVERS TODAY

Both Paul and Job understood a very important truth: We must allow our Lord to be sovereign. God is sovereign—absolutely—over every area of our lives. Because of His nature He will never allow His sovereignty to cause us harm. Yielding to the Lord is always paramount in spiritual matters.

In Christ we have full authority to resist Satan and force him to leave our presence. Yet, at the same time we must be willing to accept our Lord's sovereign purpose for allowing us to experience the battle, even if it is prolonged. No matter how fierce the battle becomes, no matter how much pressure Satan brings to bear, no matter that from the human perspective it seems otherwise, we will remain triumphant as we utilize what God has provided.

Ephesians 6:10–14: *Finally, be strong in the Lord and in his mighty power. Put on the full armor of God so that you can take your stand against the devil's schemes. For our struggle is not against flesh and blood, but against the rulers, against the authorities, against the powers of this dark world and against the spiritual forces of evil in the heavenly realms. Therefore put on the full armor of God, so that when the day of evil comes, you may be able to stand your ground, and after you have done everything, to stand. Stand firm then, with the belt of truth buckled around your waist, with the breastplate of righteousness in place.*

How are we to be strong?

_____

_____

How many times is the word *stand* used in this passage?

_____

_____

After we have done everything, what then happens? Circle all the letters that apply:

    A. The battle is over.

    B. God throws a big victory party.

    C. We stand firm in Christ whether the battle ends or continues.

    D. We rejoice in the Lord.

If the battle continues to rage, what are we supposed to do? Circle all the letters that apply:

    A. Run away and hide.

    B. Give up on God because He's a liar.

    C. Stand firm in Christ.

    D. Trust in God's sovereignty.

Who *always* knows what's best for us? Circle all the letters that apply:

    A. I do

    B. My pastor

    C. My best friend

    D. My parents or my spouse

    E. My boss or my teachers

    F. God

Review/Conclusion:

A few years before his death someone challenged Francis Schaeffer, a great twentieth-century theologian, with a provocative question. Schaeffer was battling with cancer and the whole world knew it. The visitor asked him how he viewed his illness: Was it against God's will? His answer came without hesitation and was to the point: "Who am I to question where God puts me or what He allows in my life?"

Every time we encounter a hard circumstance, even when we perceive the Enemy is behind it, Schaeffer's words should come back to us. James said, "Consider it pure joy, my brothers, whenever you face trials of many kinds, because you know that the testing of your faith develops perseverance. Perseverance must finish its work so that you may be mature and complete, *not lacking anything*" (James 1:2–4, italics added).

LESSON 3: *Who We Are*

Scripture for Meditation:

So God created man in his own image, in the image of God he created him; male and female he created them. God blessed them and said to them, "Be fruitful and increase in number; fill the earth and subdue it. Rule over the fish of the sea and the birds of the air and over every living creature that moves on the ground." (Genesis 1:27–28)

A Beginning Prayer:

Dear heavenly Father, as deep calls to deep, so that which You have created within me calls to You. In You I live and move and have breath. Who I am comes from You and rests in You. Thank You for securing my identity in Your image and grace. Let Your glory shine in my life that others will be blessed by who and what You have made me. Amen.

Lesson:

Knowing who we are in biblical terms—the way God sees us—is critical to our ability to deal effectively as Christians in the world. It is foundational. The fact that we are creations of God should be enough to assure us of the high value we possess before Him.

He cares for every aspect of His creation, and Christ declares, "Are not two sparrows sold for a penny? Yet not one of them will fall to the ground apart from the will of your Father. And even the very hairs of your head are all numbered. So don't be afraid; you are worth more than many sparrows" (Matthew 10:29–31).

In fact, before we were born, God took infinite pains to interest Himself intimately with every detail of our existence: "For you created my inmost being; you knit me together in my mother's womb. I praise you because I am fearfully and wonderfully made; your works are wonderful, I know that full well. My frame was not hidden from you when I was made in the secret place. When I was woven together in the depths of the earth, your eyes saw my unformed body. All the days ordained for me were written in your book before one of them came to be" (Psalm 139:13–16).

And an even more profound revelation of our immense value before God is found in the very beginning of His Word: "Then God said, 'Let us make man in our image, in our likeness, and let them rule over the fish of the sea and the birds of the air, over the livestock, over all the earth, and over all the creatures that move along the ground.' So God created man in his own image, in the image of God he created him; male and female he created them" (Genesis 1:26–27).

WHO ARE YOU?

- You are made in the image of God, granted authority, and blessed by God (Genesis 1:26–30).
- You are a person of great value and dignity, granted the dignity of personhood before the Lord, and are equal with others (Genesis 2:15–25).
- As have all people, you have inherited a sinful condition resulting from the fall of man (Genesis 3:1–13). Among other things, to be sinful means you inherited a nature that wants to sin (Romans 5:12–21; Galatians 5:17–21; Colossians 3:5–8).
- You are redeemed if you have accepted Jesus Christ as your personal Savior and Lord. Redeemed persons are lifted above fallen condemnation and are of great value:

    A. They are spiritual persons (John 3:6; 1 Peter 2:9–10).

    B. They are holy persons (1 Corinthians 1:2; Colossians 3:12; Hebrews 10:10, 14).

    C. They are gifted persons (Ephesians 4:7; Romans 12:6–8).

    D. They are valuable persons (Isaiah 43:1, 4; Colossians 3:12; Romans 5:8).

    E. They are persons loved and graced by God (John 15:9–10; 17:23).

    F. They are chosen for important service (1 Peter 2:5–9).

Look up and write out each Scripture reference in the section just above. Then, for each of the items, write a one- or two-sentence statement of what it means to you. Finally, write out a one-paragraph Personal Value Statement expressing how you believe God values you based on what you know to be true from His Word and your experience. Write your Personal Value Statement below:

_____

_____

While we are incredibly valuable before God, we are also incredibly fallen. Our very nature is sinful from birth because of the Fall—the sin of Adam and Eve in the Garden of Eden (Genesis 3). In the beginning, man was created perfect in every way—physically, emotionally, spiritually, and intellectually. However, using the free will implanted by God, first Eve and then Adam chose to disobey God and, as a result, allowed Satan to gain a foothold within all of creation. When Adam and Eve fell under the influence of sin in the garden, all of creation also fell—every molecule and atom is affected by the degenerative rust of sin.

Do you believe those of the world—those who are not biblical Christians—view themselves and others as inherently good or inherently bad? Why or why not?

_____

_____

If we believe that we and others are naturally good people—that our natures are not corrupted by sin—what are some of the results, consequences, and impacts of this view on our legal system, societal values, and business ethics?

_____

_____

Because of the Fall we are now susceptible to pain, toil, disease, and various afflictions and sufferings. Our senses and capacities are bent toward pursuing self-interest and evil. Without God's intervention, our minds are incapable of knowing or serving Him. Our emotions are corrupted and deceitful. These are only a few of the consequences we are now exposed to because of the Fall.

Circle **T** for True or **F** for False and then discuss your answers:

T   F   Some parts of creation are not affected by the Fall.

T   F   Sin is behind all disease.

T   F   Some parts of my life (my total being) are not affected by the Fall.

T   F   I cannot know God unless I'm enlightened by the Holy Spirit.

T   F   Being sinful is not necessarily being evil.

T   F   The Fall infected genes, molecules, atoms—all of creation—with sin.

T   F   I can be good without God's help.

GOD'S REDEMPTIVE PLAN

While the Fall in the garden was and is tragic, throughout the history of God's dealings with mankind we see the evidence of redemption at work. Throughout the Old Testament stories, God patiently, painstakingly, and persistently teaches and exhibits mercy, forgiveness, and reconciliation with His people. The culmination of this activity is in the redemptive power of the birth, life, death, and resurrection of Jesus Christ, which was then sealed at Pentecost.

Redemption reverses the effects of the Fall and through the given grace of God ushers us into His presence. Here, in Him, no longer lost but found, the process of our regeneration begins. John 3:5–8 states, "Jesus answered, 'I tell you the truth, no one can enter the kingdom of God unless he is born of water and the Spirit. Flesh gives birth to flesh, but the Spirit gives birth to spirit. You should not be surprised at my saying, "You must be born again." The wind blows wherever it pleases. You hear its sound, but you cannot tell where it comes from or where it is going. So it is with everyone born of the Spirit.'"

Does being "born again" mean that all of our problems are over? Why or why not?

_____

_____

_____

What parallels are there between growing up physically from babies to adults and growing up spiritually after we become new babes in Christ?

_____

_____

Our first birth was a result of the union between our parents. Our second birth is a result of the union between God's Spirit and our spirit. Just as genetic physical and behavioral characteristics pass on from generation to generation as a result of our first birth, so do we begin to exhibit the character traits of our heavenly Father as we grow in the Lord.

This dividing line between flesh and spirit is also the battle line where we will fight against the Enemy of our souls. God's Holy Spirit will nurture our spirit (Psalm 51:12), transforming us through the renewing of our minds (Romans 12:2), and building us into a holy dwelling (Ephesians 2).

Satan, however, will seek to distract us from our spiritual regeneration through the Spirit by degeneration in our flesh. His attacks will center on our bodily appetites (physical), our desires (emotional), and our thoughts and beliefs (intellectual and spiritual).

Circle **T** for True or **F** for False and then discuss your answers:

T   **F**   Salvation solves all my problems.

T   **F**   Struggling spiritually is sinful.

T   **F**   Accepting Christ as my Savior is only the beginning of spiritual regeneration in my life.

T   **F**   If I have specific areas of sinful struggle that may be a result of genetic predisposition (i.e., addictions, sexual orientation, etc.) I am no longer accountable for sin in those areas.

T   **F**   In Christ I have all the power I need to avoid all sin and am responsible to resist all sin, even despite potential genetic predisposition.

T   **F**   Christians never sin.

T   **F**   God sees my life in Christ as completely holy.

Review/Conclusion:

Jesus stated, "All that the Father gives me will come to me, and whoever comes to me I will never drive away. For I have come down from heaven not to do my will but to do the will of him who sent me. And this is the will of him who sent me, that I shall lose none of all that he has given me, but raise them up at the last day. For my Father's will is that everyone who looks to the Son and believes in him shall have eternal life, and I will raise him up at the last day" (John 6:37–40).

Satan will do all he can to focus your attention on your sinfulness. He will work on your emotions to get you depressed or angry with yourself. He will work on your mind to get you to think too highly or too little of yourself. He will work on your appetites to get you to fill your life with too much lethargy or too much activity. With your heart, mind, and body off balance, he'll try to convince you that your spirit is just as muddled and cluttered. Then he'll hit you with the killer lie that you are not loved by God, that you are no good at all, that it's hopeless to resist sin—just give in.

How do you deal with that? Remind him of who you are in Christ and pull out your sword: "Who shall separate us from the love of Christ? Shall trouble or hardship or persecution or famine or nakedness or danger or sword? As it is written: 'For your sake we face death all day long; we are considered as sheep to be slaughtered.' No, in all these things we are more than conquerors through him who loved us. For I am convinced that neither death nor life, neither angels nor demons, neither the present nor the future, nor any powers, neither height nor depth, nor anything else in all creation, will be able to separate us from the love of God that is in Christ Jesus our Lord" (Romans 8:35–39).

LESSON 4: *Battling the Flesh, the World, and the Devil*

Scripture for Meditation:

Submit yourselves, then, to God. Resist the devil, and he will flee from you. Come near to God and he will come near to you. Wash your hands, you sinners, and purify your hearts, you double-minded. Grieve, mourn and wail. Change your laughter to mourning and your joy to gloom. Humble yourselves before the Lord, and he will lift you up.
(James 4:7–10)

A Beginning Prayer:

Lord, thank You for providing all the wisdom, power, and insight I need to overcome the devil. Thank You that I am enabled to endure and prevail over the temptations of the flesh. Thank You also that you equip me to perceive and discern the pressures of the world that I might not be ensnared by alliances that would make me Your enemy. Amen.

Lesson:

Is it accurate to blame all of our struggles and trials on the direct attacks of the devil? In the book of James, the apostle presents three sources of our problems: the flesh, the world, and the devil. Though they interface and work together, each is unique and requires a proper biblical approach to deal with its particular pattern of temptation.

THE FLESH

The flesh is the *internal* enemy that causes fights, wars, lusts, and murders and can even corrupt our prayers. It is that sinful potential for doing evil that we inherited from the fall of man (see James 4:1–3).

List seven to ten specific examples of fleshly battlegrounds (note Galatians 5:19–21; Colossians 3:5–10):

_____

_____

_____

_____

THE WORLD

The world is an *external* enemy. The world—which encompasses philosophies, culture, entertainment, business, societies, worldviews, fashions, trends, religious orders, political systems, and so forth—tries to befriend us and win us over as allies and coconspirators. Choosing the world makes us an enemy of God. Remember, the world is as much under the curse of the

Fall as is humanity. The world offers us what our flesh wants and presents Satan's lies to us in appealing packages.

List seven to ten specific examples of worldly battlegrounds:

_____

_____

_____

_____

_____

SUPERNATURAL EVIL

The final enemy is supernatural evil (James 4:7–10 NKJV). Believers are commanded to "resist the devil." Scriptural imperatives such as "submit to God," "draw near to God," and "humble yourselves in the sight of the Lord" make clear that when we are in proper attitude to Him, our defeats by "infernal evil" will be minimal.

List seven to ten specific examples of demonic battlegrounds:

_____

_____

_____

_____

Ephesians 2:1–2 and other verses state clearly that Satan, for now, rules over this physical earth and has influence over everything on the earth. Not only does he seek to control the world, but he will use every worldly resource to threaten our spirit and soul. With his help, such seemingly innocent worlds as fashion, finance, entertainment, and even religion can turn us from God toward our own self-advancement.

(For further insight into resources available to the believer in resisting Satan, see *Raising Lambs Among Wolves,* pages 124–25, in Appendix A: Supplemental Readings.)

Circle **T** for True or **F** for False and then discuss your answers:

T **F** To walk in freedom requires the aggressive application of the provided victory and not just passive assumption.

T **F** Satan tempts believers to excuse their fleshly sins in order to take advantage of them.

T **F** Though Satan is not omnipresent like God, he functions with a diverse, organized kingdom of spirit-beings who can communicate with him instantaneously from any geographic location in the world.

T **F** The world is a global conspiracy that puts pressure on the believer to conform to its value system.

T **F** As personal spirit-beings, Satan and his host of fallen angels are able to project thoughts, emotions, and a rebellious attitude into the mind, will, emotions, and body of a believer.

T **F** It is always easy for believers to discern the difference between their own thoughts, emotions, and will from those of satanic origin.

T **F** If ground is given to the kingdom of darkness by a believer, internalized affliction, rule, and control will be experienced in that believer's life.

    T   F   Believers are provided ample resources available at any local Christian book-store for defeating Satan and walking in freedom from Satan's rule.

Every day believers are confronted with an endless stream of opportunities to opt out of faithful living and concede to the world's godless beliefs, attitudes, and philosophies. Sometimes the influences are so insistent and subtle, we accept, practice, and express views and ideas that are actually in conflict with the pure truth of the Gospel.

List and discuss examples of how you are being influenced by unscriptural ideas and beliefs:

_____

_____

What are some defenses you can deploy to resist and counter these influences?

_____

_____

Review/Conclusion:

While Satan may work to cause the forces of our flesh and the world to conspire against us, he and they are distinct forces we need to be aware of and stand guard against. Hanging Christian pictures and slogans around our home, listening only to Christian music, reading only Christian books, and watching only Christian videos are all OK things to do, but they alone will not protect us from the wiles of the Enemy. In fact, He can use these things to distract, insulate, and sedate us into complacency and error.

Our minds and lives need to be actively engaged in serving God, learning all that His Word offers, fellowshipping with genuine believers, and keeping ourselves prepared at all times to resist and defeat Satan and his kingdom.

LESSON 5: *You Are a Winner*

Scripture for Meditation:

My eyes have seen the defeat of my adversaries; my ears have heard the rout of my wicked foes. (Psalm 92:11)

A Beginning Prayer:

Lord Jesus Christ, in You I have success, sustenance, and security. I am seated with You in heavenly realms. You clothe me with righteousness. All that I am and have You have provided. Your promises and faithfulness surround me like a shield. There is nothing or no one who can come between You and me. Thank You that I am a winner as long as I persevere in the grace and strength You give me. Amen

Lesson:

Some final truths about who you are in Christ and where you stand.

(1) *You are a child of God.* As such you are to know your heavenly Father (Ephesians 1:17). Never are we instructed to know Satan in the same way we are to know God.

How can you know God?

_____

_____

(2) *You are to keep your eyes on Jesus* (Hebrews 12:1–2). Satan's trick is to get our eyes off of our Savior and focused on our problems, our weaknesses, our circumstances—anything other than Christ.

Where can you see Jesus?

_____

_____

(3) *You have the power of God* (Ephesians 1:19). The power we have access to as believers is God's power. His power is limitless and beyond our comprehension. It can fling mountains into the sea in a moment. It can open blind eyes at a word. It can stop storms instantly. It raises the dead to life. Don't limit what God can do in your life.

How do you limit God's unlimited power?

_____

_____

(4) *You can walk victorious* (Jude 24–25). Jim Logan says, "Getting free is easy; staying free is hard." But life's most precious trophies are those hardest won.

Have you walked victoriously this week? Give examples:

_____

_____

(5) *You will be delivered from the Enemy* (2 Timothy 4:18). God didn't create us to be homeless orphans whipped senseless by a defeated foe! Every circumstance we encounter serves a glorious purpose, and when the purpose is fulfilled, deliverance will come.

Describe times when you've experienced God's intervention and deliverance:

_____

_____

(6) *You are on the side that wins.* Satan and all those who serve and follow him are eternal losers:

> And I saw an angel coming down out of heaven, having the key to the Abyss and holding in his hand a great chain. He seized the dragon, that ancient serpent, who is the devil, or Satan, and bound him for a thousand years. He threw him into the Abyss, and locked and sealed it over him, to keep him from deceiving the nations anymore. . . . And the devil, who deceived them, was thrown into the lake of burning sulfur, where the beast and the false prophet had been thrown. They will be tormented day and night for ever and ever. (Revelation 20:1–3, 10)

Ephesians 1:15–23: *For this reason, ever since I heard about your faith in the Lord Jesus and your love for all the saints, I have not stopped giving thanks for you, remembering you in my prayers. I keep asking that the God of our Lord Jesus Christ, the glorious Father, may give you the Spirit of wisdom and revelation, so that you may know him better. I pray also that the eyes of your heart may be enlightened in order that you may know the hope to which he has called you, the riches of his glorious inheritance in the saints, and his incomparably great power for us who believe. That power is like the working of his mighty strength, which he exerted in Christ when he raised him from the dead and seated him at*

his right hand in the heavenly realms, far above all rule and authority, power and domin-
ion, and every title that can be given, not only in the present age but also in the one to come.
And God placed all things under his feet and appointed him to be head over everything for
the church, which is his body, the fullness of him who fills everything in every way.

What are some of the things God's wisdom will enable us to do, see, and be?

_____

_____

Do you really believe you're a winner in Christ? Why or why not? Discuss your answer. Be open and honest with your answer, as well as accepting and nonjudgmental of others' answers:

_____

_____

Review/Conclusion:

Wisdom for Christians is the ability to see life as God sees it. Our perspective is time-con-strained, myopic, and sin-hindered. God's vision for our lives and eternity is 20/20 and then some. God wants us to operate in His wisdom, and He makes His wisdom available to us. We need His wisdom (1) to understand who we are in Christ, (2) to see our enemy as he really is and isn't, and (3) to be able to recognize who our true allies are. Until you grasp the position, privileges, and power that are yours in Christ, you will be a candidate for defeat in spiritual warfare.

The reality, however, is that we are winners in spiritual warfare. In Him, we are covered, protected, strengthened, renewed, and blessed. God's will for us is to succeed in our Christian walk. To be victorious and strong. To defeat every fiery dart of the Enemy. God never desires for us something He will not also give us. We *have* the victory!

ETEB

*I*n the book *Maturity is a Choice,* by Karol Hess and Doug McCulley (Joplin, Mo.: College Press, 1994), Hess, the director of Beacon Light Christian Ministries in Watchung, New Jersey, describes a useful model for recognizing and defeating irra-tional thinking and behaving. The model is based on Rational Emotive Therapy as developed by psychologist Albert Ellis. The model is also known by the initials ETEB, representing the four steps: Event, Thought, Emotion, Behavior.

As Hess states, "This diagram provides a practical means of mapping our thinking processes and seeing how they affect our feelings and behavioral patterns. It helps identify thought patterns and compare them to the truth, including the truth about God and the facts of any given situation."

We've expanded and adapted the model, as shown on the next page.

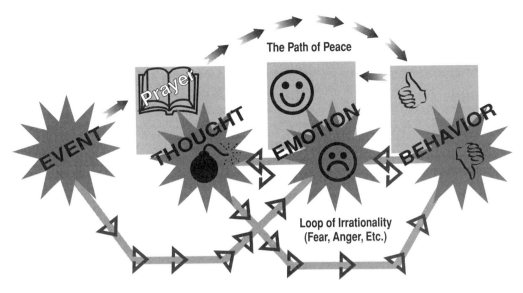

EVENT	THOUGHT	EMOTION	BEHAVIOR
We cannot control or foresee EVENTS.	We can control and change our THOUGHTS. Our MIND determines TRUTH.	We cannot control our EMOTIONS. Our EMOTIONS will come into line (tag along) with the TRUTH as we walk it out in a godly RESPONSE.	We can control and change our BEHAVIOR. Our WILL chooses our RESPONSE.
Since no man knows the future, who can tell him what is to come? –Ecclesiastes 8:7	We demolish arguments and every pretension that sets itself up against the knowledge of God, and we take captive every thought to make it obedient to Christ. –2 Corinthians 10:5 "For who has known the mind of the Lord that he may instruct him?" But we have the mind of Christ. –1 Corinthians 2:16	The heart is deceitful above all things and beyond cure. Who can understand it? I the Lord search the heart and examine the mind, to reward a man according to his conduct, according to what his deeds deserve. –Jeremiah 17:9–10	So whether you eat or drink or whatever you do, do it all for the glory of God. –1 Corinthians 10:31

To really live this model successfully when unexpected events break upon us, our entire lives must be built and maintained upon a solid FOUNDATION of being in the WORD, walking in the SPIRIT, and spending time in PRAYER and FASTING.

Stuff happens. Often we encounter situations that are unexpected and over which we have no control. Our only choice is to respond to them in Christian integrity. In the midst of these events, our emotions will be engaged and flare up automatically. These emotions can be positive or negative. In the midst of an event with our emotions on full flare-up, we have two choices:

- We can react based on our perceptions and emotions, which means to react irrationally; or
- We can choose to respond thoughtfully to the reality of the situation, with our minds and spirits fully engaged, and we can ask the Holy Spirit to fill our emotions with the fruit of His control in the truth of God's Word (Galatians 5:22–23).

Reacting irrationally will put us in an escalating "Loop of Irrationality," where emotions, such as fear, guilt, arrogance, lust, or anger, drive our behavior into irresponsible and damaging actions. These further feed our fear, guilt, arrogance, lust, anger, or other emotions, which drives more improper behavior, and so on.

Responding thoughtfully will establish us firmly on the "Path of Peace," where our minds, filled with God's truth, seek a biblical and Christlike, self-dying response, where our actions are controlled by the Holy Spirit. We focus on truth and not on emotions. As we live out this truth, our emotions settle down and come in line as well.

For example, imagine that you're at work and you're working on completing a report that has an imminent deadline. The report is related to a project that's very important to you and involving material you are fascinated by. You're totally focused on your work and your back is turned away from the entrance to your cubicle. You've purposely blocked out all the ambient office noise, concentrating intently on your work. You're in your own little world, unaware of anything else around you.

Suddenly, without warning, someone has slipped into your cubicle behind you, dropped a binder down on your desk, and said loudly, "Here's the report you were asking me about last week. Sorry it took me so long to find it!"

You have no control over this event, and your emotions—in the form of your heart in your throat—are fully engaged. Acting out of your emotions, you likely would be enraged by the insensitivity of this coworker, who seems to be totally rude and bent on causing you to miss your deadline. If you were to follow through and react, you might yell at him for being a jerk, ordering him to get out of your cubicle immediately. He might then react by shouting back at you, calling you a jerk, and so on, as you both huff and puff your way around the Loop of Irrationality.

The result would be a disrupted relationship, a disrupted workplace, and a foothold made for Satan to create increasing hostility, hurt, and resentment.

However, taking a moment to think, you realize your coworker was doing what you asked him to do (bringing you the report) and didn't realize you were so focused. You know this person and you know him to be courteous and pleasant. He would never do anything intentionally to disrupt another's success. You turn, put your hand over your heart, and say thanks. He realizes what he's done and is profusely apologetic for scaring you. You both have a small chuckle over the incident and everything is fine.

It's good in such moments to admit to yourself and the Lord that your fleshly response would have been anger. Affirm that through the Cross you are dead to the rule of your flesh and ask the Holy Spirit to replace the fleshly anger with the control of His fruit.

The reality is that your coworker didn't mean to startle you. However, your emotions are still engaged and your heart is still beating rapidly! Yet, you know there is nothing to be fearful of or angry about, and you turn back to your work. In a few minutes, your emotions and your thoughts are once again totally engaged in your project. All is well as you quietly travel the Path of Peace.

The walk of *honesty and confession* (Colossians 3:5–10); the walk *in the truth of your death with Christ* (Romans 6:11; Galatians 5:24; Colossians 3:3, 5); and the walk *in the control of the Holy Spirit* (Galatians 5:16, 18, 22–23, 25) are among the steps to follow in overcoming the fleshly responses described in Galatians 5:19–21. For a more extended discussion of this subject, see excerpts from *Raising Lambs Among Wolves*, pages 135–39, to be found in Appendix A: Supplemental Readings, readings for <u>Unit 7</u> (not this unit!). (Please note that pages 135–39 in *Raising Lambs* include more than the discussion of the three "walks," so you'll need to read a bit into the excerpt to find that material.)

Using the table below, think of types of situations and events you encounter at home, at work, at church, or somewhere else. Break down the elements of each event, and describe the emotions you would feel and the irrational and rational thoughts and behaviors you might experience and respond with. Also list additional Scriptures that illustrate the truth of each step.

EVENT	THOUGHT	EMOTION	BEHAVIOR
Situation:			
Situation:			
Situation:			
Situation:			

Satan loves to put situations before us that will inflame our emotions. He knows that the power of emotions—both good and bad—can overwhelm our reason and our faith and lead us into sinful and destructive behaviors. Whether we're caught up by the seductive lie that it just feels so good it can't be bad or we're lashing out in self-righteous anger to get even, acting out our emotions can be spiritually deadly.

Satan knows that our (E)motions can easily subvert the good intentions of our (M)ind and (W)ills. He will attempt to puff up our emotions and thus lead us into conflict, anger, hurt, disappointment, lust, addictions, and more. Only as we submit to the cross of Christ, crucifying the flesh-man, and bring our (M)ind, (W)ill, and (E)motions into subjection to Him will we find the healthy balance we need to live out our faith successfully.

THE ARMOR OF GOD

Scripture Memory Verses:

Finally, be strong in the Lord and in his mighty power. Put on the full armor of God so that you can take your stand against the devil's schemes. For our struggle is not against flesh and blood, but against the rulers, against the authorities, against the powers of this dark world and against the spiritual forces of evil in the heavenly realms.

Therefore put on the full armor of God, so that when the day of evil comes, you may be able to stand your ground, and after you have done everything, to stand.

Stand firm then, with the belt of truth buckled around your waist, with the breastplate of righteousness in place, and with your feet fitted with the readiness that comes from the gospel of peace.

In addition to all this, take up the shield of faith, with which you can extinguish all the flaming arrows of the evil one.

Take the helmet of salvation and the sword of the Spirit, which is the word of God.

And pray in the Spirit on all occasions with all kinds of prayers and requests. With this in mind, be alert and always keep on praying for all the saints. (Ephesians 6:10–18)

Unit Learning Goal:

Becoming armored and armed for warfare.

Overview of Unit 3:

Lesson 1: Taking a Stand

Lesson 2: Belt, Breastplate, and Boots

Lesson 3: A Shield of Safety

Lesson 4: Head and Hand

Lesson 5: Persistent Prayer

SUMMARY STATEMENT

Each day we need to dress for spiritual warfare and take up our sword.

Unit 3 Thought Focus:

In Ephesians 6, Paul detailed for us how we are to practically prepare for spiritual warfare. Warfare is not passive and neither is preparation. As believers we are to aggressively act in taking the armor and putting it on. In fact, this act of "being clothed" or "putting on" such elements of our faith as peace, righteousness, love, and humility is a steady theme throughout Scripture.

The Bible describes a richly varied spiritual wardrobe available to us as God's children—King's kids' clothing. Consider these verses:

> I delight greatly in the Lord; my soul rejoices in my God. For he has clothed me with garments of salvation and arrayed me in a robe of righteousness, as a bridegroom adorns his head like a priest, and as a bride adorns herself with her jewels. (Isaiah 61:10)

> Now Joshua was dressed in filthy clothes as he stood before the angel. The angel said to those who were standing before him, "Take off his filthy clothes." Then he said to Joshua, "See, I have taken away your sin, and I will put rich garments on you." Then I said, "Put a clean turban on his head." So they put a clean turban on his head and clothed him, while the angel of the LORD stood by. (Zechariah 3:3–5)

> You turned my wailing into dancing; you removed my sackcloth and clothed me with joy, that my heart may sing to you and not be silent. O Lord my God, I will give you thanks forever. (Psalm 30:11–12)

> For the perishable must clothe itself with the imperishable, and the mortal with immortality. (1 Corinthians 15:53)

And there are many, many more verses, such as Romans 13:12–14; Colossians 3:12; 1 Peter 5:5; Galatians 3:26–27; and 2 Corinthians 5:1–3. There are even descriptions of the sinner's spiritual clothing:

> Therefore pride is their necklace; they clothe themselves with violence. (Psalm 73:6)

> My accusers will be clothed with disgrace and wrapped in shame as in a cloak. (Psalm 109:29)

> For drunkards and gluttons become poor, and drowsiness clothes them in rags. (Proverbs 23:21)

> "Watch out for false prophets. They come to you in sheep's clothing, but inwardly they are ferocious wolves." (Matthew 7:15)

So, who decides which clothes we wear? In Ephesians and elsewhere, Paul says *we* are to "put off" the old and "put on" the new (see Ephesians 4:22–24; 6:11–13; Colossians 3:10, 14). Just as we choose what shirt and slacks, or blouse and skirt we'll wear every morning, so too we choose what spiritual clothing we'll wear each day and in each temptation we'll face that day.

How we dress spiritually will affect our attitudes, moods, and effectiveness. How well we dress our spirits will impact others. We need to choose to put on clothes that are washed in His forgiveness and freshly pressed by His mercy and throw out those old rags of self-righteousness.

It's a daily activity, since we can't get dressed once and for all. And if we get dirtied during the day, or start out in the wrong outfit, we can always choose to change into fresh clothes anytime.

Layering with holiness, purity, love, peace, and humility is always fashionable. And there's no better power suit than one tailored with faithfulness, righteousness, and compassion. Before you go out, check yourself in the mirror one more time. Are you dressed like the King's kid—*très chic*—or a candidate for the spiritually worst-dressed list?

LESSON 1: *Taking a Stand*

Scripture for Meditation:

I delight greatly in the Lord; my soul rejoices in my God. For he has clothed me with garments of salvation and arrayed me in a robe of righteousness, as a bridegroom adorns his head like a priest, and as a bride adorns herself with her jewels. (Isaiah 61:10)

A Beginning Prayer:

O gracious heavenly Father, You are beyond the reach of my mind, yet You are nearer to me than anyone else. On You I rely for all I need. In You I rest from all that troubles me. I lay down before Your throne all my strategies, all my plans, all my answers, all my choices. I pick up the tools of grace You provide and, on the sure foundation of Your truth, build my life as You guide my hands. Counsel me now through Your Word and Your Holy Spirit and open my understanding that my resolve to serve You would be greatly strengthened. As I am faithful to study Your Word, equip me to use Your Word effectively in battle. Amen.

Lesson:

In Ephesians 4:1, Paul states, "As a prisoner for the Lord, then, I urge you to live a life worthy of the calling you have received." Over the next two-and-half chapters or so he explains *how* we are to "live a life worthy" as individuals before the Lord and in our various relationships.

Then, about a third of the way through the last chapter, he states:

Finally, be strong in the Lord and in his mighty power. Put on the full armor of God so that you can take your stand against the devil's schemes. For our struggle is not against flesh and blood, but against the rulers, against the authorities, against the powers of this dark world and against the spiritual forces of evil in the heavenly realms. Therefore put on the full armor of God, so that when the day of evil comes, you may be able to stand your ground, and after you have done everything, to stand. (6:10–13)

Before launching into the detailed description of what the "full armor of God" is, Paul explains *why* we need to be armored: so that we can stand our ground.

Repetition is a common literary device found in Scripture. It is a natural way to emphasize the importance of something. In Scripture, anything that is mentioned three times indicates that it is of the utmost importance. And Paul refers to taking a stand *four* times within four verses.

What does it mean *to stand?* To take a stand is a frame of mind, a position, and an act of commitment. These three are tightly interrelated.

A FRAME OF MIND: ALERT AND KNOWLEDGEABLE

Throughout our lives we are called upon to take a stand for one thing or against another. What kinds of stands have you had to take in your relationships, in your home, on your job, in your community?

_____

_____

What were the outcomes of these stands, both positive and negative?

_____

_____

_____

Second Thessalonians 2:15: *So then, brothers, stand firm and hold to the teachings we passed on to you, whether by word of mouth or by letter.*

How do we learn things? Circle all the letters that apply:
   A. From reading books
   B. By going to school and church
   C. Through experiencing new things
   D. From allowing information to enter into and stay in our minds

All of the above items are correct, but the last is essential to learning. How we think about something, based on the information and truth we have received, will determine what type of stand we take on an issue. We frequently take ideological stands, or political stands, or stands on social issues. And we do so based on how we *think* about these things. And what we think is based upon what we *know.* The more we know about something, the more informed our thinking is, and the more solid our stand will be.

What are some of the big news events currently grabbing headlines nationally? In your state? In the town where you live?

_____

_____

What are your opinions about each of these current events?

_____

_____

Of these opinions, which do you hold most fervently and confidently?

_____

_____

Of the opinions you hold most strongly, are these the things you know the most about? Are these opinions truly informed, fact-based opinions? Since they are fed by facts, aren't you more convinced of the validity of your opinions?

_____

_____

When we put on the armor of God, it will be useless to us if we are not convinced in our own minds of its power. To be "strong . . . in his mighty power," I must know God. To stand firm upon the Word of God, I must be familiar with the Scriptures. To fight successfully against my enemy, I must understand who the Enemy is and the tactics and strategies my enemy relies on. In the King James Version, 1 Peter 1:13 declares, "Gird up the loins of your mind." To be effective in warfare, we must have a proper frame of mind. Being "strong . . . in his mighty power" is also a direct reference to the inner work of the Holy Spirit (see Luke 24:49; Acts 1:8).

A POSITION: STANDING

Romans 5:1–2: *Therefore, since we have been justified through faith, we have peace with God through our Lord Jesus Christ, through whom we have gained access by faith into this grace in which we now stand. And we rejoice in the hope of the glory of God.*

Stand also refers to position, and position can mean both our physical position and our spiritual position in Christ. Just as we must be upright before the Lord (which we are through grace), we have to stand up to get dressed!

To defend yourself in a battle, which position do you believe is the most effective? Circle all the letters that apply:

        A. Hiding behind a tree

        B. Lying down on your back

        C. Standing up

        D. Sitting comfortably

If you're covered with the rags of your sinfulness, can you stand before the gaze of the Lord? No! In fact, when we have fallen and have failed to quickly confess our sin to the Lord, we are downcast and burdened. Our sin literally bends us over with the weight of the guilt. We focus our eyes down and keep our heads lowered. Our shoulders stoop. Our whole demeanor is listless. The energy and joy is sapped from our lives. When we are in this state, it's difficult enough getting dressed in the clothes from our closet, let alone trying to put on our spiritual armor!

Complete the blanks in this verse and change the incorrect words using the NIV:

_____ we _____ our sins, he is _____ and just and will _____ us our sins and _____ us from some of our unrighteousness. (1 John 1:9)

In 1 John 1:9, who is it that forgives our sins? Circle all the letters that apply:

        A. The pastor

        B. The judge from People's Court

        C. The people we've sinned against

        D. God

In 1 John 1:9, how much of our sin does God cleanse us from? Circle all the letters that apply:

        A. Only as much as we confess

        B. Just a little bit

        C. Most of our sin

        D. All of our sin

Circle **T** for True or **F** for False and then discuss your answers:

  T   **F**   Once I've confessed my sin, I am always in right standing before God as far as that sin/those sins are concerned.

T   F   Before I'm truly cleansed from sin, I have to confess them all over and over again, whether they're old sins or new sins, until I really *feel* like I'm forgiven.

T   F   I'm only forgiven and cleansed from my sin if I feel forgiven, even if I've fully confessed my sin.

A COMMITMENT: NOT TO MOVE

Exodus 14:13–14: *Moses answered the people, "Do not be afraid. Stand firm and you will see the deliverance the Lord will bring you today. The Egyptians you see today you will never see again. The Lord will fight for you; you need only to be still."*

Proverbs 10:25: *When the storm has swept by, the wicked are gone, but the righteous stand firm forever.*

Finally, taking a stand means making a commitment not to move. It means resolving to be firm even when doing so may seem irrational to the natural mind. So often we're confronted with an attack of the Enemy that seems impossible to overcome. We panic and run! Or, the attack comes directly against our character. We flail out in anger!

In our flesh, when we are confronted, we tend to want to *do* something. We'll defend ourselves, justify our behavior, explain ourselves, push back, accuse someone else, cast blame, and on and on. We are compelled to take some sort of defensive action. Often, the most effective defensive action is the one that never comes to mind because it makes absolutely no sense to our fleshly minds: *stand still.* Wait on the Lord.

And this is exactly what God calls us to time after time. When we stand still, or stand firm in the Lord, control of the outcome of a situation is taken completely out of our hands and placed in God's hands. It means fully trusting in Him to deliver us from the storm no matter how loud or how hard the storm rages. Before we can stand firm in the Lord we have to know Him and be convinced in our minds of who He is—and you need to be standing upright before Him.

The results of standing firm in the Lord—just standing—will be dramatic. First, it will be readily evident to you and to everyone else that the results came from God's efforts on your behalf, not from your own efforts. Second, it will defeat the Enemy because he has no answer to God's doings.

Think about this a minute. When a situation becomes chaotic and confusing, and you are getting upset and loud with someone, yet they remain cool, calm, and collected in the midst of your turmoil, how does that make you feel? It makes you crazy! "How can you just stand there and not react?" you yell.

When Satan comes against us he wants us to react. He wants us to get worked up so we'll get worn down. He wants us to take the little things he's tripped us with and explode them into major, soul-killing offenses. He pushes our buttons, hoping we will self-destruct! And he will use others to push those buttons, confuse our words, misinterpret our actions, and remind us of our failings.

Can you think of situations where you "got crazy"? List them:

_____

_____

How *should* we respond? By confessing our sin, accepting God's forgiveness, and standing firm in the reality that we are hidden in Christ. When the storm passes, Satan and his wicked agents will be swept away, and we will still be standing.

Describe and discuss a recent situation where, instead of standing, you reacted and made the situation worse. Then, think and pray quietly, and ask the Holy Spirit to reveal to you an alternative response you could have made that would have been a way of standing still in the Lord:

_____

_____

To take a stand means what? Circle all the letters that apply:

   A. It involves having the right frame of mind.
   B. It is my spiritual position in Christ and verbalizing that in resistance.
   C. It means to make a sure commitment to something.
   D. It means standing up on my feet.
   E. It means being upright in my spirit before the Lord.

Standing involves

   1. our union with Christ "in the Lord" (Ephesians 6:10a);
   2. the working of the Holy Spirit "in his mighty power" (v. 10b);
   3. the "full armor of God" (vv. 11–17); and
   4. the all-encompassing nature of prayer (vv. 18–20).

It's good in a crisis situation where Satan's pressures are very powerful to state aloud, "I resist this power of darkness in my union with my Lord Jesus Christ. I resist you in the power of the Holy Spirit. I resist you in the whole armor of God and in the power of prayer."

Review/Conclusion:

To take a stand is a frame of mind, a position, and an act of commitment. As Christians, standing in the authority and power of God is our call, our duty, and our right. Just as in the business world dressing for success is about more than the clothes we wear but also involves the attitude we project through our actions, words, and demeanor, all of which enhance our success, so to in the spiritual realm.

God's desire is to make us into His bride, clothed in robes of righteousness (Isaiah 61:10), "a radiant church, without stain or wrinkle or any other blemish, but holy and blameless" (Ephesians 5:27).

But first, we need to put on the armor and do some battle!

LESSON 2: *Belt, Breastplate, and Boots*

Scripture for Meditation:
You are all sons of God through faith in Christ Jesus, for all of you who were baptized into Christ have clothed yourselves with Christ. (Galatians 3:26–27)

A Beginning Prayer:
Lord Jesus Christ, I take off the garment of my self and clothe myself with You. Amen.

Lesson:

THE BELT OF TRUTH

The first piece of armor we are told to put on is the belt of truth. The belt, or girdle, of a Roman soldier in New Testament times was a critical item. It was wide and protected the lower torso, which is frequently referred to in the Bible as the "loins," and it held the sword. Men didn't wear pants in ancient times, but instead wore robes. While those robes were practical garb for the Middle Eastern arid climate, they were impractical for battle. So, before going into conflict, a soldier would "gird up his loins," which meant pulling the hem of his robe up between his legs, and tucking it into his belt. With his loins girded in this manner, he gained more mobility.

Why does Paul call this the "belt of truth"? Because truth is central to all things and holds all things together. To apply truth to one's life, one must understand what truth is.

How did Jesus define truth? See John 17:17.

_____

_____

Based on John 17:17, how would you now define truth? Is it a body of knowledge? A thing? An experience? A person?

_____

_____

In light of John 17:17, what does Galatians 3:26–27 mean to you?

_____

_____

Truth is a person: Jesus Christ. To buckle the belt of truth around ourselves is to put on Christ.

What power does wearing the belt of truth give us as Christians? See John 8:32; 2 Corinthians 10:4.

_____

_____

Knowing the truth gives us the confidence and freedom to destroy strongholds and stand firmly against the lies of Satan.

THE BREASTPLATE OF RIGHTEOUSNESS

The next item we are to put on is the breastplate of righteousness. The breastplate covers the upper torso, front and back. It covers some of the most vital organs, including the heart. Guarding one's heart is critical in spiritual warfare. A key tactic of Satan is to instill fear, doubt, lustful desires, and other confusing emotions into our hearts. Temptations often revolve around our emotional responses.

However, Satan knows that if he can get us focused on what we feel instead of what we know, he can lead us into all sorts of deception and sinful behavior.

What did Jesus say comes out of our hearts? See Matthew 15:17–19; Mark 7:21–23.

_____

_____

Can emotions be trusted? See Jeremiah 17:9.

_____

_____

When we open our mouths, what's in our hearts will come out (Matthew 12:34). If there are good things in us, good things come out. If there is evil in our hearts, evil things come out of our mouths (v. 35).

Righteousness is a product of salvation. Salvation is ours through the blood of Christ. When we accepted Christ as our Savior, "our hearts [were] sprinkled to cleanse us from a guilty conscience" (Hebrews 10:22). Left to our own devices our hearts would be dark as night. However, just as David called out, "Create in me a pure heart, O God, and renew a steadfast spirit within me" (Psalm 51:10), and was cleansed, so can we be cleansed. God puts in us a new heart that we guard by putting on the breastplate of righteousness every day.

A common phrase related to computers is "garbage in, garbage out," meaning that if bad data is put in, bad data will result. The same is true with our lives and hearts. List some practical ways we can guard our own hearts and the hearts of our family members from taking in garbage:

_____

_____

THE SHOES (BOOTS) OF PEACE AND READINESS

Third on Paul's list are the boots, or shoes, of peace and readiness. To be shoeless on a hot beach or bootless in a blizzard is dreadful. Hiking in dress shoes leads to blisters. Wearing high heels to go grocery shopping is vain and foolish. Wearing the appropriate spiritual shoes is critical to our ability to stand in the midst of warfare.

(Peace *with* God, the peace *of* God, and the *God of peace* are important concepts in this spiritual warfare we are engaged in. For more information, see the excerpts from *Overcoming the Adversary,* pages 85–91, printed out in Appendix A: Supplemental Readings.)

In a warfare situation, we need spiritual army boots: shoes that are rugged and thick-soled to provide traction in any terrain, protecting and supporting our ankles, and impervious to weather and wet.

In 2 John 1:6, how is the Christian life described?

_____

_____

What are the characteristics of someone who is walking with the Lord?

_____

_____

In Isaiah 52:7, how are feet described?

_____

_____

What is the message of those who have beautiful feet?

_____

_____

According to Psalm 119:105, how are we to determine where to walk as Christians? How will we be able to see the way?

_____

_____

Who will shine on our lives and guide our feet into peace? (See Luke 1:78–79.)

_____

_____

Review/Conclusion:

Truth is impotent without application. Truth applied transforms us from the inside out. Buckling the belt of truth around the sensitive areas of our lives protects us from the lies of Satan. It also enhances our appearance to others as the effects of truth emanate from our person. After all, truth is a person, and when others look at us, our desire is that they see Christ.

There are four biblical areas of truth: the *Word* of truth, the Bible; the *person* of truth, the Lord Jesus Christ; the *Spirit* of truth, the Holy Spirit; the *pillars* and *foundation* of truth, the church. (For further information on this subject, see the excerpts from *Overcoming the Adversary*, pages 67–69, printed out in Appendix A: Supplemental Readings.)

Clothing ourselves with Christ is an act of the will, not a passive happening. We choose to put on Christ, to buckle on the belt of truth, to gird up our loins with integrity and trustworthiness. And we guard our hearts and desires as we allow our lives to be hidden in Christ.

Putting on the breastplate of righteousness is like putting on a bright red blazer with a crest on the pocket. The red is the blood of Christ that covers us in power and cleansing. The crest is a sign to the Enemy that the throne of our hearts is occupied by the King of kings, and there's no room in our lives for any other would-be ruler.

Armored with truth and righteousness, we are ready "in season and out of season" (2 Timothy 4:2) to accurately, bravely, lovingly, and peacefully share the Good News of salvation with all we encounter. Our goal is to not only live in peace with others, but to share with them the peace that surpasses understanding and is found only in Christ.

With our minds set on the Lord and fitted with the belt, breastplate, and boots of God's armor, we will be able to stand firmly as the battle rages around us, waiting on God's deliverance.

LESSON 3: *A Shield of Safety*

Scripture for Meditation:

Therefore, as God's chosen people, holy and dearly loved, clothe yourselves with compassion, kindness, humility, gentleness and patience. (Colossians 3:12)

A Beginning Prayer:

Lord Jesus Christ, be my shield and my great reward. Surround me with favor as with a shield. Cover my life with Your shield of victory. Be my strength and my shield as I trust in You. Let me find refuge and safety in the shield of Your love and truth. Amen.

Lesson:

THE SHIELD OF FAITH

In the King James, Ephesians 6:16 starts out, "Above all." The soldier's shield was his defense against those things, such as flaming arrows, that flew in at him from overhead. By holding his shield up he could protect himself from a variety of angles. He could also use the shield in close combat to deflect blows from his opponent's sword or dagger. The shield was a valuable and versatile tool of defense. For the Christian, the shield of faith is essential. The Lord is our shield. He protects us from the Enemy's sword and the fiery darts and arrows he sends our way. Our faith is focused on who Christ is and on what He has done.

Faith gives us:

F = *Forgiveness* of sin
A = *Assurance* of salvation
I = *Identification* in God's family
T = *Triumph* over Satan
H = *Hope* of deliverance

Very simply, faith is believing what God has said to us in His Word. This is our strength since we stand not in what we think or feel, but on the absolute truth of what God has said. God never changes; His promises never change. However, our thinking is imperfect and shifts as we gain more knowledge and experience, and our emotions are totally fickle.

How do we defeat the flaming darts and arrows that Satan throws at us? Circle all the letters that apply:

A. By exerting the power of positive thinking

B. By daily reading our Bible and memorizing Scripture

C. By eating right, exercising daily, and drinking lots of water

D. By taking up the shield of faith

E. By feeling good about our bodies and ourselves

F. By believing in the promises of God

Some of the darts and arrows Satan fires at us include doubts, accusations, fears, misinformation, and confusion. List as many other darts and arrows as you can think of, and, including those already given, discuss specific ways you can apply faith to quench these attacks:

_____

_____

_____

_____

THE DART SLINGERS

Satan's organization is structured much like the military. In Ephesians 6:12, Paul mentions four general groupings of demonic spirits we battle against.

(1) First are the *rulers (principalities,* KJV*)*. Much like a prince is appointed as a ruler of a municipality, so this level of demons are appointed to govern over specific geographical areas.

This concept is raised in the book of Daniel, chapter 10. Daniel had been praying for twenty-one days without response. Finally, an angel actually made an appearance and explained to Daniel that his prayers had been heard from the first day. However, the angel had been delayed by the demonic prince of Persia until the archangel Michael came to his aid.

Read Daniel 10. What are some of the things we can learn from this story? Circle all the letters that apply:

A. The prayers of a righteous person can accomplish a great deal.

B. Praying without ceasing brings results.

C. Daniel was somehow more special than we are.

D. Angels, both good and bad, are just make-believe.

E. Spiritual warfare requires both prayer and fasting.

F. Angels will always visit us in answer to our prayers.

(2) The second group of demons are the *authorities* (*powers*, KJV). These demons seek to exert power and authority over individuals' lives. Their goal is to insinuate themselves into the lives of believers especially and to influence them into wrong behavior in order to destroy them.

(3) Third are the *powers of this dark world* (*rulers of the darkness of this world*, KJV). This group of demons is assigned to those in leadership roles, including pastors and other church leaders. These demons attempt to influence the behavior and decisions of politicians, kings, presidents, corporate executives, and others who have positions of influence and power.

Circle **T** for True or **F** for False and then discuss your answers:

T   F   One of Satan's clever strategies against us is to keep us in ignorance of his power and working.

T   F   Those under persistent demonic attack often become preoccupied with thoughts about the temptations and oppression being pressed on them rather than meditating on the victory Christ has won.

T   F   Christians should be fearfully preoccupied with Satan and his kingdom, rebuking demons in every shadow.

T   F   Satan loves to plant wicked thoughts and desires in our minds and then accuse and taunt us for being such a terrible person to entertain such horrible thoughts.

T   F   While Satan can never tell the whole truth, there are moments when demons are totally honest and truthful when they are confronted.

(4) Finally, Paul mentions *spiritual forces of evil in the heavenly realms* (*spiritual wickedness in high places*, KJV). These appear to be demons associated with religions. These are responsible for perverting the truth and leading people into deceptions. They are at the heart of cults, New Age philosophies, and other alluring false ideas. Irrational fanaticism that often leads to self-destruction is a common result of the work of these demons.

List and discuss the characteristics of modern-day groups that most likely have been influenced by this fourth group of demons:

_____

_____

Review/Conclusion:

Satan and his demons are cut from the same cloth. They are all liars all the time. They will do anything and everything they can, using every means of subtle deception to steal our peace, kill our joy, and destroy our freedom. They can never be trusted to tell the truth. Even when they quote the Scripture they distort it. Their fiery darts and arrows will come at us fast, furious, and nonstop from all directions.

But as we stand firmly, clad in God's grace-provided armor and wielding the shield of total faith in Him and His promises, we never have to worry about or fear hell's attacks. God is love and perfect, and perfect love removes all fear. In Him we can stand confident and steadfast in the face of every spiritual opponent that is sent against us.

Just as the Enemy is persistent, we must pray without ceasing and build each other up in holy faith. Faith is active and aggressive. And we have a vast resource of help on which to depend. For every demon in service to Satan, there are two heavenly angels backed by an all-powerful God to stand in their way.

By keeping our eyes on Jesus, who is the way, the truth, and the life, and who is the author and perfecter of our faith, our feet will stay firmly on the path of righteousness. Our focus is on Him. Our energies are to be expended on living fruitful lives and walking in wisdom. Fear has no place in our lives.

LESSON 4: *Head and Hand*

Scripture for Meditation:

"Now arise, O Lord God, and come to your resting place, you and the ark of your might. May your priests, O Lord God, be clothed with salvation, may your saints rejoice in your goodness." (2 Chronicles 6:41)

A Beginning Prayer:

Dear Lord Jesus Christ, let Your salvation cover me and protect my thoughts from the Enemy. Wash me with Your Word. Renew my life through the transforming power of Your redemption and holiness. Teach me how to wield Your Word wisely and effectively in all areas of my life. Amen.

Lesson:

THE HELMET OF SALVATION

In Ephesians 6:17 Paul speaks of putting on the helmet of salvation. A helmet is simply a head covering of hard material, such as leather, metal, or plastic, worn to protect the head.

List as many instances as you can think of where helmets are worn today (for example, by football players, firemen, etc.):

_____

_____

Frequently the news media will carry stories about motorcyclists, bicyclists, or skiers who have sustained serious head injuries or died in an accident due to their not wearing helmets. Many states now have laws requiring that helmets and protective headgear be worn to operate a motorcycle or ride a bike. Injuries to the head are serious and often life threatening.

A head injury can be the root cause behind some mental impairment, chronic headaches, distorted vision, and other serious problems. While infections in any part of the body need immediate treatment, an infection in a head wound (the head being everything from the neck up) requires prompt and proper treatment to prevent the infection from reaching the brain.

Below, check the items and activities that are related to the head. Discuss your responses.

❑   1. Thinking
❑   2. Eating
❑   3. Praying
❑   4. Seeing
❑   5. Hearing
❑   6. Deciding
❑   7. Understanding
❑   8. Feeling
❑   9. Loving
❑ 10. Learning
❑ 11. Speaking
❑ 12. Caring

How important is our head? Protecting and caring for our heads is critical, particularly in spiritual warfare. Satan's forces can and do project thoughts into our minds that tempt us to act independently of the will of God. However, since all angels, both good and bad, lack omniscience, only God can read our thoughts and see into our hearts.

How do we fight against thoughts planted by Satan? Paul says in Romans 12:2, "Do not conform any longer to the pattern of this world, but *be transformed by the renewing of your mind.* Then you will be able to test and approve what God's will is—his good, pleasing and perfect will" (italics added). And further, in 2 Corinthians 10:5, he says, "We demolish arguments and every pretension that sets itself up against the knowledge of God, and we take captive every thought to make it obedient to Christ."

Below, check the items/activities that will help us guard our heads. Discuss your responses.

❑   1. Thinking pure thoughts
❑   2. Eating God's Word
❑   3. Praying for our enemies
❑   4. Viewing violent television shows
❑   5. Listening to gossip
❑   6. Choosing to die to ourselves daily
❑   7. Understanding God's will
❑   8. Feeling secure in Christ
❑   9. Loving our own comfort more than that of others
❑ 10. Learning the truths of the Gospel
❑ 11. Speaking to others about salvation
❑ 12. Caring about what God cares about

Putting on the helmet of salvation means filling our minds with the truth of God's Word. We wash our minds through the cleansing of the Word (Ephesians 5:26), and we are set free by knowing the truth (John 8:32).

What does *salvation* mean?

The American Heritage Dictionary offers some insightful definitions: It means to be saved or rescued! It means to be preserved or delivered from destruction, difficulty, or evil. It means deliverance from the power and penalty of sin. It means extrication from danger or confinement. In a word, it means *redemption.*

Exodus 15:2 says, "The Lord is my strength and my song; he has become my salvation. He is my God, and I will praise him, my father's God, and I will exalt him." David states in Psalm 27:1, "The Lord is my light and my salvation—whom shall I fear? The Lord is the stronghold of my life—of whom shall I be afraid?" Finally, in Revelation 12:10, John declares, "Then I heard a loud voice in heaven say: 'Now have come the salvation and the power and the kingdom of our God, and the authority of his Christ. For the accuser of our brothers, who accuses them before our God day and night, has been hurled down.'"

Ask Him to protect your mind from Satan's intruding thoughts and to put His mind within you and think His thoughts.

Based on the previous few paragraphs, discuss and write out your own definition of biblical salvation and what salvation means to you as a Christian:

_____

_____

Now, based on what you've discussed and written above about salvation, discuss and describe practical ways you can put on and keep on the helmet of salvation (see also 1 Thessalonians 5:8–9):

_____

_____

THE SWORD OF THE SPIRIT

In Ephesians, Paul also directs us to take up "the sword of the Spirit, which is the word of God" (6:17). Knowing the truth and Word of God is not enough. We must also renounce "the hidden things of dishonesty, not walking in craftiness, nor handling the word of God deceitfully; but by manifestation of the truth commending ourselves to every man's conscience in the sight of God" (2 Corinthians 4:2 KJV).

We are called to handle the Word of God with integrity and honesty. As with any weapon, the Word of God can be used for good or evil. It's vitally important that when we apply biblical truths to our own lives, or to the situations of others, that we do so accurately and lovingly.

Can you think of some ways the Word of God has been misused by Christians resulting in error and hurt? List them and discuss them:

_____

_____

Satan knows the Bible. He used Scripture to try to tempt Christ. He distorted God's words to confuse Eve in the garden. And even today, Satan will stir up all manner of wickedness under the guise of God's Word. There are many cults and ungodly organizations, such as the KKK and other racist groups, who twist and distort the truths of Scripture to fit their own ends.

Using the sword of God's Word with precision, we can strike deadly blows to the enemies of our soul. Paul writes in Hebrews 4:12, "For the word of God is living and active. Sharper than any double-edged sword, it penetrates even to dividing soul and spirit, joints and marrow; it judges the thoughts and attitudes of the heart." Revelation 12:11 says, "They overcame him by the blood of the Lamb and by the word of their testimony." In the story of David's encounter with Goliath (1 Samuel 17) we are given a powerful and encouraging example of how we can slay our spiritual enemies. Read 1 Samuel 17 and discuss and answer these questions:

What was David's weapon of choice to go out to battle with?

_____

_____

How many stones did David select for his sling? Why?

_____

_____

How did David kill Goliath?

_____

_____

After David killed Goliath, what did he do to the giant?

_____

_____

What weapon did David use to kill and behead Goliath?

_____

_____

Whose sword did David use to kill Goliath?

_____

_____

Is there any doubt that God was behind David's victory?

_____

_____

The Enemy of our souls may carry a sword in knowing God's Word. But Satan is always a liar, and when he tries to wield this sword, it is powerless. In his hands, it is always dulled and bent. It may look huge and intimidating—but that's part of his lie. However, when the same sword is used correctly—which only those who know the truth and have the Holy Spirit in them can do—it can be turned against Satan and destroy the power of his attacks.

Review/Conclusion:

The "sword of the Spirit, which is the word of God" is the only piece of armor listed that is an offensive weapon. It is a tool with which to strike down our enemy. All the other pieces are protective. To use the sword correctly—to discern and fully understand the Word of God—we need to be filled with the Holy Spirit. Only as the Spirit of God indwells us will our minds be fully quickened and our inner man adequately strengthened to deal with Satan's attacks.

To do the will of God and live according to the Spirit requires that we know the Spirit of God and walk in daily relationship with our Lord and Savior. Combat training comes in our walk with Him. Understanding what countermeasures are required to walk in victory involves intimate knowledge of the Captain of our soul.

He is our salvation and our strength. Being clothed with the righteousness of Christ means having our lives totally armored in Him. To keep our armor in good shape requires the oil of daily prayer.

LESSON 5: *Persistent Prayer*

Scripture for Meditation:

You turned my wailing into dancing; you removed my sackcloth and clothed me with joy, that my heart may sing to you and not be silent. O Lord my God, I will give you thanks forever. (Psalm 30:11–12)

A Beginning Prayer:

Lord, teach me to walk continually in Your presence and to develop a prayer life that is effective and powerful. Draw me to my knees, not just to pray for my own needs, but to intercede for and lift up those around me. May the Holy Spirit focus my praying on the specific needs and hurts of others. And show me those areas of my life that are most vulnerable to attack that I might reinforce them with more truth from God's holy Word. Amen.

Lesson:

PRAYER IN THE SPIRIT

As he closed out this section on God's armor, Paul wrote, "And pray in the Spirit on *all* occasions with *all* kinds of prayers and requests. With this in mind, be alert and *always* keep on praying for all the saints" (Ephesians 6:18, italics added). At first glance this may seem almost like an afterthought, not part of the package. The little conjunction *and* at the very beginning clearly indicates, however, that this, too, is part of our armor. And the *alls* and the *always* indicate that persistence of this application is crucial.

How frequently are we supposed to pray? Circle all the letters that apply:

A. Every morning

B. Before every meal

C. Only when we need something

D. All the time

What are we supposed to pray about or for? Circle all the letters that apply:

A. Difficult decisions

B. To have an easy, carefree life

C. That the sick will be healed

D. Everything that the Holy Spirit lays on your heart

How are we supposed to pray? What kinds of prayers? Circle all the letters that apply:

A. On our knees

B. Short prayers with simple words

C. Spoken prayers

D. Unspoken heart prayers

Prayer is focused conversation with God. We talk to Him and we listen to Him talking to us. Just as His written Word cannot become clear to us without the unction of the Holy Spirit, so too we need to pray in the Spirit to effectively communicate with our heavenly Father.

How important is prayer? We need look only at the life of Christ to see the crucial significance prayer plays in the life of a Christian.

Read Matthew 14:23; 19:13; 26:36; Mark 1:35; 14:32; Luke 5:16; 6:12; 9:18; and 18:1. Discuss and describe the prayer life of Jesus:

_____

_____

PRAYER TARGETS

A specific application of praying in the Spirit is developing prayer targets. Prayer targets are ways to deflect our reaction to a temptation or attack and channel our energies into effective prayer for another. It is also a way to strengthen our wielding of God's Word, as it helps us to focus on something positive outside our situation rather than becoming totally focused on our own need or failure.

First, in whatever areas of weakness that you are most vulnerable, develop a good arsenal of memorized Scriptures dealing with those issues. Choose verses to fortify against all three of the major categories of temptations as stated in 1 John 2:16 (KJV): "the lust of the flesh, and the lust of the eyes, and the pride of life" (or the flesh, the world, and the devil).

In addition, select a prayer target for each of your weak areas. A target is a person you know—believer or unbeliever. Whenever the Enemy attacks you with a destructive temptation, counterattack by praying for your targeted person. Pray that this person will be lifted up and strengthened in the Lord and enabled to do great damage to Satan and his kingdom.

For example, if you have a problem with anger, each time you are tempted to explode in anger, remember your memorized verses and begin praying for one of your targets. Bring your thoughts into captivity to Christ as you listen to the Spirit direct you in your prayer. As the Holy Spirit prompts you, pray for specific areas of this person's life. It's very difficult to remain angry while praying for someone else.

By choosing to pray in the Spirit this way, you will divert your own attention away from the issue prodding you to anger, and you will confound the attacker by engaging in activity that is totally the opposite of what's expected and around which demons cannot stand. Prayer repels hell since it brings us into the presence of our almighty, heavenly Father.

Below, list five areas of weakness, references to verses to memorize, and a prayer target for each area:

1

Area of weakness: _____

Prayer target for this area: _____

Verses to memorize for this area: _____

_____

_____

2

Area of weakness: _____

Prayer target for this area: _____

Verses to memorize for this area: _____

_____

_____

3

Area of weakness: _____

Prayer target for this area: _____

Verses to memorize for this area: _____

_____

_____

4

Area of weakness: _____

Prayer target for this area: _____

Verses to memorize for this area: _____

_____

_____

5

Area of weakness: _____

Prayer target for this area: _____

Verses to memorize for this area: _____

_____

_____

Review/Conclusion:

Effective spiritual warfare begins, ends, and exists in prayer. The Holy Spirit will guide us in effective prayer. The Bible provides us powerful models and words for building invincible prayers. The whole armor of God is not put on the same way we put on clothes. Each piece is prayed on daily and prayed on all day long. And once on, the armor is oiled and polished through continual prayer and supplication and all kinds of prayers. Since prayer is direct communication with God and brings us into His holy presence, the more we pray the more the powers of darkness stay away!

RECOGNIZING THE DIFFERENCE

*S*atan is a master at producing false guilt. Some individuals have difficulty knowing when they are experiencing the conviction of the Holy Spirit as opposed to facing the condemnation of the Enemy. Here are some simple, basic guidelines that will help you recognize the difference. These are especially good to share with young people and new believers.

THE WORK OF THE HOLY SPIRIT	THE WORK OF SATAN
The Holy Spirit aims to help you grasp your infinite value and worth to God. The goal is to draw you into closer fellowship with God.	Satan aims to convince you that you are bad, wicked, and unworthy of God's love and forgiveness. The goal is to push you away from God.
The Holy Spirit wants to help you realize that there is forgiveness and restoration available to you, no matter how horrible you think your sin is. The aim is confession and repentance.	Satan tries to deny the reality of forgiveness, making you feel as if whatever you've done is the unpardonable sin. The goal is to keep you in condemnation.
The Holy Spirit will speak God's Word into your mind and heart, offering encouragement. The goal is to provide solid assurance and hope of God's forgiveness based on His absolute promises.	Satan will throw into your mind pieces of Scripture twisted and ripped out of context so that they become accusations. The goal is to rob you of hope.
The Holy Spirit seeks to build up your faith, your sense of hope, and your love for the Lord and others. The goal is to increase your confidence and faith and firmly establish you in truth.	Satan is intent on seeding into your heart and mind feelings of doubt, despair, resentment, and anger toward God, toward His people, and toward His Word. The goal is to make you feel that no one as bad as you could ever be saved or used by God.
The Holy Spirit is insistent but gentle in His prodding of our hearts. The goal is to see us grow and mature in the Lord and to be vitally involved in fellowship with other believers.	Satan is nagging, forceful, and demanding in hurling his fiery darts. His goal is to deceive us and destroy our confidence, keeping us isolated from others except those who want to indulge in sinful behavior.

ANGELS AND THEIR ROLES

Scripture Memory Verses:

So Moses went down to the people and told them. And God spoke all these words: "I am the Lord your God, who brought you out of Egypt, out of the land of slavery. You shall have no other gods before me. You shall not make for yourself an idol in the form of anything in heaven above or on the earth beneath or in the waters below. You shall not bow down to them or worship them; for I, the Lord your God, am a jealous God." (Exodus 19:25–20:5a)

Unit Learning Goal:

Developing a proper, biblical view of angels and the part they play in our lives.

Overview of Unit 4:

Lesson 1: The Angel of the LORD *and Messenger Angels*

Lesson 2: Agents of Concern: Ministering Angels

Lesson 3: Protectors of Souls: Guardian and Warrior Angels

Lesson 4: Deceivers and Destroyers: Fallen Angels

Lesson 5: Angels at Work in the Bible

SUMMARY STATEMENT

The evidence is that the Angel of the LORD **(Angel of Jehovah) is not a created angel but the preincarnate Son of God visibly manifesting Himself to Old Testament personages. Not all angels are sent from God to effect His purpose and will in our lives. We need to understand how God uses His holy angels for His glory and our benefit. And we need to develop discernment to recognize angels who are merely masquerading as servants of righteousness.**

Unit 4 Thought Focus:

Angels are everywhere today! They're on television, calendars, bumper stickers, posters, product packaging, checks, and T-shirts. Books about angels abound. Believing in and talking about angels has exceeded mere faddishness—it's approaching worship!

On the one hand, as Christians we can rejoice in the opportunities afforded to share openly about spiritual things because of this intense interest in and acceptance of angelic hosts. Yet we must also be cautious on two fronts.

First, we must avoid getting caught up in the frenzy of angel-talk. Decorating our homes with a few angel images as reminders that God has created holy spirit-beings and assigned them to watch over us is a good thing. However, we need to guard against placing our faith in either the angels or the representations of angels. Our faith and trust should be in God and God alone. Ascribing undue authority or power to angels or to the representations of angels moves us into worshiping false gods and idols.

Second, we need to understand who our enemy is. We need to call to mind frequently 1 Peter 5:8, which states, "Your enemy the devil prowls around like a roaring lion looking for someone to devour." Angels don't roar and don't devour, we reason. Angels are nice, sweet things, and therefore must always be godly beings. And that's exactly how Satan would want us to always think about all angels.

However, Paul issued a clear warning in 2 Corinthians 11:14–15: "Satan himself masquerades as an angel of light. It is not surprising, then, if his servants masquerade as servants of righteousness. Their end will be what their actions deserve."

Not all angels are godly angels. Much of what is occurring around us, often under the banner of New Age thinking, is being directed by Satan and worked out through his demonic angels. Such things as channeling; sightings of UFOs; purported encounters with aliens; some forms of "advanced" meditation; psychic phenomena, such as astral projection; and more are clear portals into the demonic.

Cloaking these elements in the guise of angels is an especially insidious maneuver of Satan. It's spiritual camouflage targeted to deceive and entrap believers and nonbelievers.

To guard ourselves and our families against these fatal deceptions, we need to understand how God uses His holy angels to effect His will in our lives. Although we need to recognize our enemies, it's just as critical that we recognize who our allies are.

LESSON 1: *The Angel of the LORD and Messenger Angels*

Scripture for Meditation:

Then Manoah inquired of the angel of the LORD, "What is your name, so that we may honor you when your word comes true?" He replied, "Why do you ask my name? It is beyond understanding." (Judges 13:17–18)

And there were shepherds living out in the fields nearby, keeping watch over their flocks at night. An angel of the Lord appeared to them, and the glory of the Lord shone around them, and they were terrified. But the angel said to them, "Do not be afraid. I bring you good news of great joy that will be for all the people. Today in the town of David a Savior has been born to you; he is Christ the Lord. This will be a sign to you: You will find a baby

wrapped in cloths and lying in a manger." Suddenly a great company of the heavenly host appeared with the angel, praising God and saying, "Glory to God in the highest, and on earth peace to men on whom his favor rests." (Luke 2:8–14)

A Beginning Prayer:

Dear heavenly Father, thank You for creating Your heavenly hosts to serve You in bringing Your words of hope and truth to the shepherds at Christ's birth. Help me to see and acknowledge the work of Your holy angels as You assign them to protect me and keep me under Your watchful care. Amen.

Lesson:

THE ANGEL OF THE LORD

Although, generally speaking, the angels are created beings, one angel, the Angel of the LORD (Angel of Jehovah), appears not to be. The scholar C. Fred Dickason says that his title, identity with Jehovah, distinction from Jehovah, identity with Christ, and ministries all argue in favor of his being the preincarnate Son of God. Excerpts from Dickason's book *Angels: Elect and Evil* (Chicago: Moody, 1975, 1995), 81–87, follow:

- The title *Elohim* ("the mighty one") was used of both the true God and the gods of the heathen. But the title *Jehovah* (Heb. *Yahweh*) was reserved for the God of Israel, the eternally self-existent One who made heavens and earth and who entered into covenant relationship with His people. The angels in general are called "the sons of God" *(bene elohim),* but never "the sons of Jehovah." Therefore, since this one [angel] has a singular and peculiar title, "the Angel of Jehovah" *(malak Yahweh),* we may suspect that he was more than an angel, perhaps Jehovah Himself. (81–82)

- This angel found Hagar (Genesis 16:7) and promised to do himself what God alone can (v. 10). Moses, the writer, identifies the angel as "Jehovah that spake unto her" (v. 13 ASV). (82)

- When this angel appeared to Moses "in a flame of fire out of the midst of a bush" (Exodus 3:2 KJV), verse 4 says, "God called unto him out of the midst of the bush" (KJV). The one who spoke with Moses is called the God of Abraham, Isaac, and Jacob; and with this announcement, Moses hid his face for fear of looking upon God (v. 6). Upon this historic occasion, God revealed His name as I AM THAT I AM (v. 14 KJV), the eternal, unchanging One. Would God entrust this unique personal revelation to a mere angelic creature? Acts 7:30–34 seems to identify the angel as the Lord (Yahweh, Exodus 3:2–7), "the God of Abraham and Isaac and Jacob." (82)

- The record of Gideon's commission identifies the one who spoke to him as "the angel of Jehovah" (Judges 6:12 ASV) and as "Jehovah" (v. 14 ASV) without any notice of change of speaker. Manoah and his wife saw the Angel of Jehovah; and upon recognizing him, Manoah feared they would die because they had seen God (Judges 13:21–22). That this angel was Jehovah is also implied in the vision of Zechariah when the angel in [Zechariah] 3:1 seems clearly to be called Jehovah in the next verse (v. 2). (82)

- He intercedes to Jehovah. In Zechariah 1:9–11 we see that the man among the myrtle trees was the Angel of Jehovah, and that Jehovah had sent the horsemen who were to report to this angel. [The separate identity of Jehovah and the Angel of Jehovah] also appears in verses 12–13 where the Angel of Jehovah intercedes for Jerusalem as he speaks to Jehovah. (83)

- He calls upon Jehovah. In the vision of the cleansing of Joshua, Zechariah saw the Angel of Jehovah defending this priestly leader of Israel against the accusations of Satan in the presence of Jehovah (3:1–2). The angel (v. 1) is called Jehovah: "And Jehovah said unto Satan, Jehovah rebuke thee, O Satan; yea, Jehovah that hath chosen Jerusalem rebuke thee" (3:2 ASV). The angel called Jehovah was speaking to a separate person called Jehovah. How can there be more than one person called Jehovah? (83)

- [There] are four considerations that help to identify the Angel of Jehovah as Christ in preincarnate appearances. (1) The second person of the Trinity, the Son, is the visible God of the New Testament (John 1:14, 18; Colossians 2:8–9). Accordingly, the Son was the visible manifestation in the Old Testament also. (2) The Angel of Jehovah no longer appeared after Christ's incarnation. A reference such as Matthew 1:20 does not identify the angel and should be understood as an angel of the Lord. (3) They both were sent by

God and had similar ministries, such as revealing, guiding, and judging. The Father was never sent. (4) This angel could not be the Father or the Spirit. They never take bodily form (John 1:18; 3:8). (83)

- The angel confirmed the covenant with Abraham (Genesis 22:11–18). God had previously promised Abraham great personal, national, and universal blessings (Genesis 12:1–3). Abraham had believed God (15:5–6), and God "cut a covenant" unconditionally with Abraham (15:8–21). So great was his faith that he would have sacrificed Isaac, his only son; but the Angel of Jehovah stopped him and confirmed God's promises (22:15–18). It is in this connection that the angel is identified with Jehovah as He who made an unbreakable covenant with Israel (Judges 2:1). Christ was sent to confirm the promises to Israel for their deliverance and the forgiveness of sins for all (Matthew 26:28; Romans 15:8–9; Hebrews 9:15). (85)

- At times the angel brought judgment. When Satan had provoked David to number Israel to revel in his military might, God was displeased and sent the Angel of Jehovah to partially destroy Jerusalem (1 Chronicles 21:1, 14–15). David saw him with a drawn sword in his hand stretched out over Jerusalem and fell on his face in repentance and intercession (vv. 16–17). Then the angel commanded him to build an altar, which later became the site of the Solomonic Temple (21:18, 24–29; 22:1, 6). During the Great Tribulation, the Lord Jesus shall judge His people Israel along with unbelieving earth-dwellers (Matthew 24:44–51; 25:32–42; 2 Thessalonians 1:5–10; Revelation 5:5; 6:1–17). The purging done, the temple will be rebuilt for worship (Ezekiel 20:37–42; 43:2–5, 12). (85–86)

- The Angel of Jehovah has been shown to be equal in essence with Jehovah and yet distinct from Jehovah. The only answer to this seeming contradiction is that he is a preincarnate appearance of our Lord Jesus, the eternal Son. Indeed, he is the most frequent Christophany in the Old Testament. His ministries are varied and extensive and well known in Old Testament times from the days of Abraham to Zechariah. Some of his ministries are those that only God Himself can do and are so extensively parallel with Christ's ministries that they argue further for his identity as the preincarnate Christ. (87)

MESSENGER ANGELS

The Greek word for angels literally means messenger. Throughout the Bible, angels served in this role, bringing vital information to God's prophets, priests, and people. The chief of the messenger angels is Gabriel.

Read Luke 1 and 2 then discuss and answer the following questions:
What were the events about which Gabriel brought good news?

_____

_____

What were the messages delivered to each of these people:
Zechariah: _____
Mary: _____

When not serving as messenger, where is Gabriel; where does he stand?

_____

What other angelic visitation is recorded in Luke 1 and 2?

_____

_____

When confronted by a heavenly host, whether it was one or a group, the common reaction was a combination of fear, amazement, and even reverence. In Luke 1 and 2, Zechariah, Mary, and the shepherds all initially reacted this way.

Of the following words, circle the ones used in Luke 1 and 2 to describe the reactions to seeing angels (use the NIV for reference):

startled   gripped with fear   troubled   wonder   happy   fear   rejoicing   terrified   curious

In each instance, what immediate reassurance was offered to calm the fears of those being visited?:

      A. Bow down and worship.

      B. Don't be silly.

      C. Don't be afraid.

      D. God has sent me/us.

THE BEARERS OF GOOD NEWS

God's goal in sending His angels as messengers was not to instill fear, but to offer good news of hope and joy and promise. Although the Christmas messenger angels didn't say explicitly, "We are from God," they did not hesitate to indicate that it was He who sent them. Further, their messages and actions glorified God and specifically furthered His purpose. All of the information imparted had already been heralded ages earlier through the written histories and prophecies that make up the Old Testament. Essentially, these angels brought no new revelation, but were bringing insight and understanding to existing revelation. They told the specifics of fulfillment of prophecies. Only on very special occasions in the Bible did God send angels to speak to His servants. God typically speaks to believers through His word, illuminated by the Holy Spirit.

Circle **T** for True or **F** for False and then discuss your answers:

T   **F**   God frequently uses angels to bring new revelation to individuals.

T   **F**   Any message spoken by an angel of God will never contradict the written Word of God.

T   **F**   Seeking to be touched by an angel is an appropriate pursuit for Christians.

T   **F**   Sometimes "angels" appear as people allowing themselves to be used by God to do His will and bring blessings to others.

ENHANCERS OF OUR MINISTRY TO OTHERS

Further, although the news imparted by angels in the Bible impacted the hearers and affected how they would live their lives and make their choices, the news was not just for that person. Rather, the news was directed to the hearers in their God-given role in carrying out His preordained will as it would impact others around them. Although individuals were blessed and strengthened by angelic visitations, the ultimate purpose was to enhance the individual's ministry to others.

Circle **T** for True or **F** for False and then discuss your answers:

T   **F**   God sends His angels only for individual personal benefit.

T   **F**   Praying to angels is OK for Christians to do.

T   **F**   The appropriate response to a visitation by an angel is to give lectures, write books, and focus on how special that specific event was.

T   F   Angelic visits were to facilitate the sharing of God's Word and ministry beyond those visited.

Discuss these questions in your group:

1. What kinds of events in our lives might warrant an angelic messenger?
2. What are ways one might recognize that an angel was sent from God?
3. What abiding presence is a more valuable experience than any hoped-for angelic visitation?

Review/Conclusion:

The Angel of the LORD (Angel of Jehovah) has a distinctive ministry in the Old Testament and is most probably the preincarnate Son of God. Angels in general have brought messages to God's servants. However, angelic visits were a means of learning about His will and His ways. We have been provided with the Bible, which is our foundational source of all Good News and information for living out our Christian walk. Additionally, we have the person of the Holy Spirit of God, who indwells us and illumines to us the meaning and applications of His Word. Finally, we have the special privilege of being under the direct shepherding oversight of our Lord and Savior, Jesus Christ.

LESSON 2: *Agents of Concern: Ministering Angels*

Scripture for Meditation:

Do not forget to entertain strangers, for by so doing some people have entertained angels without knowing it. (Hebrews 13:2)

If you make the Most High your dwelling — even the Lord, who is my refuge—then no harm will befall you, no disaster will come near your tent. For he will command his angels concerning you to guard you in all your ways; they will lift you up in their hands, so that you will not strike your foot against a stone. You will tread upon the lion and the cobra; you will trample the great lion and the serpent. (Psalm 91:9–13)

A Beginning Prayer:

Lord, I'm filled with gratitude and amazement that You would encamp Your angelic hosts around me and my family. Thank You for your ministering angels that, in times of trouble and hurt, are there to protect us and guard us. I thank You that, even though the Enemy and his agents seek to intrude, You assign Your holy angels to stand guard about us to protect us. Amen.

Lesson:

MINISTERING SPIRITS

In Hebrews 1:14, the author states that angels are "ministering spirits" specifically sent "to serve those who will inherit salvation." What a wonderful realization that God cares about us so much that He provides personalized messengers to minister to and care for His own.

Angels were sent to minister to those who were in great distress as a result of intense warfare. Following the temptation in the desert, angels came and ministered to Jesus (Matthew 4:11). Again, while He was in intense prayer just prior to the Crucifixion, an angel came to Him and strengthened Him as He prayed (Luke 22:43).

In the Old Testament, following an incredible display of God's power in the face of intense idolatry, Elijah fled for his life under threat from Jezebel. Exhausted and despairing, the prophet collapsed, and God sent an angel to minister to his needs (1 Kings 19:5–9).

In your Bible, look up the examples cited above. Discuss and describe the ways these angels ministered to Jesus and Elijah:

_____

_____

Do you think we are always aware of the times when angels are ministering to us or acting as our protectors and defenders? Why or why not?

_____

_____

COMFORTERS

Angels came to comfort Mary in her distress when she discovered Christ's empty tomb. There were two angels at the tomb where His body had been. With great concern and compassion, they spoke to her and asked her, "Woman, why are you crying?" (John 20:10–13).

WITNESSES TO OUR LIVES

Angels also witness our lives. Just as someone is called to witness a legal transaction, angels stand as witnesses to our lives (1 Corinthians 4:9; 11:10). They hold no power of judgment, but they can serve to stand in agreement with our Lord concerning our lives, as stated in Luke 12:8–9: "I tell you, whoever acknowledges me before men, the Son of Man will also acknowledge him before the angels of God. But he who disowns me before men will be disowned before the angels of God."

The positive side of this witness is that it's not intended to be a role of accusation. Angels serve as holy cheerleaders, as stated in Luke 15:10: "There is rejoicing in the presence of the angels of God over one sinner who repents."

Review/Conclusion:

Angels serve a significant role in ensuring that God's will is carried out, particularly concerning the protection of our lives. Though unseen, they may be all around us. However, they are not sent to us to do our bidding. They are agents of God sent to do His bidding on our behalf. We are not to worship angels or seek to speak to them. Our view of angels needs to be balanced with biblical truth. We do not serve or pray to angels, but we may enjoy the benefits of their ministering presence. We can ask the Lord to send them to us and to others in threatening times of need or distressing danger.

LESSON 3: *Protectors of Souls: Guardian and Warrior Angels*

Scripture for Meditation:
He will defend the afflicted among the people and save the children of the needy; he will crush the oppressor. (Psalm 72:4)

A Beginning Prayer:
Dear Lord, You are a mighty tower into which I can run and hide from my attackers. Thank You that You send Your angels to defend me and guard my ways. Open my spiritual eyes that I might know that Your angelic armies are there for my defense and protection. Amen.

Lesson:

PROTECTORS

Psalm 34:7 promises us that "the angel of the LORD encamps around those who fear him, and he delivers them." God sends His heavenly caretakers to *guard* and *deliver* us from evil.

Christians should be familiar with the concept of guarding angels. This comes from passages like Matthew 18:10, where Christ states, "See that you do not look down on one of these little ones [children]. For I tell you that their angels in heaven always see the face of my Father in heaven." There is great comfort and reassurance to be taken from the fact that our children's lives are guarded by angels who are in constant communication with God. Psalm 91:9–12 conveys the truth of this same angelic guarding work.

Not only do angels intervene directly in the lives of children to protect them from harm, but they can also influence others to act as protectors. Read Matthew 2 and answer the following:

Circle **T** for True or **F** for False and then discuss your answers:

T　　**F**　　Angels cannot put thoughts into our minds.

T　　**F**　　If asleep, people can't receive a message from an angel.

T　　**F**　　Only God's angels can speak to us through dreams and visions.

An angel of the Lord spoke to Joseph at least twice through dreams to warn Joseph to take action to protect the life of Jesus (Matthew 1:20–21; 2:13). Both Mary and Joseph were visited by angels, but each in a different way (for Joseph, see Matthew 1:18–25; 2:13–15, 19–23; for Mary, see Luke 1:26–38 for the visit of the angel Gabriel).

DELIVERERS

Angels also intervened directly in circumstances to effect deliverance in the lives of believers. An especially remarkable example of this is given in Acts 12:5–11.

Peter had been placed in prison for preaching the Gospel. He was sound asleep when an angel appeared, filling the cell with light. The angel roused Peter, freed him from his chains, and then instructed him to dress, put on his cloak, and follow him out of the prison. Peter followed the angel past the unseeing guards all the way to the gates of the city, which opened on their own.

Read Acts 12:5–11 and then circle all the letters to statements that are true:

A. Peter was asleep in his cell all alone.

B. The church was earnestly praying for Peter.

C. Peter recognized immediately that the angel was real.

D. The angel gave Peter very specific instructions.

If angels were always recognizable as angels, the author of Hebrews would not have issued the instruction given in Hebrews 13:2. Nearly all of us have heard stories of persons encountered one moment who were gone the next. There are reliable stories of missionaries who were encountering an especially troubling attack from Satan at a specific time and were suddenly delivered. Only later did they learn that believers on the other side of the world had been roused by the Spirit in the middle of the night and were earnestly praying.

It is also noteworthy in Peter's deliverance to see what great care the angel exercised in dealing with Peter. To be imprisoned and shackled to guards was an emotionally and physically draining event. Peter was totally exhausted and in a deep sleep. Being awakened from a deep sleep is normally disorienting, but to awaken to a light-filled cell and being addressed by an angel would be especially disarming! Yet, the angel ministered care to Peter as well as leading him out of the jail. He woke Peter by physically nudging him. He told Peter exactly what to do, step by step, and led Peter into full freedom. Only then did the angel leave, and only then did Peter become fully aware of what had transpired.

DEFENDERS

God also sends His angels to defend us and war on our behalf. Michael is a powerful protecting warrior angel. God calls him the archangel (Jude 9). In Daniel 10, Michael's help was needed to resist the "prince of the Persian kingdom," who was detaining the messenger angel sent from God. During the Great Tribulation it is Michael and his angels who throw Satan and his angels from heaven to earth.

In 2 Kings 6, we're given another example of God's warrior angels bringing protective safety. In this instance, the prophet Elisha had been helping the king of Israel thwart attacks by the Arameans. Word of this reached the Aramean king, who sent out spies to locate Elisha in order to capture him. Elisha and his servant were in the city of Dothan, so the king of Aram sent "horses and chariots and a strong force" overnight to surround the city (v. 14).

The next morning, Elisha's servant stepped outside and was horrified by what he saw: Arameans everywhere! But Elisha calmed his servant and said, "Those who are with us are more than those who are with them" (v. 16).

Elisha prayed that God would open the eyes of his servant, who then looked out again and saw "the hills full of horses and chariots of fire all around" (v. 17). God's mighty angelic army was standing alert and ready to protect Elisha and his servant.

Review/Conclusion:

All around us in the spiritual realm, a battle rages. From time to time we are given glimpses into this intense warfare. But even without seeing them, we have the assurance that God's heavenly hosts are guarding us at all times, standing with us in our defense against the Enemy's attacks and always ready to deliver us as God directs.

LESSON 4: *Deceivers and Destroyers: Fallen Angels*

Scripture for Meditation:

"I, Jesus, have sent my angel to give you this testimony for the churches. I am the Root and the Offspring of David, and the bright Morning Star." (Revelation 22:16)

A Beginning Prayer:

Heavenly Father, Lord of my life, open my eyes that I might see Your protective care of my life. Teach me Your precepts and ways that my life may be lived in faithfulness and power. Put Your discernment within me so that I can walk free from evil in all its guises and forms and remain pure in heart and mind before You. Amen.

Lesson:

THE ACTIVITIES AND STRENGTH OF ANGELS

Except for the Angel of the LORD (Angel of Jehovah), who is not a created being but is instead identified with Jehovah, angels are created spirit-beings who were all originally holy and righteous. Each angel was made by God for a specific intended purpose, with various ranks, levels of authority, degrees of power, and duties. Lucifer, Satan's angelic name in heaven, was created as one of the more powerful angels. He was possibly equal to or even above Michael and Gabriel.

When Lucifer rebelled against God, one-third of the angels who existed at that time were involved in this rebellion. These created angels were cast from heaven with Satan. Now, as fallen spirit-beings, or demons, they continue to function in their created rank and levels of authority and power, but within the forces of Satan doing his bidding. They work now to destroy God's kingdom and undermine the witness of all who serve Christ. (See Revelation 12:1–6 for a discussion of these events.)

Satan uses fallen angels to try to rob us of our freedom and destroy us, but the holy angels continue to minister and protect. These good angels assist God in helping believers to walk in triumphant victory over the schemes of the devil and his demons. Believers have also been given full authority in Christ to resist and overcome the Enemy (Luke 10:19; Ephesians 6:10–18).

Christ recognized the seriousness of the demoniac invasion, yet He always addressed demons with authority. He also alluded to the various levels of demons when, in Mark 9:29, explaining to his disciples why they were unable to cast out a demon, He said, "This kind can come out only by prayer." He further recognized that some demons were more wicked (Matthew 12:45).

Circle **T** for True or **F** for False and then discuss your answers:

T   F   Satan is an angel who was created by God.

T   F   The demons are angels who were cast out of heaven with Satan.

T   F   Every angel and demon possess the same powers and authority.

T   F   All angels who contact us are from God.

T   F   Jesus scoffed at the thought of demons, not taking them seriously.

T   F   Satan can be in more than one location at a time, just like God.

T   F   Even God's angels respect the power of Satan.

T   F   Demons can pretend to be good angels and enable false teachers or prophets.

THE DIGNITY OF ANGELS

While we have authority over Satan and demons, we are cautioned to not use this authority derisively or in a presumptive way.

Read Jude 8–13. Discuss and answer the following questions:

When the archangel Michael was debating with him, how did Michael rebuke Satan?

_____

_____

Look up Jude 8 in various translations. What other words are used in place of the NIV "celestial beings"?

_____

_____

How are those who slander angelic beings characterized?

_____

_____

What are some consequences of exaggerating the power of the demonic, thus limiting the authority we have in Christ?

_____

_____

What are some consequences of minimizing or ignoring the power of the demonic, thus limiting the authority we have in Christ?

_____

_____

MASQUERADERS

Second Thessalonians 2:9–10 states, "The coming of the lawless one will be in accordance with the work of Satan displayed in all kinds of counterfeit miracles, signs and wonders, and in every sort of evil that deceives those who are perishing. They perish because they refused to love the truth and so be saved."

Satan and his demons can and do masquerade as angels of light through those who allow themselves to be influenced by evil. There are many people who pretend to be Christians, or have chosen to believe a distorted gospel that fits their design, who attend and are active in churches everywhere. These people are self-deceived and deceiving. Instead of believing the pure truth of the Bible, they add to it, subtract from it, or rewrite it.

Only the Spirit of God can discern the true intent of a person's heart. And only those who maintain a deep and pure relationship with Him will share in His Spirit's discernment to identify those around them who may be counterfeit. However, Christians are given some good, basic guidelines to tell the difference between spiritual "goats" and "sheep."

Look up each Scripture reference. Discuss and write out (a) one practical application for sheep, and (b) one example of how goats might exhibit each of these identifiers:

Fruit: Matthew 7:15–17

Sheep: _____

_____

Goats: _____

_____

Love: John 13:34–35; 1 John 3:10–12

Sheep: _____

_____

Goats: _____

_____

Confession: 1 John 4:1–3

Sheep: _____

_____

Goats: _____

_____

Acknowledgment: Matthew 10:32

Sheep: _____

_____

Goats: _____

_____

Actions: Matthew 7:21–23; 2 Peter 1:5–8; 2:1–3

Sheep: _____

_____

Goats: _____

_____

In Matthew 10:34–39, Jesus makes some startling assertions regarding what His coming into the world means and what the cost of following Him really is. Read this passage, discuss it, and write out a statement as to how you believe this passage could relate to spiritual warfare:

_____

_____

Review/Conclusion:

Satan and his legions are determined to kill, steal, and destroy Christians any way they can. There is no deception, no lie, no trick that is outside satanic forces' ability or willingness to employ. The only protection we have is to remain in Christ and "pray on" our spiritual armor of God daily. As we yield ourselves to Christ and allow His Word to be planted deep in us, we are to resist the devil and see ourselves as overcomers and more than conquerors in the arena of daily spiritual battle.

LESSON 5: *Angels at Work in the Bible*

Scripture for Meditation:

Submit yourselves, then, to God. Resist the devil, and he will flee from you. Come near to God and he will come near to you. Wash your hands, you sinners, and purify your hearts, you double-minded. (James 4:7–8)

A Beginning Prayer:

Lord Jesus Christ, I submit myself into Your care. I seek to come near to You and to know Your holy presence. Cleanse me and clothe me in Your righteousness. Fasten my heart firmly in Your truth. Let me not be moved or swayed from single-minded devotion and service to Your perfect will. Amen.

Lesson:

Look up each of the Scripture references given below. Identify the main character(s) of each passage and discuss the ways angels interacted with them. For each, write a brief synopsis of these angelic interventions. Indicate for each event what type of angel seems to have been involved. Names like messenger, ministering, guardian, or warrior might be applied.

Genesis 3:22–24

_____

_____

Genesis 19:1–22

_____

_____

Daniel 3

_____

_____

Daniel 6:16–23

_____

_____

Matthew 24:15–31

_____

_____

Matthew 25:31

_____

_____

Matthew 28:1–7

_____

_____

Acts 1:9–11

_____

_____

Acts 8:26–40

_____

_____

Acts 10:1–11:18

_____

_____

Acts 27:1–25

_____

_____

Second Peter 2

_____

_____

Revelation 5

_____

_____

Review/Conclusion:

Throughout history, God's holy angels have been very active in the work of informing, blessing, guarding, and defending His beloved children. These heavenly beings of God's holy work serve with ready and timely efforts to spur on the completion of God's purposes for our lives. They are our allies and comrades in our stand against the defeated powers of Satan. Just as we need to recognize and take seriously the existence and activity of the demonic, so we need to be sober-minded and enlightened regarding the existence and activity of the holy angels of God.

GIVING AND RECLAIMING GROUND; OVERCOMING STRONGHOLDS

Scripture Memory Verses:

Therefore do not let sin reign in your mortal body so that you obey its evil desires. Do not offer the parts of your body to sin, as instruments of wickedness, but rather offer yourselves to God, as those who have been brought from death to life; and offer the parts of your body to him as instruments of righteousness. For sin shall not be your master, because you are not under law, but under grace.
(Romans 6:12–14)

Unit Learning Goal:

Understanding the ways we give ground to Satan and how to take it all back.

Overview of Unit 5:

Lesson 1: Stages of Yielding

Lesson 2: Devilish Danger Zones

Lesson 3: Unforgiveness and Bitterness

Lesson 4: Pride and Sexual Bondage

Lesson 5: Getting Right, Getting Free

SUMMARY STATEMENT

Christians often give ground to Satan without realizing it. Neither do we fully understand the far-reaching effects of this. We must become aware of all the ways the Enemy can gain a foothold in our lives and through these move into our families and our churches. Once recognized, we must cut off these access points through repentance and the power of the blood of Christ to make us clean. And finally, in the authority of the Lord, we can reclaim all that's rightfully ours according to the promises of God.

Unit 5 Thought Focus:

The *Amplified Bible* renders Ephesians 4:27 this way: "Leave no [such] room *or* foothold for the devil—give no opportunity to him." The word *foothold* in the original Greek can be used to imply several related meanings, such as spot, place, location, room, home, position, tract, occasion, opportunity, locality, regions, or condition. The concept in this verse is one of giving or yielding ground, or more specifically, the idea of permitting Satan to exercise influence over us by the sins and wrong behavior patterns we allow in our lives.

Anytime we allow ourselves to indulge repeatedly in any sin, that sin becomes a point of opportunity for Satan's work in our lives. It is a spot where our souls can become vulnerable to Satan's attempts at further control through his kingdom.

Putting this verse into the context of the whole chapter, Paul makes clear that Christians are to exhibit new behaviors in line with being new creations in Christ. We are to actively, moment by moment as temptations come, put off the old self and put on the new self. This is a continuous process that is the way of life for believers. There will be struggles and failures, but our overall desire and heart intent is to be focused on living our lives under the Lordship of Jesus Christ. Falling and getting up again and pursuing the goal of not falling again by using the weapons of our warfare will keep Satan from gaining a foothold in our lives.

However, refusing to fully yield any part of our lives to the control of the Holy Spirit and continuing to "dabble" purposefully in known sin is dangerous. Harboring or cultivating known sin in our lives opens us and our families to Satan's limited control. Using this area of weakness, he seeks to take other areas of our lives under his control. He will wield our fleshly desires as a means of laying claim against us for his destroying purposes.

A teenager in rebellion, a father in some form of spiritual bondage, or a mother who is harboring resentment will affect the entire family. The Enemy knows this. That is why he's working so hard to gain a foothold in your family and mine!

The good news is that we do not have to be Satan's victims! When we recognize that we have given ground, repent of our sinfulness, and turn away from it, God will enable us to be "more than conquerors." The Lord will reclaim what the Enemy has stolen.

Are there areas of your life that you feel have been yielded, where footholds or more were given over to Satan? Are you ready to take back these areas? To recover this stolen ground? Prayerfully list them here:

_____

_____

LESSON 1: *Stages of Yielding*

Scripture for Meditation:

For you did not receive a spirit that makes you a slave again to fear, but you received the Spirit of sonship. And by him we cry, "Abba, Father."
(Romans 8:15)

A Beginning Prayer:

Lord Jesus, come near to me and shepherd me to freedom. Holy Spirit of God, quicken my spirit to yield only to the righteousness of the Father. Strengthen my defenses against all forms of evil. Teach me how to defend effectively against the schemes of the Enemy and reclaim all that he has stolen from my family and me. Amen.

Lesson:

DEMONIC POSSESSION OR OPPRESSION?

One topic that is almost certain to stir up heated discussion among Christians is that of demonic activity. All have opinions as to what constitutes *possession* as opposed to *oppression.* And inevitably the debate will zero in on the question, Can a Christian be demon-possessed? We generally speak of these issues with strong emotions and convictions.

Frequently, conclusions drawn from these intemperate debates are based more on inferences and speculation rather than on interpretation of direct biblical teaching. Further complicating the issue, the Bible does not offer a clear statement concerning the degree of problem a Christian can have with demonic powers.

This is in part due to the recognized difficulty in translating some of the original Greek and Hebrew words in ways that accurately reflect the true intent of the author.

The English word *demon* comes from transliterating the Greek word *daimon.* Then, taking the word *daimonizomai,* which is another form of *daimon,* the thought would be expressed as *demonize.* In our English Bibles this word has been generally translated as *demon-possession,* as in Matthew 9:32. Translating *daimonizomai* as *demonize* would better allow us to speak of the degree to which a person could be demonized, or controlled by some evil power.

Allowing this view, we could say that being possessed implies full control and ownership. Obviously, it would be impossible for someone to be owned by both Christ and Satan. Therefore, a Christian could never be demon-possessed. However, there is biblical evidence that a Christian can be demonized to some degree, in the sense of being influenced or controlled to do specific and repeated evil. As implied earlier, control is possible because of ground that has been surrendered to the Enemy (Ephesians 4:27).

Further, although nowhere does Scripture record anyone saying, "No, you as a believer cannot be demon-possessed, but you will be oppressed!" there are several indications that this is true.

Read 1 Peter 5:8–9 and discuss and answer these questions:

Who is the Enemy? Whose enemy is he? How is this enemy characterized?

_____

_____

What are Christians called to be and do in the face of this enemy?

_____

_____

Why are we to be and do these things? Who are the others involved?

_____

_____

What kind of common experience is shared between these others and us?

_____

_____

If we fail to be and do as directed, what will the Enemy do to us?

_____

_____

Throughout the New Testament, warnings are issued to "gird up" our lives and prepare to resist and stand firm against the Enemy. We are told to work out our salvation, actively resist the devil, keep putting on the whole armor of God, and place ourselves daily under the mercy and grace of God. We are told that we will suffer wounds from the fiery darts and flaming arrows of Satan, that our lives will be buffeted, and that there is the potential for falling away.

The word *devour* means "to gobble down quickly." Ignoring our armor leaves us open to our devouring enemy. Wearing our armor will protect us from his devouring teeth. We'll feel the impact of his jaws, but we won't be devoured.

The bottom line for believers is that evil spirits are spirits of influence only. This is not true for unbelievers, for "the god of this age has blinded the minds of unbelievers, so that they cannot see the light of the gospel of the glory of Christ, who is the image of God" (2 Corinthians 4:4). Unbelievers are firmly held in the grasp of the master they serve.

Believers cannot be possessed the same way because they remain in Christ. But we can give ground to the Enemy and allow him to control us in a limited way and generally play havoc in our lives and families.

BONDAGES AND STRONGHOLDS

Giving ground to the Enemy through harboring sin can lead to bondages and strongholds being established in our lives from which Satan can exercise a level of control over us.

In warfare, spies are often sent behind enemy lines where they set up bunkers of activity against the enemy. Being inside the line of defense, these agents can instruct their comrades how to direct their attacks most effectively. Spies know where defenses are weak. Repeatedly engaging in known sin allows Satan's spies into our camp.

Romans 6:12–14: *Therefore do not let sin reign in your mortal body so that you obey its evil desires. Do not offer the parts of your body to sin, as instruments of wickedness, but rather offer yourselves to God, as those who have been brought from death to life; and offer the parts of your body to him as instruments of righteousness. For sin shall not be your master, because you are not under law, but under grace.*

Who is responsible for allowing sin to reign in a body?

_____

_____

What are the five senses?

_____

_____

What parts of your body are needed to use the senses?

_____

_____

What unseen parts of the body are involved in processing and experiencing the information gathered through your senses?

_____

_____

If I do not offer my body to sin, to whom may I offer it?

_____

_____

If I do not offer my body to God, to whom may I offer it?

_____

_____

If I do not offer my body to anyone, who will take it?

_____

_____

If I offer any seen or unseen part of my body to sin, what will sin do to my entire body?

_____

_____

If I offer any seen or unseen part of my body to God, what will God do to my entire body?

_____

_____

Will what we experience in our body affect our spirit? How so?

_____

_____

In this passage, the word *instrument* also means "weapon." In yielding ourselves to sin we literally become weapons of Satan he will use to destroy us and those around us.

Our focus, however, is not to be on Satan. It is to be on Jesus. The more clearly we see Him, the more clearly we will be able to recognize and defeat the strategies of the devil: "Let us fix our eyes on Jesus, the author and perfecter of our faith, who for the joy set before him endured the cross, scorning its shame, and sat down at the right hand of the throne of God" (Hebrews 12:2).

STRONGHOLDS AND BONDAGE

The weapons we fight with are not the weapons of the world. On the contrary, they have divine power to demolish strongholds. We demolish arguments and every pretension that sets itself up against the knowledge of God, and we take captive every thought to make it obedient to Christ. (2 Corinthians 10:4–5)

The Greek word for *weapon* in this passage *(hoplon)* is the same word that is translated as *instrument* in Romans 6:13.

A *stronghold* has been defined by Ed Silvoso of Harvest Ministries as "a mind-set impregnated with hopelessness that causes me to accept as unchangeable something we know is contrary to the will of God." A stronghold is an idea, belief, fear, feeling, desire, or anything else (arguments, pretensions against the knowledge of God) that has a *strong hold*, or a firm grip on, our mind, spirit, body, or heart—enslaving us—motivating us to act out against God's will through repeated sinful behavior. A stronghold is a believed lie we've allowed to become reality to us and hold us in bondage to sin. It's a lie that has darkened our minds to the truth of Christ.

The Greek for *demolish* is *kathairesis*, translated in other versions as *destruction*, *pulling down*, and *overthrow*. It is the root of our English word *catharsis*, which means "to purge or cleanse the emotions, a release of emotional tension, as after an overwhelming experience, that restores or refreshes the spirit, relieving tension and anxiety by bringing repressed feelings and fears to consciousness, a freeing from sin, guilt, or defilement, purification" *(American Heritage Dictionary)*.

To gain release from bondage, the lie must be seen as a lie. This requires an encounter with truth. When we bring Christ fully into our experiences, all sin will be exposed for what it is. Christ is the truth (John 14:6), and truth sets free (John 8:32). Strongholds fall as truth is consistently applied through obedience to Christ's teaching, which is God's Word (John 8:31). Being exposed to and living out the Word will wash our spirits (Ephesians 5:26), renew our minds (Romans 12:2), and set us free indeed (John 8:36).

Review/Conclusion:

Playing with sin is playing with fire. It will destroy us and hurt those around us. We are called to flee sin and resist the devil. Temptations will come and occasionally snare us. Our response should be to throw this episode of failure aside through confession and repentance, get up, and keep on pursuing holiness. However, if the episode leads to a continuing series of related behaviors and opportunities, we have opened ourselves for Satan's devouring work. Our eyes are to be fixed on the goal of our salvation, and our seeking is to be after the righteousness of Christ. In Him all ground yielded to Satan can be reclaimed. Our goal is to feast with Jesus around His holy banquet table, not to be devoured by demonic work.

LESSON 2: *Devilish Danger Zones*

Scripture for Meditation:

To the pure, all things are pure, but to those who are corrupted and do not believe, nothing is pure. In fact, both their minds and consciences are corrupted. They claim to know God, but by their actions they deny him. They are detestable, disobedient and unfit for doing anything good. (Titus 1:15–16)

A Beginning Prayer:

Heavenly Father, to You I ascribe glory and honor and power. Before Your will I bow my own. Into Your care I submit my life, my family, my future. Shape me into Your vessel to be used as You will. Holy Spirit, shine the light of pure holiness into every obscure corner of my life so that any evil thing will be exposed that I might confess it and forsake it. Let there be no hindrances in my life to full service to my God. Amen.

Lesson:

"What harm could it do? It's no big deal! It's just a game." How many times has this phrase been uttered in reference to Ouija® boards, tarot cards, fantasy games, and other pursuits tainted with the occult and wicked fantasy? In fact, the word game could be replaced with dozens of other examples, such as books, television shows, movies, and songs that are also questionable in nature, yet not always obviously so.

To understand what the harm is, let's examine some key words in three important verses.

KEY WORDS

Appearance, Kind, Abstain. First Thessalonians 5:22 states, "Abstain from all appearance of evil" (KJV). The NIV says, "Avoid every kind of evil." The *Amplified Bible* renders this verse as "Abstain from evil—shrink from it and keep aloof from it—in whatever form or whatever kind it may be." The word translated as *appearance* and *kind* is the Greek word *eidos*, which can also mean form, view, shape, sight, or fashion. The word *abstain* is defined as "to refrain from something by one's own choice, to hold oneself back, to hold off, to withhold from."

Flee, Pursue. First Timothy 6:11 states, "But you, man of God, flee from all this, and pursue righteousness, godliness, faith, love, endurance and gentleness." *Flee* means to run away; to shun; to vanish away from; to escape; to break loose and leave suddenly, as from confinement or from a difficult or threatening situation; to bolt; to fly away; to decamp; to get out. *Pursue* is especially rich in meaning and can be defined as to follow in an effort to overtake or capture; to strive to gain or accomplish; proceed along the course of; to carry on; to attempt to gain the affection of (spark, court, woo); to move behind (another) in the same direction (follow, trail, heel); to strengthen the effect of (an action) by further action; to work at, especially as a profession.

Submit, Resist. James 4:7 states, "Submit yourselves, then, to God. Resist the devil, and he will flee from you." *Submit* means to see oneself as a servant; to be in subjection to, under the authority of; to yield; to surrender; to conform to the judgment or will of another; to capitulate; to succumb. *Resist* means to strive to fend off or offset the actions, effects, or force of; to remain firm against the actions, effects, or force of; to withstand; to keep from giving in to or enjoying; to offer resistance; to oppose actively and with force (fight, withstand, combat, duel); to take a stand against (challenge, traverse, dispute, combat, buck, contest). In this context, it means to use what our Lord has provided us that forces evil to retreat and flee.

DECLARATION OF SUBMISSION AND RESISTANCE

Using words from the expanded definitions of the key words, rewrite all three verses into a personal Declaration of Submission and Resistance. This can be several sentences, bulleted points, or whatever format works best for you. Be sure to capture all of the ideas presented in each of the verses:

_____

_____

_____

_____

Share your declarations with each other, reading them out loud; then discuss what these verses, definitions, and your declarations mean to you.

_____

_____

Share new insights you've gained through this exercise and new understanding you didn't have before.

_____

_____

Give examples of instances in the past when you did not apply these verses effectively to your warfare—and the results.

_____

_____

Discuss practical ways these verses and your declarations can be carried out in warfare from this point on.

_____

_____

DABBLING IN DARKNESS: OUIJA® BOARDS AND ASTROLOGY

Evil can take on any variety of forms and shapes and, as we've seen, can appear beautiful and inviting. Eve learned this lesson the hard way in the garden. Dabbling in darkness can begin "innocently" by involvement in what seems to be a harmless activity. The Ouija® board is a perfect example of something that looks like fun on the surface but is clearly fueled by occult spirits.

Another common example is astrology. Millions of people read their horoscopes daily "just for fun." Yet, the things they read will often influence their behavior whether or not they realize it. Both the Ouija® board and horoscopes are akin to divination.

Look up Leviticus 19:26, 31; Deuteronomy 18:9–13; 1 Samuel 15:23; and 2 Chronicles 33:6. What do these verses say about divination? What other occult practices are associated with divination? What are rebellion and arrogance compared to? Discuss your answers.

_____

_____

THE DRAW OF THE OCCULT

People are drawn into the occult to obtain power, guidance, healing, and protection.

Power is sought over one's own life or over the lives of others. The goal of this power is to gain prestige, pleasure, position, or wealth, and to exercise manipulative control over others. The expression of this power is always ultimately self-serving and is frequently abusive or violent, even to the point of murder and suicide.

Escaping into unholy fantasy is a way of manipulating reality for personal pleasure. These fantasies can be expressed through fantasy games (such as Dungeons & Dragons™), sophisticated computer video games, romance novels, pornography, and even some music. All of these things are extremely powerful tools that can be used by Satan to communicate seductive and subversive lies, philosophies, worldviews, and perceptions. We can enter these areas just for fun, just to relax, and come away profoundly and perversely changed without even realizing it.

Guidance is sought through mediums, psychics, and channelers; or through mystic devices, talismans, or practices. Demonic spirits can reside in people or animals and can affect the material world and even inhabit inanimate objects that have been used for ritual evils (Deuteronomy 7:25–26). We all want to know what the future holds, but the only One who has a right to that knowledge is God. He calls us to trust our lives to Him and His Word—completely. To seek guidance from any other source is to deny God and open ourselves to evil. The goal of all guidance sought through occult methods is disobedience and selfishness. The underlying motive is to know what no other knows, to gain an edge, to take advantage of others.

Healing can come from the devil—or at least what appears to be healing. Satan can engineer sickness, disease, and injury to his advantage. Just as he can put infirmity on people, so he can take it off. The result will appear to be a miraculous healing. Or demonic spirits can enter into and enfeeble a person and express their superhuman strength through the person. Remember the Gerasene demoniac Jesus confronted who was possessed by legions (Mark 5)? The man could throw off chains by evil supernatural power. Again, those who seek healing "by any means at any cost" are seeking their own interests rather than God's. Even if it's for another, the ultimate benefit of the healing is aimed at their own interests and desires.

Protection is something we all desire for our families and ourselves. As Christians we are surrounded with a mighty tower, strong shield, and steadfast rock of protection. The protection we have from God, while extended to our lives on earth, is ultimately focused on our eternal security. No matter what happens to our physical existence, because we remain in Christ, our souls cannot be damaged or withheld from heaven (Romans 8:38; 2 Timothy 1:12). Those seeking occult-provided protection often want to be protected now in a way that would enable them to engage in a normally harmful practice. Once again, the goal of the protection is self-seeking.

List areas of potential occult operation (whether activity or thing) and the various methods these can be brought into a person's life and home. Add to the examples given:

ACTIVITY OR THING	METHODS AND MEANS OF SPREADING	
Pornography	Movies (TV and theater)	Videos
	Publications (books and magazines)	Internet

ACTIVITY OR THING	METHODS AND MEANS OF SPREADING	
Curiosity		

ACTIVITY OR THING	METHODS AND MEANS OF SPREADING OR EXAMPLES OF OBJECTS
Occult objects	

ACTIVITY OR THING	METHODS AND MEANS OF SPREADING
Music	

ACTIVITY OR THING	METHODS AND MEANS OF SPREADING
Addictive behaviors	

ACTIVITY OR THING	METHODS AND MEANS OF SPREADING

ACTIVITY OR THING	METHODS AND MEANS OF SPREADING

Review/Conclusion:

Awareness of bondage is the beginning of freedom. Once we become educated into the various ways the Enemy seeks to ensnare and destroy us, we can abide in the power of the Holy Spirit and apply the blood of Christ against these devices. We must be as relentless in emptying our lives of all forms of evil, for the Enemy is relentless in trying to put evil into us. Satan has some power, but we have *the* Power.

Our primary goal is to fully yield our wills to the will of the Father as He leads us down paths of righteousness, delivering us from evil for the glory of His name. God is able to make all grace abound toward us in all things at all times, giving us all that we need to withstand and thwart the Enemy. He can even take the harm meant by Satan and turn it around for our benefit, thus ultimately doing damage to the kingdom of evil.

LESSON 3: *Unforgiveness and Bitterness*

Scripture for Meditation:

"You have no part or share in this ministry, because your heart is not right before God. Repent of this wickedness and pray to the Lord. Perhaps he will forgive you for having such a thought in your heart. For I see that you are full of bitterness and captive to sin."
(Acts 8:21–23)

A Beginning Prayer:

Heavenly Father, may Your Holy Spirit shine Your light of holiness into every corner of my memory, soul, heart, and spirit; and reveal to me any crumb of unforgiveness that I may be harboring. Whether I feel like it or not, help me to release all unforgiveness from my life and to freely forgive *all,* all the time. Wash me and cleanse me and restore me fully to Yourself. Help me to forgive unconditionally just as You have forgiven me. Amen.

Lesson:

"Full of bitterness and captive to sin"! What a harsh judgment. But a true one. This is one of the areas that creates major problems for many Christians. Satan has a huge quiver full of fiery arrows made of anger, bitterness, unforgiveness, and associated sins that he will very accurately aim deep into our hearts.

We love to be exceptional in our faith! That is, we'll say things like "I can forgive everyone, except so-and-so." Or, "There's nothing anyone can do to make me angry, except this or that." When we feel we've been wronged, we'll often feel that we are justified in harboring anger or unforgiveness toward someone. Unforgiveness is our attempt to punish the offender. Of course, we'll cover it with grace! But God still sees it.

Anger and unforgiveness left unchecked or ignored or denied will grow into bitterness and can become rage. These will be expressed in our attitudes and behaviors. Hebrews 12:15 says that a "bitter root grows up to cause trouble and defile *many*" (italics added). Forgiveness is to be given out by us as often and as freely as we take in our daily bread. Look at the very words of Jesus:

Matthew 6:11–15: "*'Give us today our daily bread. Forgive us our debts, as we also have forgiven our debtors. And lead us not into temptation, but deliver us from the evil one.' For if you forgive men when they sin against you, your heavenly Father will also forgive you. But if you do not forgive men their sins, your Father will not forgive your sins.*"

Circle all the words below that are expressions of unforgiveness or bitterness:

Anger	Jealousy	Rage	Brawling
Dancing	Slander	Factions	Malice
Lying	Factions	Arrogance	Filthy Language
Disputing	Smoking	Immodesty	Quarreling
Gossip	Drinking	Disorder	Loud Music

List other behaviors that could be expressions of unforgiveness or bitterness:

_____

_____

Now read 2 Corinthians 12:20–21; Ephesians 4:31; Colossians 3:8–9; 1 Timothy 2:8; and James 1:19–20. Review and discuss your answers to the above two exercises with others.

THE REALITY OF SUFFERING

Accepting the reality of suffering and getting rid of bitterness are essential for living the Christian life effectively and successfully.

The Christian life is a life of suffering. However, this is not the popular message many proclaim to tickle the ears of those who want to hear the really, really "good news"! What they actually want to hear is that once you become a Christian, everything is going to be wonderful all the time. Further, those who hold to this view will insist that anyone who suffers does so because he doesn't believe enough, give enough, or doesn't *something* enough. This view of Christianity flies in the face of our God, His Word, and the life of Jesus, who suffered more than us all so that we might have eternal life.

We will suffer in this life, Christian or non-Christian. For the Christian who accepts this truth, suffering becomes a means to further spiritual maturity and intimacy with Christ. For those who reject this truth, suffering becomes a trigger to bitterness, resentment, and anger toward God. Anyone who's angry with God has believed the devil's lies.

The drive to resist suffering is strong. Our entire society is bent on avoiding pain and suffering at any and all costs. On the mundane level, we pop aspirins and antacids by the millions at the first signs of a headache or indigestion. At the farther extreme of this continuum is the move toward legalized euthanasia—the right to die with dignity to avoid pain. In between these two extremes is a whole range of activity and practice that is aimed at making us comfortable and at ease in this life.

Even our furniture, homes, cars, and clothing are all designed to go beyond merely meeting our need of basic creature comforts. They are all designed to obliterate any sense whatsoever of discomfort. If our pants are too tight, the car doesn't handle well, the house isn't big enough, or the furniture is too hard, we will experience what we will define as "suffering," and it will annoy us!

But, not only are Christians called to suffer, we are told that we need to *rejoice* in our suffering (Romans 5:3)! Why? Because this is the life the Lord has given us to live for now; and in the context of eternity, "our present sufferings are not worth comparing with the glory that will be revealed in us" (Romans 8:18).

What happens when you focus on something that hurts? Does it get better? Does it hurt more, or less? Explain.

_____

_____

If a child is hurt, do the parents attempt to focus the child's attention on the "owie," or do they attempt to distract his attention? Why?

_____

_____

Kids are amazingly resilient. Many times when they hurt themselves, initially, staring horrified at blood oozing from a cut or scrape, or just beginning to feel the sting from the pain, they will cry hysterically. Parents, recognizing that the injury is not life threatening, will lovingly and playfully direct the child's attention away from the wound. Often they'll focus attention on caring for the wound and make a pleasant game of cleaning it and applying a cartoon bandage. With ointments, bandages, hugs, and kisses applied, what was moments before a shriek of pain and outrage becomes giggles of delight and joy.

Read Matthew 5:11–12; Romans 5:3; Philippians 4:4; and 1 Peter 1:6. In light of the above example, how should we as Christians react to suffering in our lives?

_____

_____

_____

GETTING RID OF BITTERNESS

Accepting the reality of suffering and getting rid of bitterness are essential for living the Christian life effectively and successfully. Eliminating bitterness involves three steps. Underlying these steps is the concept of forgiveness. A lack of forgiveness is our subtle attempt to punish the offender (see the parable on forgiveness in Matthew 18:21–35). The Lord requires us to let Him carry out the punishment (Romans 12:10–15). The Lord even seems to use Satan to discipline an unforgiving Christian (Matthew 18:32–35).

(1) *Identify and release.* We need to identify those who have hurt us and release them to God. Dealing with those who have wronged or hurt us is God's job, not ours. Holding grudges against others is attempting to put ourselves in the place of God over that person! It's both sinful and an affront to God, for He's the one who disciplines and judges. It's sinful because God says unforgiveness is a sin. It's harmful because unforgiveness gives Satan a foothold. Grudges burn the hearts of those who hold them. If unforgiveness is held too long, the heart not only becomes cold but may become controlled by demonic torments (Matthew 18:34–35).

Take a moment and ask the Holy Spirit to reveal to you in your mind the people you've held in bitterness and unforgiveness. Write each name down as it is revealed. If you've held bitterness against God, include His name on your list. No one else needs to see this list—this is a private matter between you and God.

_____	_____
_____	_____
_____	_____
_____	_____
_____	_____
_____	_____

Now, one by one, go through your list and prayerfully release each person to the Lord. You may even want to lift up and open your hands in a gesture of release as you focus on each name. Let the resentment, bitterness, grudge, and other negative thoughts and emotions fly away, and invite the Lord to put His Spirit's fruit within you.

(2) *Forgive from the heart.* The next step to freedom from bitterness is to forgive each of those you've released. True forgiveness embraces these truths:

- Forgiveness has no statute of limitations. The offense could have occurred decades before and the offender may even have died, but forgiveness can happen and must happen.

- Forgiveness has no exceptions. The offense could be among the most horrible, such as abuse or molestation. It makes no difference: It must all be forgiven.

- Forgiveness has nothing to do with feelings. We are not commanded by Christ to forgive when we feel like it, nor is there anything that says forgiveness when we don't feel like it is ineffective. These ideas are deceptions of the devil.

- Forgiveness is a once-for-all act. Not only will offenses against us occur throughout our lifetime, often at the hands of the same people, but memories of past and forgiven offenses will recur. The response is always to be the same: forgiveness. In the face of each new offense, and every time memories of old offenses surface, we are to release the incident and the offender to the Lord and forgive him.

Go through your list again. This time, for each name, pray this prayer: "God, I forgive _____ (the offender) for _____ (the offense)."

(3) *Accept the consequences.* This final step may be the most difficult. Once you've identified, released, and forgiven each of your offenders, you now must be willing to live with the consequences of their actions. This can only be done with the help of the Holy Spirit. But it's also the way God forgives us.

Below, list some serious offenses. For each offense, indicate some of the potential consequences the offended party may have to live with. Add to the examples given:

OFFENSE	CONSEQUENCE
Alcoholism	Dysfunctional family life
Physical ailments	

OFFENSE	CONSEQUENCE
Rape	Pregnancy/illegitimate child
	Sexually transmitted disease

OFFENSE	CONSEQUENCE
Physical Abuse	

OFFENSE	CONSEQUENCE

OFFENSE	CONSEQUENCE

Think about it. Our sins—all of them—are horrible offenses against God. We seldom fully realize how horrible. Yet, God not only forgives us, He provided the costly means for us to have access to His forgiveness—He gave His Son to die on the cross. And when He forgives us, our sins are taken completely away as if they never existed. He never calls us to account for them again. Further, not only does He live with the consequences of our sin, He enables us to endure whatever consequences our sinfulness has created for us. Ephesians 4:32 says, "Be kind and compassionate to one another, *forgiving each other, just as in Christ God forgave you*" (italics added).

Note two things in this verse. First, we are to be forgiving, implying an ongoing action. God, however, forgave us once and for all when Christ died. His action of forgiveness is done and forever. All that remains is for us to accept and walk in the grace that is ours already. We, on the other hand, being clothed in these fleshly bodies and working out our salvation in this life, will always need to be forgiving of those around us daily.

Second, we are to forgive just as God forgives: without exception, hesitation, or excuse. Only as we forgive will we escape Satan's trap of bitterness.

For each name you wrote above, list the person again on the chart below and indicate if there's an ongoing consequence of his or her behavior you will have to live with. This may not be the case for all of the names. For those you identify, go over their names one at a time, prayerfully releasing both the offender and the consequence into the hands of God. Ask God to give you grace to accept and live with each consequence. Trust the Lord to deal with each offender according to His wisdom, mercy, and grace. This is the grace of forbearance (Ephesians 4:2).

OFFENDER	CONSEQUENCE

Review/Conclusion:

Forgiveness is a choice, not a feeling. It's also a command of God and a requirement for enjoying the full measure of His forgiveness in our lives. A root of bitterness and unforgiveness in our lives is often the root of a number of other issues that we may deal with on a regular basis.

James 4:1–3 states, "What causes fights and quarrels among you? Don't they come from your desires that battle within you? You want something but don't get it. You kill and covet, but you cannot have what you want. You quarrel and fight. You do not have, because you do not ask God. When you ask, you do not receive, because you ask with wrong motives, that you may spend what you get on your pleasures."

Clearing our hearts of unforgiveness begins to clear the way for us to ask according to the will of God. It opens our heart to the healing work of the Holy Spirit and closes off major access from the Enemy.

Forgiving whether we feel like it or not, releasing even the greatest offender into God's hands and accepting the consequences of their forgiven behavior without complaint, will baffle, confound, and damage the whole realm of Satan. Just as all of heaven rejoices when we accept Christ, so all of hell impotently rages as we reclaim lost ground.

LESSON 4: *Pride and Sexual Bondage*

Scripture for Meditation:

We know that we all possess knowledge. Knowledge puffs up, but love builds up. The man who thinks he knows something does not yet know as he ought to know. But the man who loves God is known by God.
(1 Corinthians 8:1–3)

A Beginning Prayer:

Heavenly Father, open my heart to Your loving gaze that I may see myself as You see me. Enable me to lay down my life and take up Your cross. Show me daily those areas of pride that I need to confess and release. Fill me with Your Holy Spirit. Amen.

Lesson:

THE HEART OF PRIDE: "I WILL"

In God's created universe, pride was the original sin. Before Adam and Eve, before the Garden of Eden, before the earth existed, sin was birthed in the heart and mind of Lucifer. That same sin—pride—is often the base from which Satan attacks our lives.

The heart of pride is epitomized in the heart of Satan. Read Isaiah 14:13–14 and complete the five statements below:

I will _____

I will _____

I will _____

I will _____

I will _____

Who was Satan speaking to when he made these statements?

_____

_____

Look up Proverbs 23:7 in the King James Version or the *New American Standard Bible* and write it out.

_____

_____

In his final "I will" statement, Satan says he will make himself like the Most High. This is a translation of *El Elyon*, which means literally "the sovereign one who reigns in heaven and in earth." It could be said that Satan wanted to be like God in the sense of having godlike power and control, but not possessing any of the character of God. Satan's focus was on himself and what he could gain through the power of God.

Look up these verses and discuss what each reveals about the nature and effects of pride:

Psalm 10:4	Proverbs 29:23
Psalm 101:5	Isaiah 13:11
Proverbs 11:2	2 Timothy 3:2–5
Proverbs 13:10	1 Peter 5:5
Proverbs 15:25	

THE PRESCRIPTION FOR PRIDE: TO DIE DAILY

How do you deal with pride? Paul's prescription for pride is dying: "I die every day—I mean that, brothers—just as surely as I glory over you in Christ Jesus our Lord" (1 Corinthians 15:31). Paul was merely echoing Jesus' own command: "If anyone would come after me, he must deny himself and take up his cross daily and follow me. For whoever wants to save his life will lose it, but whoever loses his life for me will save it" (Luke 9:23–24).

Paul reiterated further, stating, "I have been crucified with Christ and I no longer live, but Christ lives in me. The life I live in the body, I live by faith in the Son of God, who loved me and gave himself for me. I do not set aside the grace of God, for if righteousness could be gained through the law, Christ died for nothing!" (Galatians 2:20–21).

Pride isn't something that can be plucked out once and never dealt with again. Every day, and many times each day, we must choose to die to our own desires, needs, wants, wishes, dreams, likes, and hopes, taking on those of God. Each day we walk with Him the Holy Spirit will faithfully reveal to us new areas of pride we must lay down. We either sacrifice pride on the altar of confession and the work of Christ on the cross, or pride will sacrifice us on the altar of sin.

Take a moment now, and as the Holy Spirit guides you, identify key areas of your life, such as work, finances, reputation, friends, entertainment, future choices, and others, where your pride operates. Personalize these areas by including the name of the company you work for, the names of your family members, and so on, writing these names in the spaces of the "altar" below:

MY ALTAR OF SELF-SACRIFICE

Now sincerely pray, "Heavenly Father, I want to place all the areas of my life under Your control. I want to truly say with Paul, 'For to me, to live is Christ.'" Ask God's forgiveness for the areas of your life you have built around self, and surrender them to God. Ask Him to take back any ground you have surrendered to Satan.

SEXUAL BONDAGE

Closely linked to the problem of pride is another major area of bondage. This is an area that still primarily afflicts men, but it is more and more taking women, teens, and children into its grip. Sexual bondage is an ever-increasing stronghold in the lives of many Christians. The expressions of this bondage are multifaceted, ranging from masturbation fantasies and erotic romanticism to gross perversion and violence.

How is it linked to pride? Because sexual bondage means that a person seeks physical, sexual pleasure for his own satisfaction at the expense of another. It operates in the areas of power, control, and manipulation. Sexual fantasies always manipulate the character to the fantasizer's whims. The use of pornography supports the abuse of those portrayed (male and female) by the demons who oppress them. It uses others without regard to their well-being, dignity, or humanity. Since all persons are created in the image of God, this amounts to abusing the image of God as it is expressed in another human being.

Sexual bondage sets one up against the laws of God, against the laws of nature, and even against the laws of man. It is a high expression of pride and arrogance. Further, pride feeds the bondage in that those who are entrapped and struggling to get out constantly deny their weakness and in their pride refuse help and refuse to avoid the very people, places, and things that support their bondage. After a momentary victory through avoiding a specific act, they'll say to themselves something like, "I'm strong now. I can go in that newsstand and walk by the pornography rack without a worry. I can even sneak a peak if I want, and it won't bother me!"

Bondage to a stronghold means believing a lie, or a whole series of lies, that causes us to deny the truth and power of God. The lie is that we can be strong over a stronghold while we are still in bondage. The truth is that this area is a weakness, and probably always will be a weakness, that we need to bring under the blood of Christ. Instead of trying to stand up to it, we need to flee from it by claiming death to its control through Christ's work on the cross and inviting the Holy Spirit to replace the temptation with the fruit of His control (Galatians 5:22–23).

FREEDOM FROM SEXUAL BONDAGE

If you are enslaved to sexual bondage, here is a way to find freedom through Christ.

(1) Thank God that He made you a sexual being and that He has a holy plan for your sexuality that glorifies His name and brings good to humankind.

(2) Ask the Holy Spirit to help you remember the first sexual experience you had that violated God's law and began the process of giving ground to Satan. Prayerfully, allow the Lord to lead you through your life and acknowledge to Him all the areas and events He brings to your awareness.

(3) Confess all that needs to be confessed. Seek His forgiveness and ask Christ to reclaim any surrendered ground and restore you to fellowship with Him in these areas.

(4) Ask God to take back all the ground given to the Enemy through each moral failure.

(5) Dedicate your body "as a living sacrifice" to the service of God and the carrying out of His will and purposes. Acknowledge that "you are not your own" and that "your body is the temple of the Holy Spirit." Pray that the Holy Spirit will control every area of your life, beginning with your mind and including your sexual desires. Pray, "I thank You, Lord, that You created me and gave me my sexual drive. I surrender to Your purpose and control all of my sexual desires."

(6) Be vigilant and on guard for renewed attack from your flesh and spiritual oppressors. These may not be obvious, but subtle. Be ready to resist any unclean spirit (fully armored at all times). When a temptation arises, focus on your freedom through the Cross and the fruit of the Holy Spirit. Invite Him to replace the temptation with His control.

(7) Set your mind on Christ and His righteousness. Fill your mind with memorized Scriptures, which God will use to renew your thought life and provide you with weapons of defense. Refuse to give any more ground to Satan through being ruled by sexual lusts.

Review/Conclusion:

Our pride will try to tell us that we should be able easily and permanently to do away with this or that sin. Our pride will taunt us as "weaklings" if we admit that we do have areas of weakness. Our pride will try to make us feel like we are stronger than we really are. And then our pride will lead us to that very thing we need to avoid and will tell us, "Go ahead! You deserve it!"

Pride goes by many names and is expressed in many degrees: ego, selfishness, arrogance, haughtiness, narcissism, conceit, egotism, insolence, presumption, vanity and vainglory, and more. Under whatever banner it marches, it always leads to destruction.

Being puffed up with pride will cause us to drop our guard. The Enemy will find the foothold and seek to establish a stronghold in our lives. Replace pride by keeping your focus on Christ. Knowing that we are nothing and He is everything provides a shield of safety.

"Carry each other's burdens, and in this way you will fulfill the law of Christ. If anyone thinks he is something when he is nothing, he deceives himself. Each one should test his own actions. Then he can take pride in himself, without comparing himself to somebody else, for each one should carry his own load" (Galatians 6:2–5).

LESSON 5: *Getting Right, Getting Free*

Scripture for Meditation:

But whatever was to my profit I now consider loss for the sake of Christ. What is more, I consider everything a loss compared to the surpassing greatness of knowing Christ Jesus my Lord, for whose sake I have lost all things. I consider them rubbish, that I may gain Christ and be found in him, not having a righteousness of my own that comes from the law, but that which is through faith in Christ—the righteousness that comes from God and is by faith. (Philippians 3:7–9)

A Beginning Prayer:

Lord Jesus Christ, with You in my life I can do all things to Your glory. With You, nothing is too difficult to deal with. Help me as I seek to honestly confront my past, seek where appropriate to make amends, and freely offer full restitution as You direct. Amen.

Lesson:

KEEPING OUR CONSCIENCE CLEAR

If we don't keep our conscience clear, the Enemy gains an advantage over us. A clear conscience is absolutely essential for us as Christians. In fact, Paul wrote that the "goal of this command"—or the purpose of ministry or teaching—is a life that flows "from a pure heart and a good conscience and sincere faith" (1 Timothy 1:5).

A pure heart looks at the present, a clear conscience at the past, and genuine faith to the future. If your heart is pure and the past is taken care of, you can look to the future with assurance.

You can't move forward looking back. A burdened conscience is always looking over its shoulder at what's behind. Paul said, "Forgetting what is behind . . . I press on toward the goal [of] Christ Jesus" (Philippians 3:13–14). This doesn't mean you pretend that things didn't happen. You just let go of them and move on. In this verse, "forgetting" means to "disregard the significance of." We can't forget what's happened in our past: those things we've done and those things done to us. But we can refuse to allow the memories to sting our hearts whenever they surface. Once forgiven, these events are dead, and death holds no sway over us in any form.

Satan is an ace archeologist when it comes to digging up our pasts. He loves to delve into the dirt of our lives and bring up old, stinking, dead issues and shove them under our noses. His goal is to accuse us and make us think this is how God views these past, confessed, forgiven sins. It's a lie!

Look up each of the following references and answer the question or complete the phrase:

Psalm 103:12: How far from us have our sins been removed, and who removed them?

_____

_____

Jeremiah 31:34: What are two promises of God stated in this verse?

_____

_____

Hebrews 8:12: "For I will _____ their _____ and will _____ their sins _____."

Hebrews 10:17: When will God bring up our sins again?

_____

_____

Are any exceptions to the phrase "no more" stated in any of these verses?

_____

_____

What is Satan the father of? (John 8:42–47)

_____

_____

Is there any truth in Satan? Can he ever be believed?

_____

_____

If memories surface and we feel condemned, is this from God?

_____

_____

What's the difference between condemnation and conviction? Which is from God and which is from Satan? What are the results of each?

_____

_____

A good practice when memories of the past surface is to pray: "Thank You, God, for reminding me through this memory of what happens when I try to run my life instead of yielding to the control of Your Holy Spirit. Again, I release this event and those involved into Your hands. I forgive those involved, and I forgive myself and accept Your forgiveness. I reaffirm my commitment and dedication to living my life for You, and I look forward to the future with hope and excitement. As I remain in You and allow You to remain in me, I know that I will not do those kinds of things anymore."

The devil will resurrect old memories to accuse us and bring us down. Instead, if we lift Jesus up and resist Satan, he flees and the power of the memory is broken.

Clearing our conscience can involve selective acts of restitution and reconciliation. These acts may involve contact with those we have offended. For example, if theft of money was involved, the money plus interest should be returned. If we slandered someone and caused them harm, then we will need to confess and apologize.

However, caution needs to be exercised. First, we do not need to confront those who have offended us. We release them to God and forgive them, then walk away from the incident. In some instances, we may walk away from the person forever.

Second, restitution and reconciliation is not something to rush into. It's not about making ourselves feel better, especially not at the expense of making the other feel worse! We do it as an act of obedience to our Lord, so we should act only as the Holy Spirit clearly and insistently directs.

Our goal is to clear our conscience before the Lord. There are times when some things, as far as other people are concerned, are better left unsaid. If we share things about ourselves with those who are neither part of the problem nor part of the solution, we may live to regret it. The scope of forgiveness sought need be no greater than the scope of the offense—and that includes the people we tell.

Discretion is critical. If we force ourselves back into the lives of those we offended and they don't welcome the revisiting, we will only be creating a new offense. We don't have a right to spill out all of our confessions if that will wreak needless pain and havoc in someone else's life. If there are people from your past you need to forgive, God is big enough to bring them back into your life.

Follow these steps to clear your conscience from guilt:

(1) Imagine other people making a list of those who had offended them. Would you be on their list? Prayerfully go before the Lord and ask the Holy Spirit to reveal those on whose list your name would appear as an offender. Write their names below as they are revealed to you:

_____	_____
_____	_____
_____	_____
_____	_____
_____	_____

(2) For some of those on your list, you may already have resolved the situation, having sought their forgiveness. Put a line through their names, thanking God for the healing in each case. Those names remaining are those persons you have offended and never sought forgiveness from. Write their names below in the left column, and indicate the offense in the right column:

PERSON	OFFENSE
_____	_____
_____	_____
_____	_____
_____	_____
_____	_____

(3) With a trusted counselor or mature Christian friend, go through your list, briefly stating each offense. With the agreement of your partner, ask and receive God's forgiveness for each of your offenses toward these people. Ask God to reveal to you those you need to approach in person, and put a star by their names. Cross out the names of the others. Rule out

those people in whose lives your reappearance now would cause serious difficulty, for example, someone you once dated who is now married.

(4) For each of the names you have starred, call the person on the phone, if possible. Be brief and to the point. State that as you've been examining your past you realized you had failed them in _____ (name the offense). Ask for forgiveness.

(Note: All you can do is ask for forgiveness. You may not get it from them. You can't force it from them. And you really don't deserve it from them. If they refuse to forgive you, let it go, since you've done your part by owning the offense. Be courteous and friendly, wish them well, and gently hang up the phone. Release them to the Lord and move on, never looking back.)

(5) Make restitution where needed.

(6) If there are those from whom you have benefited and you've never expressed your gratitude, tell them thank you now. Call them, send them thank-you notes, and spread your appreciation around generously.

(7) Ask God to reclaim all the ground given to Satan related to these situations which have now been brought under the blood of Christ.

Review/Conclusion:

Our hope is set before us, not behind us. Our goal is heaven, not here. Our view should be of eternity, not history. Looking back and fretting over things we fear may catch up to us will only drag us down into the mud of despair. It will give the Enemy foothold after foothold to climb into our lives, establish strongholds, and hold us in bondage. This is not God's desire for His children. He wants us free, clean, and without baggage. He provides all we need for the journey to glory. All the stuff we cling to will only hold us back from all He wants us to have. We can't hold on to our "stuff" and receive the riches of His grace at the same time. We need to let go and let God!

RECOGNIZING AND RENOUNCING

How can one tell if a child is becoming involved with evil? How can one know if a behavior the child has struggled with for years could be from demonic influence? The following lists will help you answer these questions. Also included is a brief questionnaire to help you determine the areas in which you may need to renounce past involvement in damaging activities.

The behaviors in the first list could indicate potential occult involvement. However, they could also indicate behavior problems related to other factors, such as stress, grief, loss, disappointment, or failure. View any unusual or problematic behavior in the context of the person's whole life and character. Take into account all the things that are going on around the individual, as well as the personal struggles that may be going on inside them. Pray for discernment and insight.

SIGNS OF POTENTIAL INVOLVEMENT IN THE OCCULT

- Alienation from family, church, and Christianity in general
- A drastic drop in grades and a lack of school involvement
- Evidence of increasing rebellion against society and authority
- Cut or tattoo marks on the body; the little or middle fingernail of the left hand painted black indicates a dedication to evil
- Heavy involvement in fantasy or role-playing games
- Compulsive interest in heavy metal or any music containing satanic, suicidal, obscene, or despairing lyrics
- Increasing involvement with alcohol and illegal drugs
- Growing interest in the occult and the use of occult/satanic symbols drawn on the hands or arms and on books and other possessions
- Possession of occult books and magazines, black candles, ceremonial knives, a chalice, altars, robes, animal or human bones, and other ritual paraphernalia
- Heavy interest in horror (fright, slash, etc.) videos, television programs, movies, and books
- A lack of humor; smiles are rare
- Seeming pleasure regarding the suffering of animals or people
- A fascination with death or dying

As with the above, the list on the following page is not exhaustive or absolute. The items listed are not meant to be conclusive evidence of demonic activity or affliction but are merely indicative that the potential exists. Again, pray for discernment and insight.

SIGNS OF POTENTIAL DEMONIC AFFLICTION

- A compulsive desire to curse the Father, the Lord Jesus Christ, or the Holy Spirit
- A revulsion toward the Bible, including a compulsion to deface or destroy Bibles
- Strong suicidal or other compulsive, violent thoughts
- Deep-seated, irrational feelings of intense bitterness and hatred toward individuals or groups (i.e., ethnic groups)
- Any compulsive temptation that forces you to think or act in a way you truly do not want to think or act
- Compulsive desires to destroy the reputations of, attack the character of, and lie about other people; using vicious and cutting remarks to injure those perceived as a threat to a problem area in your life
- Terrifying, persistent, and overwhelming feelings of guilt and worthlessness even following sincere confession to the Lord of known sins
- Physical symptoms that appear suddenly and pass quickly for which there is no medical or other basis; these might include choking sensations, pains that move around the body, feelings of tightness around the head and eyes, dizziness, blackouts, or fainting seizures
- Deep, persistent despondency and depression
- Recurring dreams and nightmares that are especially horrifying and disturbing, or clairvoyant dreams of things that later take place
- Sudden, unprovoked surges of violent rage, uncontrollable anger, or seething hostility
- Debilitating and persistent doubt regarding one's salvation

SIGNS OF POTENTIALLY SERIOUS DEMONIC ACTIVITY

- Inability to live normally
- An expressed or exhibited kinship with death and the dead
- A proneness to violence; exhibiting unusual strength when violent
- Severe behavior and personality problems
- Persistent restlessness, agitation, and insomnia
- A sense of intense inner anguish and torment
- Self-inflicted injuries (i.e., cutting, burning, etc.) or recurrent injurious accidents

Exposure to the occult can be so subtle or have occurred far enough in our past that it is not easily recalled. The following questionnaire is useful in pinpointing those experiences so that they can be renounced in prayer. Check off each item that applies even if it's something you don't do now. If something comes to mind that's not included, write it in at the end of the list.

OCCULT AND RELATED ACTIVITY QUESTIONNAIRE

Occult Activity

_____ Have you ever visited a fortune-teller who told your fortune by:

        ___ cards   ___ tea leaves   ___ palm reading

        ___ Other _____

_____ Do you or have you ever read or followed horoscopes?

_____ Have you ever played games of an occult nature, such as:

        ___ ESP?   ___ Kabul?   ___ Other _____

_____ Have you ever consulted out of curiosity or interest:

        ___ Ouija® board?   ___ planchette?   ___ crystal ball?   ___ tea leaves?

        ___ Other _____

_____ Have you ever had a life or reincarnation reading?

_____ Have you ever   ___ had your handwriting analyzed?

                        ___ practiced mental suggestion?

                        ___ cast a magic spell or curse?

                        ___ sought a psychic experience?

_____ Have you practiced mystical meditation?

_____ Do you now or have you ever had a spirit guide?

_____ Have you ever seen or been involved in Satan worship?

_____ Are you now or have you ever been a practicing witch?

_____ Have you ever had an imaginary playmate?

_____ Have you practiced any of the martial arts (karate, etc.)?

_____ Have you practiced mind control, as in Sylon Pathways, Zen Buddhism?

Cult Activity (Direct or Indirect)

___ Hare Krishna   ___ Unitarian   ___ Spiritual Frontier Pathways

___ Scientology   ___ Church of Jesus Christ   ___ Jehovah's Witness

___ Zen Buddhism   ___ Children of God   ___ LDS (Mormons)

___ Unification Church   ___ Christian Science   ___ Meher Baba

___ TM   ___ Theosophy   ___ Baha'i World Faith

___ Hippie-ism   ___ est   ___ Inner Peace Movement

___ Unity   ___ Rosicrucianism   ___ Gurdjieff Foundation

___ Religious Research of America (The Fourth Way)   ___ The Way International

___ The Local Church

___ Others _____   _____   _____

RITUAL PRACTICES, READINGS, OR USE OF OBJECTS

_____ Have you ever sought, or been subject to as a child, healing through magic conjuration and charming, for things such as the removal of warts and burns, treatment of disease, etc., through:

___ a spiritualist?	___ metaphysical use of a pendulum?
___ Christian Science healer?	___ hypnosis?
___ spirit healer?	___ trance for diagnosis?
___ psychic healer?	___ Other _____

_____ Have you ever received or worn an amulet, talisman, or charm for luck or protection?

_____ Have you ever sought to locate missing persons or objects by consulting someone with psychic, clairvoyant, or psychometric powers?

_____ Have you or has anyone on your behalf practiced water witching (aka dowsing or diving) to locate water, etc., using a twig or pendulum?

_____ Do you read or possess occult or spiritualist literature such as books on:

___ astrology?	___ fortune-telling?	___ dream interpretation?
___ black magic?	___ ESP?	___ clairvoyance?
___ cultic literature?	___ self-realization?	___ psychic phenomena?

_____ Have you ever experimented with or practiced

___ extrasensory perception (ESP)?	___ telepathy?

_____ Have you practiced any form of magic charming or ritual?

_____ Do you possess any occult or pagan religious objects, relics, or artifacts which may have been used in pagan temples and religious rites or in the practice of sorcery, magic, divination, or spiritualism?

CONSCIOUSNESS PROBLEMS

_____ Have you ever lost awareness of time (minutes or hours) ending up somewhere and not knowing how you got there?

_____ Do you or have you ever experienced extreme drowsiness during sermons or discussion of Christian spiritual things?

_____ Have you ever exhibited extraordinary abilities, such as ESP or telekinesis?

_____ Have you ever or do you hear voices in your mind that mock, intimidate, accuse, threaten, or bargain?

_____ Do you (or a relative) speak about yourself (himself) using the third person (we)?

_____ Have you ever had supernatural experiences or encounters, such as hauntings, movement or disappearance of objects, etc.?

WIELDING THE SWORD: WARFARE PRAYERS AND MORE

Scripture Memory Verse:

During the days of Jesus' life on earth, he offered up prayers and petitions with loud cries and tears to the one who could save him from death, and he was heard because of his reverent submission. (Hebrews 5:7)

Unit Learning Goal:

Recognizing the centrality of prayer and the Word to successful warfare.

Overview of Unit 6:

Lesson 1: The Power of the Word

Lesson 2: Reading and Studying the Word

Lesson 3: Memorizing the Word

Lesson 4: Praying the Word

Lesson 5: Psalm 18

SUMMARY STATEMENT

God has lovingly provided us with two immensely powerful tools that enable us to know how to live our lives in Christ and communicate with our heavenly Father. Through the Word we learn the path to righteousness, and through prayer we gain the power to live in righteousness.

Unit 6 Thought Focus:

The Bible has been called God's love letter to His children. It's also been called the Christian's Handbook. The Word of God is both and more—it provides practical instruction, reveals the character and nature of God, yields accurate historical accounts, and gives practical biographical examples. God has gone to extraordinary lengths to ensure that His Word was faithfully recorded, translated, printed, and passed on from generation to generation. The Bible is a great treasure for all believers.

Prayer also is a powerful gift from God. Not only can we read about Him, He has also provided this marvelous means through which we can communicate directly with Him. We are enabled to know Him and be in a close, communing relationship with Him. We can talk to Him, and we can invite Him to talk to us through our prayers.

Combine heavy ingestion of the Word with copious periods of prayer, and you have the formula for success in your Christian walk and in spiritual warfare.

LESSON 1: *The Power of the Word*

Scripture for Meditation:

Preach the Word; be prepared in season and out of season; correct, rebuke and encourage—with great patience and careful instruction. (2 Timothy 4:2)

A Beginning Prayer:

Dear heavenly Father, instill Your Word deep in my being. Let Your truth permeate my being and become truth and life to me. Let the Words of Scripture bubble up in my thinking all day long and become actions taken and words spoken. Let all I do, all I say, and all that I am emerge from the ground of Your powerful Word at all times. Amen.

Lesson:

THE ABSOLUTE TRUTH OF THE BIBLE

Basic to the victory of believers over Satan, the flesh, and the world is the absolute truth of the Bible and its doctrine. There has never been a time when the soundness of solid biblical doctrine was more critical than now. Why? "For the time will come when men will not put up with sound doctrine. Instead, to suit their own desires, they will gather around them a great number of teachers to say what their itching ears want to hear. They will turn their ears away from the truth and turn aside to myths" (2 Timothy 4:3–4).

Below, check the items that are examples of believers with "itching ears." Discuss your responses.

☐ 1. Church-hopping—never settling into a body

☐ 2. Chasing the latest fads in worship

☐ 3. Reading the Word daily

☐ 4. Listening to radio call-in shows on conspiracies and plots

☐ 5. Looking to "new truth" outside the Word for direction

☐ 6. Praying and fasting and walking in humble faith

All around us we see people throwing off all constraint, pushing the Bible out of schools, courtrooms, businesses, and more. All the while, masses run after the newest hot idea being proclaimed by the latest best-selling guru. When the Bible is quoted, it is torn and twisted out of context and misapplied to support immoral and ungodly ideas and behaviors.

The only protection we have against false doctrine is to be totally immersed in God's doctrine. And the best defense we have against all the lies of the Enemy is the Word of God. Satan backs off from nothing but the absolute truth and fact of God's Word. Doctrine is not just something we learn in church or Bible college. Sound doctrine is what we are to live out every day.

Steady emotions, enlightened minds, the sincerest desires, and the strongest wishes are no match against the wiles of the devil. In fact, these are the areas he'll attack first. With all of my being I can want and wish to love and serve the Lord and avoid being defeated by Satan, but I will fail sincerely if I fail to use the truth of God as a source of strength and defense. My own devices are powerless against Satan. Without the Word we aren't equipped.

THE BIBLE AS A SOURCE OF STRENGTH AND DEFENSE

Look up the Scripture references and fill in the blanks or answer the following questions:

Second Timothy 3:16–17: _____ *Scripture is _____ and is useful for teaching, rebuking, correcting and training in righteousness, so that the man of God may be _____ equipped for _____ good work.*

What parts of the Bible aren't useful, so therefore can be ignored?

_____

_____

What areas of Christian living will the Bible *not* equip or will only *partially* equip me to deal with?

_____

_____

If men wrote the Bible and men aren't infallible, why can I trust the Bible?

_____

_____

According to the verse above, what are the four areas the Bible is useful for? Circle the correct words:

confusing	berating	correcting	washing	teaching
shielding	training	rebuking	saving	

Hebrews 4:12: *For the word of God is _____ and _____. Sharper than any double-edged sword, it penetrates even to dividing soul and spirit, joints and marrow; it _____ the thoughts and attitudes of the heart.*

Is God's Word dead or alive? Active or inactive? What difference does it make?

_____

_____

What is the difference between a thought and an attitude of the heart?

_____

_____

What truth exists in the world that is sharper and more penetrating than God's Word?

_____

_____

Read this verse in *The Amplified Bible* and then write your own paraphrase of the verse:

_____

_____

Second Peter 1:3–4: *His divine power has given us* _____ *we need for life and godliness through our* _____ *of him who called us by his own glory and goodness. Through these he has given us his very great and precious promises, so that through them* _____ *in the divine nature and escape the corruption in the world caused by* _____.

Circle **T** for True or **F** for False and then discuss your answers:

T   **F**   God has provided only a few of the tools we need to live an effective Christian life.

T   **F**   We attain godliness in character through feeling really good about God and ourselves.

T   **F**   The promises of God are precious and are found in His Word.

T   **F**   Corruption in the world is caused by our evil desires.

T   **F**   We can know about God, but we don't have a share in His divine nature.

T   **F**   Escape from sinning can be found through application of God's promises to our lives.

Review/Conclusion:

How many Bibles do you have in your home? How many different translations do you own? How many of these Bibles have dust collecting on them and have few or no verses underlined? How many show virtually no evidence of having been opened or read recently?

We are a spoiled people when it comes to the riches of God's Word. Translations, paraphrases, and supporting references abound. All the tools and more that we need in order to fully delve into the bottomless treasures of Scripture are readily available to most of the population of the world. Yet, we spend far more time being busy with our lives, watching sitcoms on television, reading current best-sellers, or just relaxing than we spend reading the Bible.

And then we complain bitterly to God when circumstances well up against us, when we're confronted with a dilemma, when our families begin to crumble. We suddenly feel lost, abandoned, and adrift in the midst of trials. This should not be!

We have been given *all* we need, *everything* we need to live godly lives and escape the debilitating effects of a sinful world. What do *all* and *everything* mean? They mean *all* and *everything!* It means an amount or quantity from which nothing is left out or held back! God has withheld *no* good thing from us, but we have withheld much from Him, including total devotion to His Word.

The Word energizes, purifies, washes, renews, heals, clarifies, banishes confusion, sets our minds at peace, grounds us solidly on the eternal rock of our salvation. Without the Word buried deep in our hearts we're allowing Satan access to our lives. We're fair game! And as a result, we'll become his trophy of defeat and spiritual bondage.

We need daily large infusions of the Word if we want to defeat the enemy of our soul. There are no shortcuts to victory.

LESSON 2: *Reading and Studying the Word*

Scripture for Meditation:
In the beginning was the Word, and the Word was with God, and the Word was God.
(John 1:1)

A Beginning Prayer:
Dear heavenly Father, fill me with an unending hunger and an unquenchable thirst for Your Word. Amen.

Lesson:

UNDERSTANDING GOD'S WORD

The Bible can be an intimidating book since it's actually sixty-six books in one! It's understandable and reasonable that people might have a difficult time knowing where to start in learning the Word. Not only is the amount of information provided in the Bible intimidating, but the nature of some of the passages also can be alternately confusing and tedious. The "begats" passages aren't very exciting, and much of Revelation is baffling.

Add to these challenges the call to systematically study or even memorize Bible passages and one can be filled with hopelessness and frustration. Of course, this is exactly the goal of Satan! He wants us to believe the lie that we can't ever hope to understand God's Word.

What's the whole truth? First, on our own we can't understand the Bible. Our natural minds are unable to appreciate the mighty and truly mysterious truths of Scripture. To a worldly mind, the Word of God is foolishness (1 Corinthians 1:18). Without Christ, our minds are unregenerate and worldly, and this is where the devil would leave us. To this kind of thinking, Paul says, "Are you so foolish? After beginning with the Spirit, are you now trying to attain your goal by human effort?" (Galatians 3:3).

Here's the rest of the truth: We begin in Christ through the Spirit, we continue in the Spirit, we will end in the Spirit. Understanding God's Word does not come through our human effort. It comes through the empowerment and enlightenment of the Holy Spirit.

The books of the Bible are listed in the following table, but not in order. Plus there are "extra" books listed (not really in the Bible). Cross out the names of fake books. For the others, in the column after the book name write either OT for Old Testament or NT for New Testament (without looking in your Bible's table of contents!). Check your work with your group:

Hezekiah		Revelation		Jude	
Matthew		Haggai		1 Samuel	
Titus		Genesis		2 Samuel	
Exodus		Philemon		Ephesians	
Ezra		Malachi		Jeremiah	
Psalms		Leviticus		Lamentations	
Philippians		Jonah		Micah	
Isaiah		Nahum		Daniel	
Luke		Phoebe		Zephaniah	
Ezekiel		Nehemiah		1 Corinthians	
Proverbs		Hebrews		2 Corinthians	
1 Kings		Acts		Obadiah	
2 Kings		James		Habakkuk	
1 Israel		Joshua		Nathan	
2 Israel		Jezeniah		1 Peter	
1 Chronicles		John		2 Peter	
2 Chronicles		1 John		Galatians	
Joel		2 John		Amos	
Numbers		3 John		Colossians	
Hosea		4 John		Deuteronomy	
Romans		1 Thessalonians		Judges	
Song of Solomon		2 Thessalonians		Phyllis	
Zechariah		1 Timothy		Ruth	
Ecclesiastes		2 Timothy		Esther	
Mark		Job		Episcopals	

Too tired to read the Word? Ask the Spirit to give you endurance and alertness. Confused about where to begin? Ask the Holy Spirit to direct you into a course of reading and study. Don't understand a difficult passage? Ask the Spirit of God to open your mind and your heart that you might understand. As you keep reading the Bible, you will keep growing in His understanding.

PRECONDITIONS OF EFFECTIVE BIBLE STUDY

In his book *How to Study the Bible*, R. A. Torrey lists eight preconditions for effective Bible study:

(1) *You must be born again.* This seems obvious. However, many have picked up the Word and come away unimpressed because they had not been drawn by the Holy Spirit. We've already learned that Bible study will be unprofitable without the Holy Spirit's help.

Are you a Christian? Do you have Jesus in your heart? Do you want and need to be born again? If so, stop right now and with a sincere heart pray this simple prayer of faith, asking Jesus to become Savior of your life:

Dear Lord Jesus Christ, I acknowledge that I am a sinner and that I need Your mercy, grace, and cleansing in my life. On my own effort I cannot be good enough to become holy. Forgive me of all my sins. Wash me inside and out with Your blood. Make me a new creature in You. Place Your Holy Spirit in my heart to enable me to walk worthy after You. Give me a hunger and desire to read and do Your Word. Be Lord of my life completely. Thank You for Your forgiveness and salvation. Thank You, Jesus, for coming into my heart even now. I place my life in Your hands and desire to do Your will at all times in all ways. Amen.

(2) *You must have a love for the Bible.* If you're eating food you like, you'll enjoy your meal much more than if the food is not to your liking! Again, the Spirit of God will instill in you a hunger for His Word, if the Spirit is in you. Plus, the more you enter into the Word, the more your love for the Word will grow.

(3) *You must be willing to work hard.* If you're looking for quick, pat answers to life's problems, you're not going to find them in the Word. Why? All the answers you need are there, but they reveal themselves to those who dig for them. Just as the earth will yield gold and diamonds when it is mined, so effort must be expended to extract the Bible's treasures. If you're not willing to think and use the intellectual and reasoning capacities God gave you, the Word will ever remain a mystery to you.

Which has been more valuable to you, an experience that came easily or one that involved great effort and endurance? Why?

_____

_____

(4) *Your will must be wholly surrendered to God.* Says Torrey, "A surrendered will gives that clearness of spiritual vision necessary to understand God's Book. Many of the difficulties and obscurities of the Bible rise simply because the will of the student is not surrendered to the will of the Author of the Book."

(5) *You must be obedient to the teachings of the Word as soon as they are encountered.* James exhorts us to be doers of the Word, not just hearers (James 1:22). To read the Word and then not do what it says is to be self-deceived and easy prey for Satan.

(6) *You must have a childlike mind.* "God reveals His deepest truths to babes," says Torrey. "A child is not full of his own wisdom. He recognizes his ignorance and is ready to be taught." So many approach the Word ready to tell it what it says! To reap a rich harvest from the Word, it's vital that we possess a teachable heart and fully lay aside our own preconceived notions. A childish mind talks back to God; a childlike heart welcomes instruction from the Father.

How does a healthy child view the world around her as she encounters things for the first time? Circle all the letters that apply:

    A. With wide-eyed wonder and awe

    B. Arguing against every new thing and discounting its value

C. With endless curiosity

D. With innocence and complete trust

E. With constant fear, doubt, and insecurity

(7) *You must study the Word of God as the Word of God.* What does this mean? It means we accept the commands and teachings presented without question. We rely absolutely on all the promises of God as totally true. We are quick to adjust our lives to the truths we encounter. We recognize that the Bible *is* the Word of God, and we enter His presence as we read.

(8) *You must read prayerfully.* Torrey suggests even reading the Bible on your knees. Or, he says, "Never open the Bible without at least lifting your heart to God in silent prayer that He will interpret it and illumine its pages by the light of His Spirit."

CHOOSING A BIBLE

So where do you begin? First, you'll need a Bible in a reliable translation that is readable. Every person's individual tastes vary. Go to a bookstore that sells Bibles and read the same three passages in each translation (for example, Psalm 23; Matthew 6; or Ephesians 6) until you find a style you're comfortable with. Good translations include the historic King James Version, the *New International Version*, the *New King James Version*, the *New Living Translation*, and the *New American Standard Bible*, to name a few. A popular and enjoyable paraphrase is *The Living Bible.*

Any of these versions published in a study edition will be especially helpful. Study Bibles include useful tools, such as book outlines, introductions, commentary, and more, that will enhance your reading and study immensely.

STUDY OF A BIBLE BOOK OR PASSAGE

Next, you need to pick a place to begin. Some good books to start with are Psalms, Mark, John, or 1 Thessalonians. Once you've settled on a place to begin, here are some simple steps to follow to gain fuller appreciation of the Word.

(1) *Read the book.* Read the entire book through two to three times, preferably in one sitting. In the case of Psalms, which is actually four books in one, you'll need to take it in sections. Just reading a book of the Bible all at once will be very enlightening.

(2) *Outline the book.* Most Bibles today are already broken into various sections. Even so, try to write out your own outline in your own words as to how you believe the book is structured.

(3) *Study the points.* Work your outline and study in more detail one major point at a time. Reread the verses in these sections. Look up the cross-references that are listed. If you're using a study edition, read all the associated commentary and notes.

(4) *Meditate on the meaning.* Prayerfully ask the Holy Spirit to illuminate the passage to your spiritual mind. Think about how you can apply the truths stated or what the passage could mean to you and your family.

(5) *Journal your insights.* Keep a notebook handy when you read or study the Word. Write down all the things that come to mind as you read, including insights, practical application ideas, and questions you have about the passage. Ask the Holy Spirit to answer your questions at the proper time as you continue with your study.

TOPICAL OR WORD STUDY

This type of study involves using your concordance or a topical Bible reference book to examine all that the Bible has to say on a specific topic or word. For example, a topic would be "the character of God." A word study would look at all the references to one word, such as "love."

List five words or topics you want to study:

_____

_____

CHARACTER STUDY

This is the same as a topical or word study, only you'll look up every reference you can find on a specific biblical character, such as Paul or Moses.

List five names of biblical characters you want to study:

_____

_____

There! That's not so difficult, is it? These methods are a start, a few of the many approaches to Bible reading and study. Your local Christian bookstore will have a variety of study aids that can prove to be very valuable. Your pastor can also direct you to especially useful tools. As you grow in your appreciation and love for the Word, you'll want to tackle more and more challenging approaches to Bible study.

Review/Conclusion:

If you're planning a trip, you'll never arrive if you never start. You'll never read the Bible unless you pick it up, open it, and start reading! Good intentions are useless if never acted upon. If you truly love the Lord, no person or thing will be able to hold you back from the pages of the Bible. If your heart is not drawn to the Word of God, pray to the Holy Spirit for help. Pray simply, "Holy Spirit, fill me with an unending hunger and an unquenchable thirst for the Word of God. Place in my heart an unyielding passion and burning desire to read and study the Bible." Ask Him, and He will give you what you ask!

If you can do nothing else, exercising your control of yourself, make yourself at least read in the Psalms every day. Even in the worst periods of stress, crisis, despair, and illness, Christians everywhere will testify to the soothing power and comforting strength that can be found in the Psalms. God will honor your effort, and you will be lifted up as the Word goes into you, even a little at a time. But you must make the choice to read it daily.

LESSON 3: *Memorizing the Word*

Scripture for Meditation:

The Word became flesh and made his dwelling among us. We have seen his glory, the glory of the One and Only, who came from the Father, full of grace and truth. (John 1:14)

A Beginning Prayer:

Dear heavenly Father, I can never know enough of Your Word or get too much of it in me. Help me now to set myself to taking in Your Word more seriously and more memorably than ever before. As I work to read and study the Scriptures, burn them into my very being. Write Your truths on my heart and mind. Shut my ears to the claim of Satan that I can't memorize Your Word—that's a lie. I can do all things as You give me strength! Strengthen me now in this endeavor. Amen.

Lesson:

SCENARIO #1: SAM AND THE CHURCH SOLO

Sam agreed to sing a solo at church for the Sunday morning worship service several weeks in advance. However, instead of going right out to a music store and selecting a song and accompaniment tape, he said to himself, "I've got plenty of time. I'll do it later." As the date for him to sing approached, Sam kept putting the preparation off. Finally, it was the Monday before the Sunday he was to sing, and Sam still didn't have a tape. Going through his CDs he came across a song he thought he could sing and began calling area stores for the accompaniment tape. None of the stores in town had what he needed. He dug out a mail-order catalog and called the company. Fortunately they had the tape in stock, and for the cost of the tape plus twice more for shipping, they could have it to him by Thursday. The tape came Friday, which gave Sam enough time to learn the song, but not to memorize the words. He would need to refer to the words on Sunday morning. When Sunday came, as he was leaving the house in a hurry since he was running late for church, he bumped into the door and knocked his glasses off. The impact on the porch broke them. He would have to wear an old pair to drive to church. Since the ones that broke were the only bifocals he had, there was no way he'd be able to read the words to the song. When he got to church, he approached the music director and explained that he would not be able to sing that morning. Since there was no backup, there was no special music for the morning worship.

How many things went wrong for Sam that prevented his singing? What were they?

_____

_____

Is there any course of action Sam could have taken that would have ensured his being able to sing despite his breaking his glasses? If so, what could he have done?

_____

_____

What did Sam's lack of preparation cost him? Money and what else?

_____

_____

What impact did Sam's lack of preparation have on the body of Christ? What difference could there have been had he been able to sing?

_____

_____

If we aren't memorizing the Word, this is how Satan will trip us up—by placing us in everyday annoying circumstances that build from little molehills into seemingly impossible-to-overcome mountains. With the Word in our hearts and minds, deep spiritual foundations begin to build within us. Through memorized texts, each temptation can be met with a verse that defuses the confusion and clears our minds. Each fiery dart is quenched by the inward store of truth.

SCENARIO #2: JANE AND THE DRIVER'S MANUAL

Jane was excited about getting her driver's license but hated having to study for the test. She disliked tests and would do nearly anything to avoid them. The thought of having to memorize nearly the entire driver's manual did not appeal to her at all. But she *did* want to drive! A friend from school, Ellen, had recently taken the test, and Ellen's uncle, Bill, worked in the Department of Motor Vehicles. Jane found out that Ellen's uncle had told her there were only two versions of the test, and only certain questions were covered. Ellen marked the items in Jane's book she would need to study in order to pass either version of the test. Jane focused only on those items, which represented about a third of the main points of information covered in the manual. She took the test, passed, and got her driver's license.

She was so excited she convinced her parents to let her take the car out on her own. She picked up her friend Ellen to celebrate. As they were driving to a popular hangout across town, they were suddenly confronted with an exceptional traffic situation neither had expected. It terrified both of them. "What do I do?" shrieked Jane. "I don't know!" cried Ellen. "But wasn't there something in the manual about these kinds of situations?" shouted Jane frantically. "Yes, I think so!" Ellen screamed back. "But I didn't read that part! It wasn't on the te . . . !" Ellen wasn't able to complete the sentence, as the car had gone completely out of control. They crashed forcefully into an oncoming truck. Both girls died instantly. Jane hadn't read that part of the manual either.

This scenario is a bit exaggerated, but how do you think it relates to memorizing God's Word?

_____

_____

How did Jesus deal with Satan when confronted and tempted by him in the wilderness? Did Jesus have a written copy of the Jewish Scriptures with Him?

_____

_____

Is there any way for us to know when, where, and how Satan will attack or tempt us?

_____

_____

Even if you always have a Bible with you, do you know exactly where to look for the specific Scriptures you'll need to thwart *every* confrontation with hell?

_____

_____

Is it reasonable to expect the privilege of results (blessings) without the experience of the effort?

_____

_____

A KEY TO MEMORIZING SCRIPTURE

These examples are both a bit amusing and tragic, yet both are realistic in their use as metaphors for how we frequently arm ourselves for warfare. In both examples, there were real costs. In the second example, the costs were extremely high. We never know when, where, or how Satan will come against us. We don't know what person or circumstance he will try to influence to bring us down. The attack could come from any direction at any time and be directed toward any number of weaknesses present in our lives. The only way to be prepared to counter these attacks is through the reading and memorization of Scripture. The more we read and memorize, the better we'll be armored.

Now, if merely reading and studying the Bible is intimidating to many people, the concept of memorization is triply so! When confronted with such a vast volume of information, how can we possibly memorize all of it? For reasons known only to himself, it's been reported that a man once ate an entire car. When asked how he had done such an awesome thing, he replied simply, "One bite at a time."

He literally had taken just a few ounces of metal and plastic and other material off the car at a time, ground it all up, and sprinkled it on top of normal food. The process of eating an entire car took a few years. But, ridiculous as it seems, he did it!

And this is the key to memorizing Scripture: *Do it one bite at a time.* The two key words are *bite* and *time. Bite* is especially appropriate since the Word offers a spiritual feast for the true believer. And, as you know, you are what you eat! But before you sit down to eat, you need to (a) set aside regular, recurring blocks of time for the meal and (b) plan the meal.

Take some time right now to covenant with God to begin a course of Scripture reading and memorization. Prayerfully complete the following declaration. Be reasonable and realistic in setting times. These can be blocks of fifteen minutes or more. Don't overcommit yourself, which will only lead to failure and disappointment. You can always set aside more time later.

Dear heavenly Father, on this day _____ *(date), I,* _____ *(your name), commit to setting aside the following times and days each week to faithfully devote myself to the reading and memorization of Your Holy Word:*

DAYS OF THE WEEK	TIMES (START AND END TIMES)
_____	_____
_____	_____
_____	_____
_____	_____
_____	_____
_____	_____

By Your Holy Spirit, help me seal this commitment in my heart. Set my will to the successful completion of this commitment each week. Lord, go before me in time, and clear the obstacles the Enemy will send in an attempt to divert me from this plan. Make my path clear and level and unobstructed. Amen.

Signed: _____

A well-balanced diet will be planned around nutritional needs. The same is true for Scripture memorization. You may want to start with Scriptures that address your specific needs and areas of weakness. This will allow you to apply the truth against the Enemy where you're getting hit the hardest over and over.

Many Bibles have sections that will point you to several verses that address a particular topic. Such references can help you build a checklist of Scriptures to begin memorizing. Or you may want to use the results of a topical or word study you've done. Below are a few examples of shorter and longer passages to which you may add other verses:

TOPIC: PROTECTION

Joshua 23:10	1 Samuel 2:9	Job 5:19
Psalm 9:9	Psalm 27	Psalm 91:9–13
Psalm 121:8	John 17	2 Thessalonians 3:3

TOPIC: MONEY

Psalm 23:1	Proverbs 11:28	Proverbs 19:1
Proverbs 21:20	Malachi 3:10	1 John 3:17

TOPIC: LUST

1 Kings 11:3	Matthew 5:27–29	Luke 11:33–36
1 Corinthians 13:4–7		

Below, for each block of time you've set aside, select one topic to focus on and find appropriate verses to memorize. Ask the Holy Spirit to help you as you complete these charts. You may want to get ideas from your friends or your pastor.

Review/Conclusion:

To be successful in any venture you need to be prepared. To become prepared, you need a plan and you need to work that plan faithfully. This is true whether you're learning a new subject in school or a new skill on the job. Once you've completed your memorization commitment, schedule, and topics, you'll have the plan! As you begin working that plan, you'll be amazed at how easily memorization will come. God will respond to your commitment by strengthening you, quickening your mind, and sealing His Word in your heart and soul. It will become part of you and part of your armor as you stand ever more firmly and fearlessly in the face of Satan's onslaughts. Learning longer portions of the Word and praying them back to God can be most rewarding.

LESSON 4: *Praying the Word*

Scripture for Meditation:

That which was from the beginning, which we have heard, which we have seen with our eyes, which we have looked at and our hands have touched—this we proclaim concerning the Word of life. (1 John 1:1)

A Beginning Prayer:

Dear heavenly Father, thank You for the grace given to me in Jesus. Thank You for enhancing my life in every way—in my speaking and in my understanding—as the reality of Christ is confirmed in me. You have equipped me with every spiritual gift, and I eagerly look forward to my Lord's return. I know You will keep me strong to the end. Thank You for calling me into fellowship with the Lord Jesus Christ. I know He is faithful. Amen.

Lesson:

Most believers are familiar with the disciplines of reading, studying, and memorizing Scripture, but many may not be familiar with another very powerful use of the Word: *personalizing* and *praying* it.

PERSONALIZING SCRIPTURE

An effective method for applying the Word to your life and making it really come alive is to personalize passages as if they were written specifically to you! In fact, God's Word was written just that way since every verse has a purpose to help *you* grow in *your* faith. The Word is living and active. Its purpose is to teach, correct, rebuke, and train *you* in righteousness.

Personalizing passages of Scripture will be a powerful source of comfort and reinforce your efforts of memorization. Below is 1 Corinthians 1:4–9. In each of the blanks, write in your first name, then read the passage aloud. Imagine that this is a letter you've just received from Paul!

Dear _____,

    I always thank God for you because of his grace given you in Christ Jesus.

    For in him you, _____, have been enriched in every way—in all your speaking and in all your knowledge—because our testimony about Christ was confirmed in you.

    Therefore you do not lack any spiritual gift as you eagerly wait for our Lord Jesus Christ to be revealed. He will keep you strong to the end, so that you, _____, will be blameless on the day of our Lord Jesus Christ.

    God, who has called you into fellowship with his Son Jesus Christ our Lord, is faithful.

    Maranatha, _____!

                   Yours in Christ,
                   Paul

PRAYING SCRIPTURE

Another powerful use of the Word is to pray it. How often have you sensed a need to pray over a specific problem or issue in your life, yet felt you just didn't know the right words? This is a common experience. The solution is right in God's Word. There are prayers scattered throughout the Bible that can both serve as models for your own prayers or be adapted to your specific need. Probably the most well-known Scripture prayer is the model Christ gave to His disciples:

> "This, then, is how you should pray: 'Our Father in heaven, hallowed be your name, your kingdom come, your will be done on earth as it is in heaven. Give us today our daily bread. Forgive us our debts, as we also have forgiven our debtors. And lead us not into temptation, but deliver us from the evil one.'" (Matthew 6:9–13)

Every time you speak the Lord's Prayer, you are praying Scripture. In addition to specific prayers, all Scripture can be used in prayer. It's perfectly acceptable for believers to take various passages, modify the wording, and put them together to form a prayer. Doing this is not a rewriting of Scripture or tampering with the Word. Rather, it is applying the Word in practical, biblical warfare.

The only caution: We must never create any prayer that misuses or misrepresents God's established Word. Our prayers are to be doctrinally correct and biblically accurate. That's their very power! Satan cannot stand against the doctrinally correct Word-based prayer because it is absolute truth.

Let's take another look at 1 Corinthians 1:4–9 and rewrite this passage into a warfare prayer:

> Dear heavenly Father, I always thank You because of Your grace given to me in Christ Jesus.
>
> For in Christ, I have been enriched in *every* way—in *all* my speaking and in *all* my knowledge—because Your testimony about Christ is confirmed in me.
>
> Therefore I do not lack *any* spiritual gift as I eagerly wait for my Lord Jesus Christ to be revealed. He *will* keep me strong to the end, so that I *will* be *blameless* on the day of our Lord Jesus Christ.
>
> God, You have called me into fellowship with Your Son Jesus Christ my Lord, who is faithful. Amen.

Read 1 Corinthians 1:4–9 in its original form in your Bible, and then reread the personalized and the prayer versions above. Can you begin to see how much more God's Word comes alive using these methods? Can you see how useful praying these truths in the midst of a spiritual battle can be? This brief passage is full of rich truths about who you are in Christ, how God has called you to Himself, and how you can be absolutely assured that He can and will faithfully sustain you in all things! (Remember: *all* means *all!*)

Again, read 1 Corinthians 1:4–9 in its original form in your Bible. Then reread the personalized and the prayer versions above. Finally, answer these questions:

Circle **T** for True or **F** for False and then discuss your answers:

**T   F   ** God's grace has absolutely been given to me in Christ.
**T   F   ** In Christ, my life is better in only a few areas.
**T   F   ** I have every spiritual gift I need to live a victorious Christian life.
**T   F   ** God may or may not keep me strong until the end.
**T   F   ** My pastor brought me into fellowship with Jesus.
**T   F   ** Jesus is faithful, absolutely.

Rewrite each of the False statements to make them True statements:

_____

_____

_____

_____

_____

_____

You can develop Scripture prayers for all kinds of situations and needs. You can pray the Word as protection over your children. You can pray the Word over illness for healing. You can pray the Word over your financial situation for guidance. You can pray the Word over any situation, person, and need in your life at any time!

Where do you begin? First, you can take the results of your reading, study, and memorization efforts and begin to build Word prayers around the topics, subjects, and verses you've become familiar with. If you've done topic or word studies, these are the most likely areas around which you need to pray the Word.

Another wonderful source of Word prayers is the book of Psalms. Virtually every psalm was written as a prayer, song, or responsive reading. In the next section, we're going to take an extended look at Psalm 18 as it applies to spiritual warfare.

Keep in mind that praying the Word is not an incantation, mantra, or magic formula that in mere repetition will force God to move and make things happen the way you want. Rather, it is a way to put God's Word into practical use against the Enemy. Praying the Word will reinforce its truth in your heart and mind and will build your faith. Our faith is in God, not in repeating certain arrangements of words. Our trust is in Him and the truth He has provided us to walk in freedom. Our goal is not to attempt to force God to do what we believe He should do. It's asking Him to do His will. Faith is not a formula; it is a walk—a way of life.

Review/Conclusion:

One of the most common excuses offered for not praying is the same complaint spoken by the disciples: "I don't know how to pray." As Jesus quickly illustrated to the Twelve, it's not that hard. Prayer is simply talking the truth. When directed at God, it is to honor and worship Him and share our hearts with Him—our true hearts. When used in warfare, it is to beat back the lies of Satan and force him to retreat. Truth is powerful. God's Word is all truth, and it's available to us all the time. The more we read and study the Word, the more we'll want to read and study. The more time we spend memorizing, the easier memorization will become. And as we read, study, and memorize more of God's Word, praying it in the face of demonic distress will become second nature. As we yield ourselves completely to the Holy Spirit and pray in the Spirit, we will see that the Spirit will frequently pray the Word through us. Then strongholds will crumble!

LESSON 5: *Psalm 18*

David is a remarkable character. In his lifetime he confronted a variety of flesh-and-blood enemies, both man and beast. He also suffered a great deal of personal tragedy, some caused by others and some caused by his own sinfulness. Even though anointed to be king at a young age, David did not come into his kingship for many years. In fact, he was betrayed and forced to go into hiding to preserve his life. David was familiar with warfare and was a valiant warrior. He was also a man of deep emotion and intense creativity. The life of David offers a rich variety of stories, examples, and experiences. We can all find many things from David's life with which we can identify.

David's psalms are poetry, praise, prayers, songs, and beautifully literate statements of doctrinal truth. When put into the context of spiritual warfare (i.e., our battle is not with flesh and blood), David's writings can take on new power and insight. Psalm 18 is an excellent example. We're going to use this psalm as a beginning place for you to launch your program of organized Bible study and reading. You're also going to have an opportunity to develop a personalized portion from this psalm, as well as a warfare prayer.

In the tables below, the verses of the entire psalm are in the left column. In the right column are insights and commentary, questions, and space for you to make your own observations. You should first work through this lesson on your own and then discuss your insights and answers in your group. But before you begin writing anything, be sure to read through the psalm two or three times. Prayerfully ask the Holy Spirit to prepare your heart to see and receive new truth as you look into God's Holy Word.

(1) For the director of music. Of David the servant of the Lord. He sang to the Lord the words of this song when the Lord delivered him from the hand of all his enemies and from the hand of Saul. He said:

I love you, O Lord, my strength.

(2) The Lord is my rock, my fortress and my deliverer; my God is my rock, in whom I take refuge. He is my shield and the horn of my salvation, my stronghold.

(3) I call to the Lord, who is worthy of praise, and I am saved from my enemies.

• • •

(4) The cords of death entangled me; the torrents of destruction overwhelmed me.

(5) The cords of the grave coiled around me; the snares of death confronted me.

(6) In my distress I called to the Lord; I cried to my God for help. From his temple he heard my voice; my cry came before him, into his ears.

• • •

(7) The earth trembled and quaked, and the foundations of the mountains shook; they trembled because he was angry.

(8) Smoke rose from his nostrils; consuming fire came from his mouth, burning coals blazed out of it.

(9) He parted the heavens and came down; dark clouds were under his feet.

(10) He mounted the cherubim and flew; he soared on the wings of the wind.

(11) He made darkness his covering, his canopy around him—the dark rain clouds of the sky.

(12) Out of the brightness of his presence clouds advanced, with hailstones and bolts of lightning.

(13) The Lord thundered from heaven; the voice of the Most High resounded.

(14) He shot his arrows and scattered the enemies, great bolts of lightning and routed them.

List on the left the words David uses to describe God, on the right how you think God is these things:

_____ _____

_____ _____

_____ _____

_____ _____

_____ _____

_____ _____

What do these verses speak to your heart?

Who holds the power of death? (Hebrews 2:14) _____

Who sets snares (traps, deceptions, lies) to trap us? _____

When we pray, does God hear? _____

What do these verses speak to your heart?

On your first reading, who did you think God was angry at (v. 7)?
Why did you think He was angry? _____

_____
Who is God really angry with? Who is He coming against on David's behalf? _____

God is a jealous God. He doesn't like it when someone hurts us or tries to hurt us. Especially when that someone is Satan. What would your reaction be if you saw someone abusing or hurting your child or someone you loved? You'd be angry! You'd "thunder" to their aid! And that's exactly what God is doing here. And this is exactly what He does when we are being demonically abused and call on His name! This vision is what the demons see—God in His wrath, which is focused on the devil and his demons, not on you—coming at them from the heavens.

Seeing this vision, do you think the demons will stand or flee? ____

_____
What do these verses speak to your heart?

(15) The valleys of the sea were exposed and the foundations of the earth laid bare at your rebuke, O Lord, at the blast of breath from your nostrils.

• • •

(16) He reached down from on high and took hold of me; he drew me out of deep waters.

(17) He rescued me from my powerful enemy, from my foes, who were too strong for me.

(18) They confronted me in the day of my disaster, but the Lord was my support.

(19) He brought me out into a spacious place; he rescued me because he delighted in me.

• • •

(20) The Lord has dealt with me according to my righteousness; according to the cleanness of my hands he has rewarded me.

(21) For I have kept the ways of the Lord; I have not done evil by turning from my God.

(22) All his laws are before me; I have not turned away from his decrees.

(23) I have been blameless before him and have kept myself from sin.

(24) The Lord has rewarded me according to my righteousness, according to the cleanness of my hands in his sight.

(25) To the faithful you show yourself faithful, to the blameless you show yourself blameless,

(26) to the pure you show yourself pure, but to the crooked you show yourself shrewd.

(27) You save the humble but bring low those whose eyes are haughty.

• • •

(28) You, O Lord, keep my lamp burning; my God turns my darkness into light.

(29) With your help I can advance against a troop; with my God I can scale a wall.

Without God's help, could this enemy be defeated? _____

Was the enemy attacking when David was strong or when he was weak? (v. 18) _____

Did God's rescue hold any conditions (I'll only rescue you if you do such-and-such)? _____

What do these verses speak to your heart?

David doesn't say that God helped him according to his self-righteousness, but according to his righteousness.

Who is our righteousness? _____

Can a person sin yet still have a heart after God? _____

Can anything separate us from the love of God? (Romans 8:35, 38–39) _____

Even if we're being attacked by hell because we've sinned and given Satan a momentary foothold, if we humble ourselves, confess, and repent, we are *immediately* cleansed, restored to fellowship, pure, and blameless in Christ. When we turn to God, crying out to Him, He is faithful and just to *always* come to our defense! The righteousness we claim is the righteousness God gives us through His Son, Jesus Christ.

What do these verses speak to your heart?

Who arms us for warfare? _____

Who provides us with strength for battle? _____

Who gives us a shield of protection? _____

Who makes our path straight? _____

Who is mightier than our God? _____

(30) As for God, his way is perfect; the word of the Lord is flawless. He is a shield for all who take refuge in him.

(31) For who is God besides the Lord? And who is the Rock except our God?

(32) It is God who arms me with strength and makes my way perfect.

(33) He makes my feet like the feet of a deer; he enables me to stand on the heights.

(34) He trains my hands for battle; my arms can bend a bow of bronze.

(35) You give me your shield of victory, and your right hand sustains me; you stoop down to make me great.

(36) You broaden the path beneath me, so that my ankles do not turn.

• • •

(37) I pursued my enemies and overtook them; I did not turn back till they were destroyed.

(38) I crushed them so that they could not rise; they fell beneath my feet.

(39) You armed me with strength for battle; you made my adversaries bow at my feet.

(40) You made my enemies turn their backs in flight, and I destroyed my foes.

(41) They cried for help, but there was no one to save them—to the Lord, but he did not answer.

(42) I beat them as fine as dust borne on the wind; I poured them out like mud in the streets.

(43) You have delivered me from the attacks of the people; you have made me the head of nations; people I did not know are subject to me.

(44) As soon as they hear me, they obey me; foreigners cringe before me.

(45) They all lose heart; they come trembling from their strongholds.

• • •

(46) The Lord lives! Praise be to my Rock! Exalted be God my Savior!

(47) He is the God who avenges me,

What do these verses speak to your heart?

It makes no difference what the Enemy puts on us, when we stand firmly on the rock of Christ, we will overcome in all our problems. Besetting sins, habits, wrong behaviors, emotional pain, mental confusion—whatever our "enemies" are—God will empower us to turn and pursue them, crush them, and beat them fine as dust.

Think of "the nations" (v.43) as your life, your family. Think of "people"(v. 43) as those areas of your life that were once out of your control because of the enemy's influence—those healthy qualities of your character held captive in the strongholds of the enemy and perverted to work against you. The people you "did not know" (v. 43) were the positive expressions of your character qualities. Think of "foreigners" (v. 44), "foes" (v. 48), and "violent men" (v. 48) as demons and others being used by Satan against you.

What do these verses speak to your heart?

God inhabits the praises of His people! Satan hates it when we praise God and will not stand in the presence of holy praise. Praise reflects a heart and attitude of gratitude. Offered in the presence of who subdues nations under me,

(48) who saves me from my enemies. You exalted me above my foes; from violent men you rescued me.

(49) Therefore I will praise you among the nations, O Lord; I will sing praises to your name.

(50) He gives his king great victories; he shows unfailing kindness to his anointed, to David and his descendants forever.

adversity and trial, especially when deliverance isn't immediately discernible to our fleshly eyes, it is a sweet sacrifice that pleases God. If we can do nothing else, praise is always appropriate. "Rejoice in the Lord always. I will say it again: Rejoice!" (Philippians 4:4).

Who is the King of Kings? _____

Who wins a great victory in Revelation? _____

Are you anointed in Christ? (2 Corinthians 1:21–22) _____

What do these verses speak to your heart?

Select several verses from Psalm 18, and write out a personalized version below. Be sure to use your name in appropriate places:

Dear _____,

_____

_____

_____

_____

Sincerely,

David

Select several verses from Psalm 18 (they can be the same or different from the ones you chose for your personalized version), and write out a warfare prayer below that you can use to stand against an attack of the enemy:

_____

_____

_____

_____

Review/Conclusion:

These are your tools—your weapons of warfare. Feel free to write the personalized version and the prayer out on separate pieces of paper and expand them. As the Holy Spirit opens deeper truths to you, revise them often. Make versions specifically for your children, your spouse, or a friend as the Lord leads you. Add truths from other passages to them. Use them daily to defeat every fiery dart of the Enemy!

DEALING WITH THE FLESH: SEXUAL AND OTHER BONDAGES

Scripture Memory Verse:

"If you do what is right, will you not be accepted? But if you do not do what is right, sin is crouching at your door; it desires to have you, but you must master it." (Genesis 4:7)

Unit Learning Goal:

Understanding the origin, extent, and effects of sin in creation.

Overview of Unit 7:

Lesson 1: Original Sin and the Sinful Nature

Lesson 2: Sins of the Intellect

Lesson 3: Sins of the Emotions

Lesson 4: Sins of the Body

Lesson 5: When Sins Are Spirits

SUMMARY STATEMENT

Unresolved sin problems of the flesh open the door for footholds of unique satanic control of any person's life. A stronghold in one individual's life can affect others around them. Sins of the flesh can become some of Satan's most powerful weapons against us.

Unit 7 Thought Focus:

Everyone—from the brand-new believer to the mature Christian patriarch—battles daily against a variety of flesh-related sins. These fleshly sins range from anger and jealousy and self-advancement to more outward and obvious sexual sins, as well as to the further extreme of criminal and violent behavior. The Word of God provides us with definitive lists of fleshly sins: Mark 7:20–23; Galatians 5:19–21; and Colossians 3:5–10. It is good to memorize a list like Galatians 5:19–21 so that when we are tempted by these sins we will know that the source is the flesh.

It is through the flesh—our senses, our sensual nature—that sin becomes tangible. What starts as an alluring thought moves to a compelling desire and ends with a sinful act. And each sinful act defies God, defiles our lives, and leads us a step closer to spiritual bondage.

Sensuality is rampant in our society and most world cultures. Freedom of expression in every area, from speech to dress (or undress), yields to nothing. Discretion is dead. Morality is relative. The will of the masses rules. Being a Christian and maintaining purity, an ethical lifestyle, and biblical morality is becoming increasingly difficult.

The influences working against us are subtle and many, requiring ever-growing diligence in our faithfulness. Staying close to God is the only way to be free of the world's pollution.

LESSON 1: *Original Sin and the Sinful Nature*

Scripture for Meditation:

Then the eyes of both of them were opened, and they realized they were naked; so they sewed fig leaves together and made coverings for themselves. Then the man and his wife heard the sound of the Lord God as he was walking in the garden in the cool of the day, and they hid from the Lord God among the trees of the garden.
(Genesis 3:7–8)

A Beginning Prayer:

Dear heavenly Father, deliver me from evil. Protect me from all harm. Keep my whole person safe in Your care at all times. In Jesus' precious name. Amen.

Lesson:

In the beginning, God created humans after His own image who were perfect and sinless and walked in intimate fellowship with Him. It was a beautiful world, idyllic in every sense. Then sin entered, pride swelled up, and self-worship was chosen over God-worship. In clearly understood disobedience to God, Adam and Eve willfully chose to worship the pleasuring of their flesh, both as desire and senses, and ate of the forbidden fruit. All that was perfectly good now became corrupted by that which was evil. Adam and Eve lost their fellowship with God and their ability to obey Him. Sinful desires began to rule, and righteous desires were foreign to their experience.

Two critical realities must be understood by all Christians if they are to succeed in living successful Christian lives.

First, when Adam and Eve fell in the garden, all of God's earthly creation fell. Everything that was named in Genesis as springing from God's creative desire—the earth, the plants, the animals, the stars, the sun—all of it, every atom and molecule, was instantly infected with sin's consequences. What was healthy became sick to some degree. What was perfect became flawed.

To some extent, this explains why there is so much disease and sickness in the world: Sin is at work corrupting everything in our physical world. Everything. That some believe that addictive behavior is genetically based doesn't change the fact that sin is behind it. Rather, it merely confirms the impact of the Fall on every element of creation.

Circle **T** for True or **F** for False and then discuss your answers:

T F All people are inherently good at heart—good-natured.

T F Criminals can be rehabilitated (become good) by merely changing their behavior patterns.

T F Only God can change a person's nature from sinful to holy.

T F There are no bad children or adults, just bad behaviors.

T F Our sinful nature is changed only when we enter heaven.

When we are born, we are born in sin (Psalm 51:5). We begin this life sinful and we end this life sinful (1 John 1:8). The sinfulness of our fleshly desires is always with us (Romans 7:21–23). The battle against sin is a never-ending struggle. This is the theological concept of total depravity. Goodness is not determined by behavior. Good behavior alone will not get us into heaven. Galatians 5:16–26 describes well the internal struggle believers face between their flesh and their reborn spirit.

Second, although we are born in sin with a bent toward wickedness, we still possess free will and the capacity to make choices. More important, although our essential nature has been marred, we are still created in the image of God. Every human being possesses the mark of God in him. This image is reflected in our spiritual desires. (See Appendix A, material from *Raising Lambs Among Wolves*, pages 132–33, for more on this subject.)

Even without Christ, people recognize that there's "more to life" than money, success, nice clothes, and big houses. Few people in the world would deny the existence of spiritual desires. They may pursue evil counterfeits to satisfy the longing of their souls, but in so doing they are giving tacit confirmation of the image of God in them. In this, all humanity possesses absolute, irrevocable dignity and value. All people of all "makes and models" are priceless and significant before God.

Below, circle the words that represent groups that are of *no value* in God's eyes. Discuss your answers in your group.

Muslims	Murderers	Child Molesters	Catholics
Terrorists	Politicians	Cult Leaders	Fallen Angels
Adulterers	Methodists	Hippies	Homosexuals
Women	Jews	Executives	Televangelists
Pentecostals	Idolaters	Alcoholics	Lawyers

And herein lies the human condition: We are all totally depraved, yet all infinitely precious! However, the gap between these two extremes can only be bridged through the Cross of Christ. Our own self-initiated attempts to *do* good and therefore to *be* good are hopeless. Humanitarianism will make us feel good and will provide some positive benefit to others, but it will not rescue us from our depraved state.

Hebrews 11:6: *And without faith it is impossible to please God, because anyone who comes to him must believe that he exists and that he rewards those who earnestly seek him.*

Is it possible to please God if you are not a Christian? Is faith valid if you are not a Christian? Why or why not?

_____

_____

Cross out the statements below that are *not* true based on Hebrews 11:6. For a person to please God, he must

      A. earnestly seek Him.

      B. believe that God is real and exists.

      C. have faith in God.

      D. come to God (come into relationship with God).

      E. not necessarily expect eternal reward.

Romans 7:18: *I know that nothing good lives in me, that is, in my sinful nature. For I have the desire to do what is good, but I cannot carry it out.*

On your own effort, is it possible to consistently live a good, moral life that is pleasing to God if you really, really want to?

_____

_____

What are some evidences that humans are inherently evil in their nature, even when they are "good people"?

_____

_____

Without God's intervention of grace, what do we really deserve from Him based on who and what we are on our own merits and efforts?

_____

_____

John 15:5: *"I am the vine; you are the branches. If a man remains in me and I in him, he will bear much fruit; apart from me you can do nothing."*

What can you do that will really amount to anything of value without Christ?

_____

_____

How much do you try to do on your own? To earn God's approval and blessing?

_____

_____

Matthew 19:26: *Jesus looked at them and said, "With man this is impossible, but with God all things are possible."*

Is there *any* sinful bondage, debilitating habit, addictive behavior, or evil stronghold in your life or anyone else's life that God cannot eliminate?

_____

_____

When confronted with our own weaknesses or the sinful weaknesses of others, is our attitude as forgiving, accepting, and forbearing as God's?

_____

_____

What is our attitude typically, especially as Christians looking at other Christians who are struggling, even failing, in their sins? Are those in the world more forgiving toward those who have fallen than we are as believers?

_____

_____

Titus 1:15–16: *To the pure, all things are pure, but to those who are corrupted and do not believe, nothing is pure. In fact, both their minds and consciences are corrupted. They claim to know God, but by their actions they deny him. They are detestable, disobedient and unfit for doing anything good.*

To the pure all things are _____.

As Christians, our purity and righteousness are from _____.

To not believe God or in God is to be _____.

Those who are corrupted by disbelief deny God by their _____.

They are corrupted in both their _____ and _____.

As a Christian, you have the mind of _____ (1 Corinthians 2:16).

Those without Christ are _____, _____ and unfit for doing

_____.

Review/Conclusion:

Frustration and failure will be the constant companions of those who try to bring down sinful strongholds in their lives through willpower and being good. To become free we must recognize that we are totally depraved and sinful, that we will always be sinful, and that our only hope is through Christ. Only as we bring our sinful beings into subjection to the will of God, *daily* dying to our selfishness and putting on Christ, will we find victory and release from the grip of sinful habits. This involves claiming the work of the Cross at the moment of temptation. The good news is that there *is* hope—in Christ Jesus our Lord and Savior!

LESSON 2: *Sins of the Intellect*

Scripture for Meditation:

Do not conform any longer to the pattern of this world, but be transformed by the renewing of your mind. Then you will be able to test and approve what God's will is—his good, pleasing and perfect will. (Romans 12:2)

He [who serves idols] feeds on ashes, a deluded heart misleads him; he cannot save himself, or say, "Is not this thing in my right hand a lie?" (Isaiah 44:20)

A Beginning Prayer:

Dear heavenly Father, I stand in the truth that You have placed the mind of Christ within me. I choose to bring all of my thoughts into subjection to the Lordship of Jesus Christ. Cover my mind, head, and intellect with the protective, cleansing blood of Christ. Holy Spirit, search out all wickedness, error, and any ungodly or untrue concept, idea, belief, or thought and wash it from me. Fill my mind fully and exclusively with all that is holy, true, pure, praiseworthy, and glorifying to God. Amen.

Lesson:

All of our struggles with sin originated in the Fall. The flesh, the world, and the kingdom of darkness can each be the source of any temptation. But sin's effect upon us varies. The Enemy is cunning and has devised a broad arsenal of sins that will lure us through the various parts of our being: our intellect (thoughts, mind), our emotions (feelings, desires), and our bodies (sex, addictive behavior). It is through these avenues that the Enemy will hook us into sinful, destructive choices.

Note: This is an arbitrary and simplified categorization of sins. It's done primarily as a matter of convenience for study. What is presented here is not absolute or the only ways sin can be viewed or grouped.

In nearly every instance of sin, all of these areas will be touched. Sin is all-encompassing in its embrace of our lives. Yet different kinds of sins frequently have their beginnings focused in one of these aspects.

PRIDE

Pride is never listed as a fleshly sin. It is uniquely of darkness and signifies Satan's work. Pride will focus our attention on our physical appearance, play with our emotions, and incite us to intellectually deny our shortcomings and justify our arrogant behavior. But it is primarily rooted in the thought life: I think I'm better than everyone else; therefore I am!

Read Psalm 10:4. What kind of thought is there no room for in the mind of a prideful person?

_____

_____

What kind of person is prideful?

_____

_____

What kind of person is wicked?

_____

_____

What was the sin of Satan?

_____

_____

Pride pushes God out of our thoughts and out of our lives. It seeks to set ourselves on the throne of our lives. But the reality is that when we push God out, Satan and his demonic hordes come rushing in. Pride opens the door to wickedness. Wickedness opens the door to pride. Both close the door of our hearts and minds to the presence of God and His saving grace.

What are other words that mean the same or nearly the same as *pride?* List as many as you can think of:

Synonyms for PRIDE:

_____   _____

_____   _____

_____   _____

_____   _____

_____   _____

LYING AND DECEIT

In Psalm 120 David cries out, "Save me, O Lord, from lying lips and from deceitful tongues" (v. 2). Why? Because David knew the result of lying was God's discipline: "What will he do to you, and what more besides, O deceitful tongue? He will punish you with a warrior's sharp arrows, with burning coals of the broom tree" (vv. 3–4).

Read the following references in Proverbs and answer the questions. Discuss your answers with your group.

Proverbs 10:18. What is a liar?

_____

_____

Proverbs 12:19. How long does a liar endure?

_____

_____

Proverbs 12:21. Does deceit bring true joy to the deceiver?

_____

_____

Proverbs 12:22. What does God detest?

_____

_____

What brings delight to God?

_____

_____

Proverbs 21:6. Any dishonestly derived gain will be what to us?

_____

_____

Proverbs 26:28. Who does lying hurt?

_____

_____

Do you lie to or about those you truly love?

_____

_____

Deceit is lying that is intent on misleading another. It is purposely causing another to believe what is not true. It is manipulative and abusive, whether its goal is to hide our own shortcomings or to influence another to participate in our sin.

Read Jeremiah 9:5. Who deceives whom?

_____

Who speaks the truth?

_____

Read Leviticus 19:11–13. Is deceit a sin? Why?

_____

_____

What are other words that mean the same or nearly the same as *lying* and *deceiving?* List as many as you can think of:

Synonyms for LYING:	Synonyms for DECEIVING:
_____	_____
_____	_____
_____	_____
_____	_____
_____	_____

Read Psalm 31:18; 109:2–3. What other sins are associated with lying and deceit?

_____

DISSENSION, STRIFE, AND HERESIES

Proverbs 16:28 says, "A perverse man stirs up dissension, and a gossip separates close friends." The word *perverse* carries with it a connotation that ties it to sexual perversion. But according to the *American Heritage Dictionary,* the real meaning of *perverse* is that which is "directed away from what is right or good." Or to "obstinately persist in an error or a fault and by a disposition to oppose and contradict."

Dissension is disagreement. When normal dissent and disagreement are perverted instead of settled, they turn into strife. *Strife* is heated disharmony and violent conflict. This violence can be physical, emotional, or verbal. *Heresies* are the result of persistent perversity in thinking and behaving.

Read 1 Timothy 6:3–5 (NIV) and fill in the missing words:

If _____ teaches false doctrines and _____ to the sound instruction of our Lord Jesus Christ and to godly teaching, he is _____ and understands _____. He has an _____ interest in _____ and _____ that result in _____, _____, _____, _____ and _____ between men of corrupt mind, who have been robbed of the truth and who think that _____ is a means to financial gain.

What are other words that mean the same or nearly the same as *strife, dissension,* and *heresies?* List as many as you can think of:

Synonyms for STRIFE: Synonyms for DISSENSION:

_____   _____

_____   _____

_____   _____

_____   _____

Synonyms for HERESIES:

_____   _____

_____   _____

_____   _____

THEFT AND GREED

The mantra of the 1980s and 1990s has been "Greed is good." The accumulation of wealth and the flaunting thereof has become the passion of Generation X and everyone else. As a result, *theft* is also rampant. Those who want "more" but don't have the means rob from those who do. Those who have "more" have the means but still want to rob from everyone.

Read Matthew 15:19–20. From whence does theft originate?

_____

What other attitudes or behaviors are associated with theft?

_____

What do these things do to a person?

Greed shows up in our mailboxes almost every day in the form of sweepstakes. Letter after enticing letter proclaims, "You May Already Be a Winner!" Those sending the mailings are greedy for our dollars for magazine subscriptions and more. Those responding want to get rich quick. Yet there are also victims.

The mailings of American Family Publishers and the dozens, hundreds, and thousands of others like them are blatantly, intentionally, and premeditatedly deceptive. Their goal is to confuse, beguile, and deceive, while tiptoeing just inside the fringe of legality and raking in lots of cash.

It is sad that those responding to these mailings are generally painted as greedy and shiftless hopefuls, too stupid to know better. Generally, I don't believe that's true. The greedy and shiftless are all those involved in creating and perpetrating these mailings. They are shameless hucksters sharking the mails for the innocents unaware. Offering something for nothing is the world's oldest scam—Satan used it on Eve in the garden: "Here, Eve, live forever. All ya gotta do is bite the fruit. It's free!" Right. It only cost her her soul and brought the whole world under a curse, but that's another story.

And some people have really big dreams with very little means. Those taken in by these mailings, which are designed to fog one's reason, are blinded by greed but also by hope. This hope may be temporarily misplaced, but it's hope nonetheless. There may be a desire to meet the needs of debt-burdened children, an aging and ill spouse, or a charitable organization, but, at heart, the gambling craze is greed with a capital *G*.

These mailings, akin to the phone and other scams we hear so much about, are most specifically targeted at an aging population that is too often left with nothing more than memories and Social Security to live on. These people are our older parents, grandparents, aunts, uncles, grade school teachers, and the parents of our childhood friends. Many are widows or widowers, time-orphaned and lonely. All have served us in some way, helping us become what we are.

Now, frequently feeling that they have nothing left to offer, they search for significance anywhere they can find it. Their desire is to leave behind a positive legacy. Dick, Ed, and all the others promise to help them do just that. All it takes is a stamp and a magazine subscription. Don't delay; respond today!

They are us not too far from now. Today, our brains purr merrily along, full of clear-sighted reason (usually). Tomorrow, the mail may seem to hold more promise for joy than our Parkinsoned, Alzheimered, grief-numbed, and age-warped minds can comprehend. The offers seem too good to be true, but then who knows . . . ?

The Bible, always a good guide in matters of ethics, states plainly, "Do not take advantage of a widow or an orphan" (Exodus 22:22) and "Look after orphans and widows in their distress" (James 1:27). We who know better need to protect those not so aware of these legal deceits.

Read Romans 1:28. What kind of mind does greed come from?

What will a depraved mind fill itself with?

Can someone who knows about God and knows the Bible be depraved?

_____

_____

What is one distinction between someone who gives into depravity and one who resists depravity through Christ (v. 32)?

_____

_____

Read Matthew 7:16–20; 15:18–19; Galatians 5:19–23; Colossians 3:8–9, 12; and 2 Peter 1:5–8. Below list the bad fruit to avoid and the good fruit to pursue as a Christian:

Bad Fruit of Fleshly Desires: Good Fruit of the Holy Spirit:

_____   _____

_____   _____

_____   _____

_____   _____

_____   _____

How can you tell the difference between a genuine Christian with a heart after God, yet struggling against sin, and a person who has given himself over to a depraved mind, yet pretends to be a Christian by being good?

_____

_____

What are other words that mean the same or nearly the same as *theft* and *greed?* List as many as you can think of:

Synonyms for THEFT: Synonyms for GREED:

_____   _____

_____   _____

_____   _____

_____   _____

_____   _____

_____   _____

IDOLATRY, WITCHCRAFT, AND REBELLION

Idolatry means that one gives excessive, even blind, devotion to someone or something. The object of idolatry is an idol. Anyone or anything can become an idol to us, and we may not even realize it.

A common idol among Americans is our comfort! We go to great lengths to protect our comfort and add to it. The clothes we wear, the cars we drive, and the homes in which we live are all aimed at making us comfortable. And if someone dares to mess with our comfort—*watch out!*

For example, if you've just settled down in your favorite, comfortable easy chair to watch television, and a friend calls who's in distress and needs to talk, how do you react? Is it with ease, cheer, and gladness that you turn away from your comfort to provide comforting to your hurting friend?

What are things and people that could be or may be idols in your life?

_____

_____

Read Romans 1:25. What is idolatry?

Exchanging the truth of God for a _____

Worshiping and serving _____

_____

Read Zechariah 10:2. What do idols "speak"?

_____

_____

What other practices are idols associated with?

_____

_____

What are the results of involvement with idols and these practices?

_____

_____

Read Isaiah 44:9–20. Write down your impressions of these verses. How does this passage relate to your life? Your job? Your family? Your church? Your possessions? Discuss your insights with your group.

_____

_____

Witchcraft and Satan worship are on the rise. The headlines of our newspapers frequently carry stories of the effects of someone bound up in these wicked practices. People are tortured, brutalized, and murdered in the name of Satan. Self-proclaimed witches' groups or covens seek equal rights and recognition as churches. Hard rock lyrics blast the profane and bizarre into the ears and minds of children, teens, and adults, sometimes leading them to sadistic and suicidal behavior.

It all starts in the mind, and it starts so innocently. New Age philosophy is "a way of thinking" that is related to witchcraft. Many view Satan worship as nothing more than a harmless alternative choice of worship. Evil and decadent lyrics and graphic images are simply the exercise of free speech and artistic expression. Kids playing with demonic-looking figures and emblazoning their bodies and their possessions with images of death and the devil are merely going through harmless phases.

The Enemy is subtle, cunning, and crafty in the intellectual arguments that are devised to defend and support this so-called diversity of opinion and expression.

Consulting the dead, channeling spirits, psychic hot lines, obsessions with aliens, fortunes, horoscopes, foretelling the future, healing with crystals and Eastern chants, inflicting curses, and any variation of these types of activities are all expressions of witchcraft, sorcery, satanism, and other demonic engagement.

Read Deuteronomy 18:10–12; 2 Kings 17:17; and 2 Chronicles 33:6. What are the various evil practices listed in these verses:

_____

_____

What was sold by those who practiced these evils? To whom was it sold?

_____

_____

What did they sacrifice in the fire?

_____

_____

What are modern applications of this type of sacrificing?

_____

_____

What is abortion?

_____

_____

How does the Lord view the practices listed in these verses?

_____

_____

Read 1 Samuel 15:23. What sin is like the sin of divination?

_____

_____

What sin is like the evil of idolatry?

_____

_____

What is being rejected by the sins of rebellion and arrogance?

_____

_____

Read Titus 1:10. What other sins are associated with rebelliousness?

_____

_____

Read Proverbs 17:11. What is an evil person bent on doing?

_____

_____

Read 1 Timothy 1:9–11. What other types of people does a rebellious person associate with?

_____

_____

What are other words that mean the same or nearly the same as *idolatry, witchcraft,* and *rebellion?* List as many as you can think of:

Synonyms for IDOLATRY: Synonyms for WITCHCRAFT:

_____   _____

_____   _____

_____   _____

_____   _____

_____   _____

Synonyms for REBELLION:

_____   _____

_____   _____

_____   _____

_____   _____

_____   _____

Review/Conclusion:

Sin is sticky. One sin will draw us to another, which will draw us to another, and on and on. Read Proverbs 6:16–19 and Galatians 5:19–21 to discover the truth of the interrelatedness of sin. How do we protect against this pervasive network of entangling death? In Matthew 22:37–38 and Mark 12:29–30, Jesus gave the core solution: "Love the Lord your God with all your heart and with all your soul and with all your *mind* and with all your strength" (italics added).

The battle begins in the mind and in the will. It engages and encompasses the heart, soul, and body. It calls for our entire being to be submitted to the will of the Father. To be pleasing to Him and to do His will we must have decided in our minds to be completely submitted to Him. For, as Paul states, "The sinful mind is hostile to God. It does not submit to God's law, nor can it do so. Those controlled by the sinful nature cannot please God" (Romans 8:7–8).

The answer is to take "off [the] old self with its practices" and "put on the new self," always "being renewed in knowledge in the image of [our] Creator" (Colossians 3:9–10). If, as

Paul states, we truly do "have the mind of Christ," how could we even think of doing anything but His will?

(For practical steps to follow in taking off the old self and putting on the new, see the excerpts from *Raising Lambs Among Wolves*, pages 135–39, printed out in Appendix A: Supplemental Readings.)

LESSON 3: *Sins of the Emotions*

Scripture for Meditation:

Like the blind we grope along the wall, feeling our way like men without eyes. At midday we stumble as if it were twilight; among the strong, we are like the dead. (Isaiah 59:10)

When the richest provinces feel secure, he will invade them and will achieve what neither his fathers nor his forefathers did. He will distribute plunder, loot and wealth among his followers. He will plot the overthrow of fortresses—but only for a time. (Daniel 11:24)

A Beginning Prayer:

Loving heavenly Father, may Your Holy Spirit help me to stand in the truth of God's Word and not be moved by the fluctuating fickleness of my emotions. Teach me that it is not how I feel but what You cause me to know that is important. The assurance of my salvation rests upon the firm fact of my confession of You as my Lord and Savior, not on my feeling saved. Nothing in heaven or on earth can separate me from Your love. Thank You for that absolute certainty. Amen.

Lesson:

James writes that when we are confronted with temptation we are, through our "own evil desire . . . dragged away and enticed. Then, after desire has conceived, it gives birth to sin; and sin, when it is full-grown, gives birth to death" (1:14–15). The original Greek word translated in the NIV as *evil desire* is *epithumia*. It can also mean passionate longing, lust, coveting, impulses, a longing (especially for what is forbidden), or concupiscence.

Emotions are powerful. If we let them, they can be incited in an instant and totally short–circuit our reason. Our flesh, the sinful man, loves emotions and craves emotional stimuli like a drunk craves booze. Exclusively following our feelings is to take the clear path to bad consequences and disaster. Just because something "makes me happy" or "feels so good and right" doesn't make it the way to go.

Misguided parents everywhere support their children in chosen perversions because "all that matters is that they're happy." Men and women daily dive into the destructive depths of adulterous affairs because "it just feels so right." Thousands of young lives are trashed hourly by the seductiveness of drugs, sex, alcohol, and more, all because "it feels so good." And hundreds of well-intentioned but poorly grounded Christians are headed for trouble because, instead of looking to serve a holy God in costly obedience, they run after being happy and feeling good all the time at any cost.

How could the pursuit of *feeling good* or *being happy* all the time be idolatry?

JEALOUSY

Proverbs 27:4 warns, "Anger is cruel and fury overwhelming, but who can stand before jealousy?" Did you realize that in Scripture jealousy is considered a far more powerful emotion than anger or fury? The Hebrew word for jealousy in this verse is *qinah*, which can also mean ardor, zeal, anger, envy, passion, or rivalry. Jealousy has two negative branches: fear and resentment.

A person can be jealous in that he is fearful of losing a position or someone's affection. For example, you may feel jealous of your boss who is promoted because you're afraid your position may be eliminated by his replacement. Or a child may be jealous of a new sibling because he's afraid his parents won't love him as much anymore. A person who is fearfully jealous becomes possessive, apprehensive, and clutching.

A person may also be jealous because he is resentful of or painfully desirous of another's advantages. For example, he might be jealous of his neighbor's new car because it's exactly the make and model he wants but can't afford. Or a wife may be jealous of her best friend because her friend's husband seems more caring than her own. Someone who is resentfully jealous will be envious and covetous.

Read Genesis 30:1. Why was Rachel jealous? What kind of jealousy was it?

_____

_____

Read Genesis 37:11. Who was jealous of Joseph and why?

_____

_____

Read Acts 13:45. Why were the Jews jealous?

_____

_____

In all of these examples, did the jealousy lead to good or bad results?

_____

_____

Read Romans 13:13; 1 Corinthians 3:3; and 2 Corinthians 12:20. What other sinful behavior is associated in these verses with jealousy?

_____

_____

A third aspect of jealousy conveys the idea of vigilantly guarding and watching over something or someone. Negatively applied, this would take the form of stalking or intrusive spying. Positively applied, it is the sense conveyed in Exodus 34:14: "Do not worship any other god, for the Lord, whose name is Jealous, is a jealous God."

ANGER

Holy anger is good and is justifiable. God's anger at our sin is justifiable. The anger Jesus expressed toward the money changers and the religious leaders of his day was reasonable. Our anger over the abuse or misfortune of others that leads us to act to help is good. But what differentiates holy anger from bad anger?

Good anger comes slowly and is guarded by love:

Psalm 145:8: The Lord is gracious and compassionate, slow to anger and rich in love.

Good anger does not overwhelm but remains under the control of reason:

Proverbs 29:11: A fool gives full vent to his anger, but a wise man keeps himself under control.

Good anger does not lead to sinful actions:

Psalm 4:4: In your anger do not sin; when you are on your beds, search your hearts and be silent.

Ephesians 4:26–27: "In your anger do not sin": Do not let the sun go down while you are still angry, and do not give the devil a foothold.

Good anger doesn't remain burning in one's heart or stir up strife:

Ecclesiastes 7:9: Do not be quickly provoked in your spirit, for anger resides in the lap of fools.

Proverbs 30:33: For as churning the milk produces butter, and as twisting the nose produces blood, so stirring up anger produces strife.

Bad anger is the kind that originates in our flesh. It will poison your attitude toward everything and infect your behavior.

Read Galatians 5:20–21; Ephesians 4:31; Colossians 3:8; 1 Timothy 2:8; and James 1:20. What are ways anger expresses itself in a person's life?

_____

_____

What are the results of these negative expressions?

_____

_____

What are Christians supposed to do with these things?

_____

_____

FALSE PEACE

We hate to feel bad, unsettled, anxious, pained, upset, sick, tired, achy, troubled, depressed, stressed, pressured, and a whole range of other "yucky" feelings. To resolve these feelings into a semblance of peace, we will go to great and expensive lengths from popping any number of pills to reading dozens of self-help books to running to a variety of counselors. What are we searching for? We are looking for someone to "dress [our] wound . . . as though it were not serious" and then pat us on the back and say, "'Peace, peace' . . . when there is no peace" (Jeremiah 6:14).

Seeking peace without confronting the reality of sin in the world is a form of deceit and denial. In fact, refusing to acknowledge and accept that life involves suffering and trouble is to deny the Word of God.

John 16:33: *"I have told you these things, so that in me you may have peace. In this world you will have trouble. But take heart! I have overcome the world."*

First Peter 4:19: *So then, those who suffer according to God's will should commit themselves to their faithful Creator and continue to do good.*

Read 1 Thessalonians 5:3. What happens to those who pursue peace and safety?

_____

_____

What does Matthew 24:42 say we should do?

_____

_____

Will someone who is convinced that all is "peace and safety" be vigilant and on guard against sin and living in anticipation of Christ's return?

_____

_____

The emotional sins listed above are not all-inclusive. List as many others as you can think of. Discuss your lists in your group and add items others included.

_____	_____
_____	_____
_____	_____
_____	_____
_____	_____

Review/Conclusion:

Emotions are powerful. If we allow emotions to drive our behavior rather than being self-controlled, they will "drag us" to destruction.

What will change our emotions? Choosing to think through our situation, deciding to act according to biblical truth, and filling our mind with God's Word will, over time, bring our emotions into line. This is the attitude we need to have even before encountering an emotional circumstance.

If we are not already committed to do God's will and live in His holiness no matter what, when we are faced with sudden grief, tragedy, or other mind-reeling experiences, we will falter and fall. Or we could even bump up against an occasion of intense pleasure, satisfaction, and ecstatic delight that cannot be satisfied within the moral realm. We need to be on guard, remain vigilant and sober-minded, and keep our eyes on Christ and the reward He holds out to us.

The Enemy doesn't care whether our emotions feel good or bad as long as they distract us, even for a moment, from the One in whom we live and move and have our being, so that he can deceive us into bondage, destruction, or death.

LESSON 4: *Sins of the Body*

Scripture for Meditation:

"If your right eye causes you to sin, gouge it out and throw it away. It is better for you to lose one part of your body than for your whole body to be thrown into hell. And if your right hand causes you to sin, cut it off and throw it away. It is better for you to lose one part of your body than for your whole body to go into hell."
(Matthew 5:29–30)

A Beginning Prayer:

Dear heavenly Father, sanctify my body to Your service. Wash me in Your blood and cleanse me from all impurity. Holy Spirit, search through my body and sweep clean all traces of sinfulness and demonic influence. Escort away from me all hellish powers assigned to afflict and torment me and send them to the place Christ has assigned them. Let them never return to me again. Set my mind on holiness and perseverance in righteousness. Guard my life, body, and desires against all sin. Amen.

Lesson:

In 1 Corinthians 6:18–20, Paul writes, "Flee from sexual immorality. All other sins a man commits are outside his body, but he who sins sexually sins against his own body. Do you not know that your body is a temple of the Holy Spirit, who is in you, whom you have received from God? You are not your own; you were bought at a price. Therefore honor God with your body."

SEXUAL SINS

All sin is conceived in the heart and mind and finds expression through our bodies in word and deed. However, some sins, as Paul points out, are especially body related. The foremost of these are sexual sins. These include, but are not limited to, the following:

(1) *Adultery.* This is engaging in sexual activity with someone other than your spouse while you are married. The sexual activity included in this sin is not limited to sexual intercourse but extends to all sexual activity. It can be heterosexual or homosexual activity. (Note: The term *homosexual* refers to all same-sex relations, including lesbian.)

Read Exodus 20:14; Deuteronomy 5:18; Mark 10:19; Ephesians 5:3–7; and 1 Thessalonians 4:1–8. Is there any circumstance under which adultery could be OK? Does God, Jesus, or Scripture offer any exception to this commandment?

_____

_____

In addition to physical sexual intercourse, what other activities would be included in adultery?

_____

_____

(2) *Fornication.* Generally, this is engaging in heterosexual or homosexual sexual activity outside of marriage. While a common occurrence among young people before marriage, this is an especially troubling area for divorced individuals who have not remarried. The Greek term for fornication is *porneia*, which is related to our word *pornography*. The sexual activity included in this sin is not limited to sexual intercourse, but extends to all sexual activity.

In the King James Version read Acts 15:20, 29; Romans 1:29; and 1 Corinthians 5:1; 6:18–20. Compare the King James to other translations. How else is the word *fornication* translated?

_____

_____

Several translations render the term *fornication* as *sexual immorality*. These two words actually encompass a whole range of sinful activity. What are some specific examples of sexual immorality that are common today? Check them below and discuss your responses.

☐ 1. Graphic portrayal of sexual activity on TV and in movies
☐ 2. Sexually oriented, seductive lyrics in music
☐ 3. Revealing and alluring fashions
☐ 4. Toleration of sexual indiscretions by those in public office
☐ 5. Another? _____
☐ 6. Another? _____

In addition to physical sexual intercourse, what other activities would be included in fornication? Circle all that apply and discuss others:

Mutual masturbation	Petting	Touching genitals
Deep kissing	Oral sex	Holding hands
Flirting	Phone sex	Dating

Regardless of how it is termed or where it is encountered, what is Paul's simple, straightforward instruction for dealing with all sexual immorality? Circle one:

A. Go on a television talk show and tell the world about it.
B. Be accepting and affirming of it.
C. Flee, run, escape, bolt away from it.
D. Acknowledge it as a legitimate alternative lifestyle.
E. Indulge in it without shame.

Of those answers listed above (A through E), which ones are common responses by the world to what God's Word describes clearly as sexual immorality and sin? List them and any others that come to mind:

_____

_____

PHYSICALLY ADDICTIVE SINS

There are other sins that have a dramatic physical impact. These practices stimulate powerful physical responses that turn into equally powerful cravings that result in ever-increasing need and habit.

(1) *Alcoholism* and *drug addiction*. These are two of the more obvious physically addictive sins. Not only are these substances dangerous in themselves, but under their influence

inhibitions are broken down and behavior slides into the gutter. These are sins that branch out into other sins.

Further, to fulfill the ever-increasing dependence, the one defeated by these substances will often engage in deception, lying, theft, robbery, and even murder in order to fund his habit. Abusing alcohol and drugs will rob a person of reason and restraint and feeds the heart on a deadly diet of desperation and dependency.

Read Genesis 19:30–38; Deuteronomy 21:20; 1 Kings 16:9–10; Proverbs 23:20–21; Ecclesiastes 10:17; Isaiah 19:14; Jeremiah 25:27; and Romans 13:13. In Scripture, drug addiction and drunkenness can be considered as one and the same. Is there anything positive about drunkenness or its effects?

_____

_____

(2) *Lust.* When fantasies gain a foothold in the mind and the desire to make the fantasy real fills the heart, lust is born. Lust is an intense, unrestrained sexual craving that compels an individual to feed the craving in sexual activity.

Read Proverbs 6:23–27; Matthew 5:28; Romans 1:26–27; Ephesians 4:19; 1 Thessalonians 4:4–5; 1 Peter 4:3; 2 Peter 2:18; and 1 John 2:16. Based on these verses, write in your own words a definition of lust:

_____

_____

In Ezekiel 23, the prophet characterizes Jerusalem and Samaria as two sisters who, instead of following the Lord and His ways, wantonly pursue the fulfillment of their lusts. The allegory is graphic, tragic, and fully applicable to people, whether as individuals or as entire nations. As described in Ezekiel 23 and based on your own experience and knowledge, what are consequences of lust?

_____

_____

Review/Conclusion:

The sins of the body covered in this lesson do not by any means represent an exhaustive list. Others that could be discussed include gambling, overeating, excessive spending, obsessive exercising, and many other obsessive, compulsive, excessive behaviors engaged in daily by millions of people. Many might argue whether these are sins of the body or sins of the mind. Worse, many more would argue that these aren't sins at all.

The point is to be on guard against the schemes of Satan. He will take the most innocent, God-ordained, and beneficial behaviors and acts and twist them into sinful perversions aimed at the destruction of our souls.

As Paul says, "everything is permissible," but "not everything is beneficial" or constructive, and we should not be "mastered by anything" (1 Corinthians 6:12).

LESSON 5: *When Sins Are Spirits*

Scripture for Meditation:

The Spirit clearly says that in later times some will abandon the faith and follow deceiving spirits and things taught by demons. Such teachings come through hypocritical liars, whose consciences have been seared as with a hot iron. They forbid people to marry and order them to abstain from certain foods, which God created to be received with thanksgiving by those who believe and who know the truth. (1 Timothy 4:1–3)

A Beginning Prayer:

In the powerful name of the Lord Jesus Christ, I take my place of being seated with Christ in heavenly realms far above the powers of darkness and evil. I acknowledge Jesus Christ as my Lord and Savior, who came to earth as man, died on the cross for my sins, and rules over the throne of my heart today. I reject and renounce all sinful activity against my life, which is authored by the powers of darkness. I place my will, my spirit, my heart, my mind, my soul, and my body—my whole being—under the sovereign, loving, and righteous protection and direction of the Lord Jesus Christ. I have been purchased by the blood of Christ and set apart as one made holy, to the glory and honor of God. Amen.

Lesson:

Our struggle against the world and the flesh is constant. Although these are areas Satan will use to draw us into his control, they do not in themselves indicate demonic rule. But they can become so. How do we tell the difference between that which is of the flesh or of the world and that which may indicate control by evil powers?

THE SINS AROUND US (THE WORLD)

Read 1 Timothy 4:1–3 (just above) carefully. How many reports can you recall about various cultish groups that described their practices as including restrictions on marriage or perversion of normal marriage practices? Strict dietary restrictions and other harsh demands? And of these groups, how many claim to draw at least some of their teachings from the Bible?

If you've ever thought that groups such as these were devilish in nature and origin, you were right. We are surrounded by a culture permeated with the rule of darkness, from the extreme and obvious to the subtle and nearly imperceptible. Yet it is all equally dangerous. It all leads away from God toward bondage to darkness.

Again, look carefully at the Scripture for Meditation above. Timothy plainly states that some Christians—our fellow brothers and sisters in the Lord—will "follow deceiving spirits and things taught by demons." Does this mean that these people will actually be visited and confronted by deceiving spirits and demons face-to-face? In some instances, probably this will occur. However, look at what Timothy says next: "Such teachings come through hypocritical liars, whose consciences have been seared."

Just as God expresses His grace and mercy through the godly actions of people, so will the teachings of Satan be disseminated through speaking, writing, legislating, movie-making, story telling, television show producing, magazine and book publishing, radio broadcasting, and all means of communication by sinful, godless, Satan-manipulated men and women. These people may even be our friends, acquaintances, and relatives. In some instances what they do is the result of deliberate choice. In many more instances what they do is the result of believed deceptions of darkness.

How do we guard against this kind of evil activity?

- Trust in the Lord and live in constant intimate relationship with Him.

Psalm 86:2: *Guard my life, for I am devoted to you. You are my God; save your servant who trusts in you.*

- Immerse yourself and your mind in the Word of God.

Second Timothy 2:15: *Do your best to present yourself to God as one approved, a workman who does not need to be ashamed and who correctly handles the word of truth.*

John 8:32: *Then you will know the truth, and the truth will set you free.*

- Be filled with the Spirit and walk daily in the Spirit.

First Corinthians 2:14–16: *The man without the Spirit does not accept the things that come from the Spirit of God, for they are foolishness to him, and he cannot understand them, because they are spiritually discerned. The spiritual man makes judgments about all things, but he himself is not subject to any man's judgment: "For who has known the mind of the Lord that he may instruct him?" But we have the mind of Christ.*

Based on all the things we've discussed so far in this study guide, and on all that you currently understand about God's Word, what are some other ways you can guard against demonic activity in the world and culture around us?

_____

_____

THE SINS WITHIN US (THE FLESH)

Have you ever or are you currently struggling with a recurring, enduring sin? What some refer to as a "besetting" sin? It's an area over which you feel as if you have no or very little control. You resist as best you can, yet eventually you always cave in and yield.

This struggle is your private hell and a source of continual defeat and anguish. Your repeated failures haunt your worship and dampen your fervor for prayer and the Word. Yet, whatever this thing is, you hate it and its power over you. You know that it is sin, and you want it to be out of your life forever—and at the same time it is incredibly seductive, sweet, and tempting.

Of the items listed below, circle all that could be a besetting sin, discuss, and list others:

Smoking	Eating	Oversleeping	Addictions
Laziness	Gossip	Lying	Pornography
Bragging	Fighting	Yelling	Spending
Overworking	Gambling	Ignorance	Fearfulness
_____	_____	_____	_____

The odds are that a besetting sin that has been practiced over a period of time will lead to some degree of evil spirit control. A demonic spirit has gained a foothold in your life and has built a stronghold of control. Each time you have yielded to the besetting sin the control has become stronger. While you hate this thing immensely, you have not understood how to see this control purged from your life.

Unlike us, Satan and his demons are indefatigable. They watch for every opportunity to attack us and rule us. Any weakness we yield up, no matter how slight it may seem from our viewpoint, will be claimed by the Enemy to oppress and control us.

So how do you gain victory over these repetitive sins that may have moved from being a fleshly problem to one of evil control?

First, recognize one very important but often missed point: The fierceness of the battle is not evidence of defeat. All Christians experience temptation and are in a battle—it is part of our walk with the Lord. The struggle with sin is real and to be expected. And there are moments when the struggle will be intensely sharp and heated. Just because you're battling something you thought you'd settled doesn't mean that you are defeated or weak or anything more than that you are under renewed attack by the Enemy. First Peter 5:8–9 says: "Be self-controlled and alert. Your enemy the devil prowls around like a roaring lion looking for someone to devour. Resist him, standing firm in the faith, because you know that your brothers throughout the world are undergoing the same kind of sufferings."

Circle **T** for True or **F** for False and then discuss your answers:

T   **F**   All our problems fall away when we become Christians.

T   **F**   Good Christians don't struggle with problem areas.

T   **F**   Maturity and holiness are processes that last a lifetime.

Frequently we confuse situations in our life with television episodes. We expect to be able to resolve great difficulties within thirty minutes to an hour. This thinking is totally unrealistic and unbiblical. Although some situations will be resolved quickly, many will continue over days, weeks, months, years, and even lifetimes. The focus of our devotion is not to be on the solution we want but rather on the path God has chosen for us to walk.

Read 2 Corinthians 12:7–9. What was the source of Paul's torment?

_____

_____

How many times did Paul pray to be released from this torment?

_____

_____

What was God's answer to Paul?

_____

_____

Did Paul receive relief from the torment?

_____

_____

Why did Paul say he received this torment?

_____

_____

Was the result of the torment destructive or beneficial in Paul's life?

_____

_____

Sometimes the answer we receive from God is not the answer we want, but it's always the answer we need. He allows things to enter our lives to shape us into the glorious and spotless people He calls us to become.

Second, no matter how seriously the battle rages, it is never an excuse to yield to sin or to Satan. Although Paul accepted the affliction, he still resisted Satan. Satan won no victory over Paul, for Paul turned the torment into opportunity to praise and give glory to God. He allowed the battle the Lord permitted to keep him humble.

Read Romans 8:28; 2 Corinthians 9:8; Philippians 4:4; and 1 Peter 4:12–13. What should our attitude be in the midst of suffering of any kind?

_____

_____

With these two truths in mind, here are additional steps to receiving victory over besetting sins that may have evil power involvement.

- Stand in the truth of who you are in Christ and your position in Christ. Memorize and claim and even speak out loud verses such as John 1:12; Romans 8:1–2, 16–17; and 1 John 1:9.

Look up these Scriptures and write them out below:
John 1:12

_____

_____

Romans 8:1–2

_____

_____

Romans 8:16–17

_____

_____

First John 1:9

_____

_____

- No matter how many times you give in to the sin, promptly and specifically confess your sin to God and ask for His forgiveness. Then accept and stand in the truth of that forgiveness.
- Pray with your God-given authority against the spirit behind the sin. Name it and renounce it in the mighty name of the Lord Jesus Christ. For instance, if your sin is lying, pray against the spirit of lying in this manner. An example of a prayer might be:

In the name of the Lord Jesus Christ and by the power of His blood, I come against the evil power of _____ (name symptom) and all of his host. I command you to cease your evil work; you and your host must leave my presence and go where my Lord Jesus Christ sends you. I invite my Lord Jesus Christ to replace this temptation and control with the Holy Spirit's control.

Continue exercising these steps over and over against any and all repeating sins in your life as they are brought to your attention. As the Enemy realizes that you will not give up in your pursuit of righteousness and holiness, these troubling areas of control will leave and begin to fade in intensity. As they fade, keep up the practice of resisting them just as fervently.

Review/Conclusion:

Until we reach heaven and as long as we walk in these fleshly bodies, there will never be such a thing as "victory once for all" over Satan's attacks. As we yield to his deceptions, the Enemy will renew and redirect his attacks against us. However, as we submit ourselves to Christ and walk in the power of the Holy Spirit, we will begin to walk in freedom from any control of Satan and his demons. We will become stronger and more focused on yielding to Christ and walking in moment-by-moment fellowship with Him.

THE PRINCIPLE OF THE DELAYED HARVEST

The power of generational sins is real and must be reckoned with. The impact down the family line can be as basic as dysfunctional behavior or as serious as the transference of demonic influence.

In her 1987 book *Intimate Partners: Patterns in Love and Marriage* (New York: Random), secular author Maggie Scarf cites example after example of behavior patterns in entire families that were carried over from previous generations. Individuals who experience extended struggles with such things as addictive behavior and sexual compulsion are often amazed to learn of such behavior in their forefathers. Often this is not readily apparent, as these things can skip a generation only to re-emerge later.

This issue becomes especially important in this age of blended families where in one home the generational lines of multiple heritages can come together. For example, imagine the complex genealogies in a situation where two divorced individuals with children, at least one adopted, marry and bring their families together. They bring together the family lines of their former spouses and relatives, their new relatives, and the adopted child. And often with adopted children, the full details of their blood family and preadoptive life are not known.

The passing of the sins of the forebears to subsequent generations is recognized in Scripture as a reality. However, it is not one-sided. God is merciful and forgiving. Blessings also flow from generation to generation:

POSITIVE/BLESSING	NEGATIVE /CONSEQUENCE
Numbers 14:18a: "The Lord is slow to anger, abounding in love and forgiving sin and rebellion."	**Numbers 14:18b:** "Yet he does not leave the guilty unpunished; he punishes the children for the sin of the fathers to the third and fourth generation."
Luke 1:50: "His mercy extends to those who fear him, from generation to generation."	**Hosea 8:7:** "They sow the wind and reap the whirlwind. The stalk has no head; it will produce no flour. Were it to yield grain, foreigners would swallow it up."
Hosea 10:12: "Sow for yourselves righteousness, reap the fruit of unfailing love, and break up your unplowed ground; for it is time to seek the Lord, until he comes and showers righteousness on you."	**Hosea 10:13:** "But you have planted wickedness, you have reaped evil, you have eaten the fruit of deception."
Galatians 6:8b: . . . the one who sows to please the Spirit, from the Spirit will reap eternal life.	**Galatians 6:8a:** The one who sows to please his sinful nature, from that nature will reap destruction . . .

(A more extended discussion of the transference of "the sins of the fathers" to their children can be found in *Raising Lambs Among Wolves,* pages 47–51, printed out in Appendix A: Supplemental Readings.)

DANIEL, NEHEMIAH, AND OTHER BIBLICAL EXAMPLES

Scripture Memory Verses:

"Salvation is found in no one else, for there is no other name under heaven given to men by which we must be saved." (Acts 4:12)

Therefore God exalted him to the highest place and gave him the name that is above every name, that at the name of Jesus every knee should bow, in heaven and on earth and under the earth, and every tongue confess that Jesus Christ is Lord, to the glory of God the Father. (Philippians 2:9–11)

Unit Learning Goal:

To become familiar with biblical examples of spiritual warfare.

Overview of Unit 8:

Lesson 1: Daniel

Lesson 2: Nehemiah

Lesson 3: David

Lesson 4: Job

Lesson 5: Jesus

SUMMARY STATEMENT

The Bible provides a variety of teaching through a variety of viewpoints. But the focus is always the same—on a triune God, who He is, and who we are in Him. Understanding how to deal with direct spiritual encounters comes through looking carefully at examples of those who have had these encounters. The Bible tells of many such instances. We will look only at a few.

We are surrounded by a clutter of ideas, philosophies, and experiences. We may be familiar with stories of biblical heroes from Sunday school lessons, but the power of these lessons and stories may have become diluted over time and confused with many other influences seeping into our lives.

By examining the characters and people of the Bible, we can learn how to avoid and side-step sticky situations, as well as how to defeat the wiles and schemes of Satan. More than mere theory and supposition, God's truth is worked out in the lives of Bible characters through hands-on blood, sweat, and tears living.

LESSON 1: *Daniel*

Scripture for Meditation:

Even youths grow tired and weary, and young men stumble and fall; but those who hope in the Lord will renew their strength. They will soar on wings like eagles; they will run and not grow weary, they will walk and not be faint. (Isaiah 40:30–31)

A Beginning Prayer:

Dear Father in heaven, open my heart, mind, and soul to receive the full truth of Your word. Through Your blessed Holy Spirit, speak Your infinite, loving truths deep into my being. Make me ever more conscious of Your presence and Your will. Draw me close to Your heart and keep me ever under Your watchful care. Amen.

Lesson:

Daniel walked in a high level of devoted obedience to the Lord. He allowed nothing to come between him and his time with God. He withstood royal decrees, watched his companions face a fiery furnace, resisted indulging in kingly delicacies, and spent a night fending off ravenous lions with prayer and faith. Centuries before Paul penned his admonition to put on the full armor, Daniel knew the reality of God's shielding presence.

Do you think that Daniel would have faced such intense spiritual battles had he not been such a threat to God's enemies? Probably not. The more intensely we desire to follow our Lord and live out His truth with integrity in all we do, say, and are, the greater we are a threat to Satan. Just as with Daniel, so with us the Enemy will try to defeat us through circumstances, our friends, those we work with, and others.

Daniel had a number of direct spiritual encounters. He received unique visions and revelations because he was yielded to do God's work. Chapter 10 of the book of Daniel contains one of the most familiar visions and reveals insights into Satan's kingdom as well as God's authority.

(Daniel 10:1) In the third year of Cyrus king of Persia, a revelation was given to Daniel (who was called Belteshazzar). Its message was true and it concerned a great war. The understanding of the message came to him in a vision.

(2) At that time I, Daniel, mourned for three weeks.

Today, many seek visions, dreams, and prophetic insights, not so much to better understand how they can serve God, but so they can gain special honor from others. That was not Daniel's purpose.

Why do you think Daniel received this revelation?

_____

_____

_____

(3) I ate no choice food; no meat or wine touched my lips; and I used no lotions at all until the three weeks were over.

• • •

(4) On the twenty-fourth day of the first month, as I was standing on the bank of the great river, the Tigris,

(5) I looked up and there before me was a man dressed in linen, with a belt of the finest gold around his waist.

(6) His body was like chrysolite, his face like lightning, his eyes like flaming torches, his arms and legs like the gleam of burnished bronze, and his voice like the sound of a multitude.

(7) I, Daniel, was the only one who saw the vision; the men with me did not see it, but such terror overwhelmed them that they fled and hid themselves.

(8) So I was left alone, gazing at this great vision; I had no strength left, my face turned deathly pale and I was helpless.

• • •

(9) Then I heard him speaking, and as I listened to him, I fell into a deep sleep, my face to the ground.

(10) A hand touched me and set me trembling on my hands and knees.

How did Daniel respond?

_____

_____

_____

Why do you think Daniel responded as he did?

_____

_____

_____

It seems as if everyone is seeing angels these days. On television talk shows and in sensational magazine articles, people are recounting their experiences with these "angels of light." Generally, these encounters are described as warm, peaceful, gentle, and sweet. That is not how Daniel described his experience, nor is it typical of the angelic meetings other biblical characters report.

How was Daniel affected by this angelic visit?

_____

_____

_____

How does this compare and contrast with other modern-day stories you've heard regarding angels?

_____

_____

_____

What do you think are the origins of most modern-day angelic sightings, and why do you think they seem to be occurring more frequently?

_____

_____

_____

Who do heavenly angels represent? _____

Why did Daniel tremble? _____

How do you think you would react in the presence of God's holiness?

_____

_____

_____

(11) He said, "Daniel, you who are highly esteemed, consider carefully the words I am about to speak to you, and stand up, for I have now been sent to you." And when he said this to me, I stood up trembling.

Who else in the Bible was called "highly esteemed" or "highly favored" by an angel?

_____

_____

_____

What do you think it would take to be considered "highly esteemed" by God (think of Daniel's example)?

_____

_____

_____

• • •

(12) Then he continued, "Do not be afraid, Daniel. Since the first day that you set your mind to gain understanding and to humble yourself before your God, your words were heard, and I have come in response to them.

(13) But the prince of the Persian kingdom resisted me twenty-one days. Then Michael, one of the chief princes, came to help me, because I was detained there with the king of Persia.

(14) Now I have come to explain to you what will happen to your people in the future, for the vision concerns a time yet to come."

What do you think had been Daniel's prayer that brought this angelic messenger? Do you think Daniel was asking for an angel to visit?

_____

_____

_____

The "prince of Persia" is one of Satan's ruling demonic powers. What insights does this passage give you into Satan's kingdom?

_____

_____

_____

_____

_____

• • •

15) While he was saying this to me, I bowed with my face toward the ground and was speechless.

(16) Then one who looked like a man touched my lips, and I opened my mouth and began to speak. I said to the one standing before me, "I am overcome with anguish because of the vision, my lord, and I am helpless.

(17) How can I, your servant, talk with you, my lord? My strength is gone and I can hardly breathe."

(18) Again the one who looked like a man touched me and gave me strength.

What insights do these verses give you into God's character? Into how we should respond to God?

_____

_____

_____

_____

_____

_____

_____

(19) "Do not be afraid, O man highly esteemed," he said. "Peace! Be strong now; be strong." When he spoke to me, I was strengthened and said, "Speak, my lord, since you have given me strength."

_____

_____

_____

_____

_____

• • •

(20) So he said, "Do you know why I have come to you? Soon I will return to fight against the prince of Persia, and when I go, the prince of Greece will come;

(21) but first I will tell you what is written in the Book of Truth. (No one supports me against them except Michael, your prince.

(11:1) And in the first year of Darius the Mede, I took my stand to support and protect him.)

The battle in the heavenlies is never-ending. Not only does this angel need to return to the warfare he had been engaged in, but he also indicated to Daniel that he will be in continued warfare as well.

Who is coming when the angel leaves? _____

Is this prince of God or of Satan? _____

Take a moment to reread Daniel 10 and reflect on your group discussion. Write down any new insights you received into spiritual warfare as a result of this study. Discuss these with your group:

_____

_____

Review/Conclusion:

Some Christians seek after revelations, dreams, visions, prophecies, and the like. Daniel didn't do that. He only sought the Lord's answer and became "esteemed by God." Because a person is "esteemed" by God does not exempt that person from spiritual warfare. In fact, "to whom much is given, much will be required."

Daniel was esteemed by God because of his close, intimate relationship with God. Daniel knew God and was known by Him. His entire life was bent toward worshiping, honoring, and serving obediently the God of creation—at all costs.

Daniel's prayer times were not practiced only in the heat of distress. They were continuations of an ongoing relationship and communion with God. In prayer, Daniel focused his entire attention on the Lover of his soul. This kind of reverence and devotion is much more worthy than a desire for supernatural visits and dreams. A deep, loving, intimate relationship with God will provide the best protection and the strongest defense against the wiles of Satan's attacks. Satan does try to afflict and destroy us in the physical world, but he can't touch our eternal relationship with God.

LESSON 2: *Nehemiah*

Scripture for Meditation:

"If you believe, you will receive whatever you ask for in prayer." (Matthew 21:22)

A Beginning Prayer:

Dear Lord, give me a steadfast and faithful heart. Strengthen my will and determination toward full service to You. Purify my motives and cleanse my heart of all doubt. Plant my feet firmly on the ground of Your unchanging truth. Set my face like flint against all the intrigues of the Enemy. Open my eyes that I may clearly discern the devil's trickery and cunning at work around me and against me. Amen.

Lesson:

Nehemiah served as the king's cupbearer while exiled in Persia with his people. Yet there was no conflict between his earthly position and his heavenly position. One day he received news regarding the deplorable state of his much-loved city of Jerusalem. "The wall of Jerusalem is broken down, and its gates have been burned with fire" stunned his ears and moved his heart to grief.

(Nehemiah 1:1) The words of Nehemiah son of Hacaliah: In the month of Kislev in the twentieth year, while I was in the citadel of Susa, (2) Hanani, one of my brothers, came from Judah with some other men, and I questioned them about the Jewish remnant that survived the exile, and also about Jerusalem. (3) They said to me, "Those who survived the exile and are back in the province are in great trouble and disgrace. The wall of Jerusalem is broken down, and its gates have been burned with fire." (4) When I heard these things, I sat down and wept. For some days I mourned and fasted and prayed before the God of heaven.	In this instance, unlike with Daniel, the news came via people instead of an angel, and it regarded past events, not future. But given the circumstances surrounding Nehemiah, do you think that his receiving this message was coincidence or a concert of God-directed spiritual activity? _____ _____ _____ How does Nehemiah's reaction to this news compare with Daniel's reactions to the fore-news he received? _____ _____ _____

Nehemiah recognized the spiritual significance of this situation. He also saw the intense human need of the remnant of the children of Israel. Not only did he see and understand this need, but he took on a sense of personal responsibility to do spiritual battle through prayer and fasting, seeking help from the only One who could help. In times of great need—and aren't our current times just that?—prompt action in faithful prayer can change the course of events. Yet sometimes we are not even prepared to devote the needed time and energy for our own burdens, let alone intercede on behalf of those around us.

People want push-button deliverance. We are the products of our age. We feel that if an answer isn't forthcoming quickly, there must be something wrong with our seeking one at all! But there is nothing wrong with having a burden so great that we must express ourselves in tears, fasting, and extended prayer. Such a burden can be a vital part of living out God's plan. Look at Nehemiah's prayer and the results it yielded.

(1:5) Then I said: "O Lord, God of heaven, the great and awesome God, who keeps his covenant of love with those who love him and obey his commands,

(6) let your ear be attentive and your eyes open to hear the prayer your servant is praying before you day and night for your servants, the people of Israel. I confess the sins we Israelites, including myself and my father's house, have committed against you.

(7) We have acted very wickedly toward you. We have not obeyed the commands, decrees and laws you gave your servant Moses.

(8) "Remember the instruction you gave your servant Moses, saying, 'If you are unfaithful, I will scatter you among the nations,

(9) but if you return to me and obey my commands, then even if your exiled people are at the farthest horizon, I will gather them from there and bring them to the place I have chosen as a dwelling for my Name.'

(10) "They are your servants and your people, whom you redeemed by your great strength and your mighty hand.

(11) O Lord, let your ear be attentive to the prayer of this your servant and to the prayer of your servants who delight in revering your name. Give your servant success today by granting him favor in the presence of this man."

I was cupbearer to the king.

(2:1) In the month of Nisan in the twentieth year of King Artaxerxes, when wine was brought for him, I took the wine and gave it to the king. I had not been sad in his presence before;

(2) so the king asked me, "Why does your face look so sad when you are not ill? This can be nothing but sadness of heart." I was very much afraid,

Read through Nehemiah's prayer (vv. 5–11a) and outline the structure, themes, and highlights as you see them. (Helpful reading on this subject can be found on pages 94–212 of Mark I. Bubeck, *The Rise of Fallen Angels* [Chicago: Moody, 1995].

_____

_____

_____

_____

_____

_____

Was Nehemiah praying fully expecting God to answer? Why or why not?

_____

_____

Did he pray on the authority of who he was? If not, on whose authority?

_____

_____

What was the result of Nehemiah's prayer?

_____

_____

(3) but I said to the king, "May the king live forever! Why should my face not look sad when the city where my fathers are buried lies in ruins, and its gates have been destroyed by fire?"

(4) The king said to me, "What is it you want?" Then I prayed to the God of heaven,

(5) and I answered the king, "If it pleases the king and if your servant has found favor in his sight, let him send me to the city in Judah where my fathers are buried so that I can rebuild it."

(6) Then the king, with the queen sitting beside him, asked me, "How long will your journey take, and when will you get back?" It pleased the king to send me; so I set a time.

Was Nehemiah's attitude arrogant and demanding or something else?

_____

_____

_____

Did Nehemiah flaunt his God-given authority in the face of the king? How did he deal with the king?

_____

_____

_____

Once the king responded positively to Nehemiah's request, how did Nehemiah react? What did he do next?

_____

_____

_____

Invincible warfare prayer is centered in great expectancy. Nehemiah expected God to touch the heart of the pagan king he was enslaved to. He expected to be released from service to the pagan king to do service to his King of Kings. Yet, Nehemiah didn't rest merely on expectation—he was also a man of action.

(2:7) I also said to him, "If it pleases the king, may I have letters to the governors of Trans-Euphrates, so that they will provide me safe-conduct until I arrive in Judah?

(8) And may I have a letter to Asaph, keeper of the king's forest, so he will give me timber to make beams for the gates of the citadel by the temple and for the city wall and for the residence I will occupy?" And because the gracious hand of my God was upon me, the king granted my requests.

Many Christians pray believing that when the answer comes they won't have to lift a finger themselves. This is a lazy faith and won't hold up in the face of serious warfare. Nehemiah understood that, and he was specific in his requests.

What did Nehemiah ask for?

_____

_____

What did he receive, and why?

_____

_____

_____

(9) So I went to the governors of Trans-Euphrates and gave them the king's letters. The king had also sent army officers and cavalry with me.

(10) When Sanballat the Horonite and Tobiah the Ammonite official heard about this, they were very much disturbed that someone had come to promote the welfare of the Israelites.

(11) I went to Jerusalem, and after staying there three days

(12) I set out during the night with a few men. I had not told anyone what my God had put in my heart to do for Jerusalem. There were no mounts with me except the one I was riding on.

(13) By night I went out through the Valley Gate toward the Jackal Well and the Dung Gate, examining the walls of Jerusalem, which had been broken down, and its gates, which had been destroyed by fire.

(14) Then I moved on toward the Fountain Gate and the King's Pool, but there was not enough room for my mount to get through;

(15) so I went up the valley by night, examining the wall. Finally, I turned back and reentered through the Valley Gate.

(16) The officials did not know where I had gone or what I was doing, because as yet I had said nothing to the Jews or the priests or nobles or officials or any others who would be doing the work.

(17) Then I said to them, "You see the trouble we are in: Jerusalem lies in ruins, and its gates have been burned with fire. Come, let us rebuild the wall of Jerusalem, and we will no longer be in disgrace."

(18) I also told them about the gracious hand of my God upon me and what the king had said to me. They replied, "Let us start rebuilding." So they began this good work.

(19) But when Sanballat the Horonite, Tobiah the Ammonite official and Geshem the Arab heard about it, they mocked and ridiculed us.

What did he do? What steps did he take next?

_____

_____

_____

_____

_____

_____

_____

Nehemiah's mission was ordained by God. God's favor clearly rested upon him. Why didn't he ride into town with a lot of fanfare and noise, proclaiming the news of the victory he had won?

_____

_____

_____

_____

_____

_____

Several times during his inspection tour, Nehemiah encountered obstacles. This is often the case in any situation of spiritual warfare. When the going got tough in one direction, what did Nehemiah do? Give up? Turn back? And how do his actions relate to our efforts in warfare?

_____

_____

_____

Read verses 17–18. Why do you think Nehemiah was so concerned about removing this "disgrace"? Of whom was it a reflection?

_____

_____

_____

Even though it was clearly stated and proven (he had letters) that Nehemiah had both God's and the king's approval, he encountered open opposition. In fact the opposition accused him of rebelling against the king and questioned Nehemiah's obvious authority. How does this relate to tactics used by Satan against us in warfare?

_____

"What is this you are doing?" they asked. "Are you rebelling against the king?"

(20) I answered them by saying, "The God of heaven will give us success. We his servants will start rebuilding, but as for you, you have no share in Jerusalem or any claim or historic right to it."

_____
_____
_____

How did Nehemiah respond to these outrageous taunts?

_____
_____

Nehemiah knew that he stood solidly on the full authority of God and the king. He knew his position was absolutely certain. Despite the taunts of these other "officials," Nehemiah was not budged in his faith and rebuked them on the basis of fact.

Many others would have faltered in the face of such opposition. This is partly due to the misbelief that just because we stand in an authoritative position we will not encounter resistance. This faulty logic has caused many Christians to be deflected from their callings when any opposition comes across their path. This is not a scriptural view.

Satan will use counterfeit authority to attack our position in Christ and attempt to knock us off balance. Although Satan must yield to the authority of Christ when it is properly brought to bear, he has no regard for authority in general. He will probe and prod our lives, looking for points of weakness to see if we will crack. However, if we stand on the Word that ensures our position in Christ through His death and resurrection and our confession of faith, and use the Word against Satan, just as Jesus did, then we will remain standing in the battle.

Review/Conclusion:

In Nehemiah 6, opposition and scheming against Nehemiah continues. This is the same way Satan schemes against us. He will use intimidation, subterfuge, deceit, lies, and all manner of subtlety to distract, dissuade, and destroy our progress in the Lord.

Nehemiah continued to stand firmly upon the truth. Not an imagined truth or a relative truth—but _the_ truth. He was not moved by fear, doubt, or any other emotion. He knew that what he knew was true. Standing in truth rather than getting caught up in emotion, Nehemiah was able to clearly discern the trickery being brought to bear against him. He remained steadfast, calm, and committed to the Lord's work he'd been given.

And what was the outcome? "So the wall was completed on the twenty-fifth of Elul, in fifty-two days. When all our enemies heard about this, all the surrounding nations were afraid and lost their self-confidence, because they realized that this work had been done with the help of our God" (Nehemiah 6:15–16).

This same kind of victory can be yours in spiritual warfare.

LESSON 3: *David*

Scripture for Meditation:

"For nothing is impossible with God."
(Luke 1:37)

A Beginning Prayer:

Heavenly Father, affirm in my heart the truth that nothing is impossible with You. Help me to fully grasp with all of my being the reality of absolute victory over all forms of spiritual opposition that rise up against Your plans for me. Amen.

Lesson:

Anyone who has ever been to Sunday school probably knows the story of David and Goliath. In fact, the concept of a boy giant-killer excites even the imaginations of unbelievers. And well it should. Not only is this an actual historical event and a wonderful Bible story to tell our children, it is also a powerful demonstration of victorious spiritual warfare. It's a story we need to revisit often as adults as we mature in the Lord.

The imagery in this story is rich with profound spiritual truths and insights that can help strengthen our own understanding of how to engage effectively in spiritual battle. With your study group, read through this passage, ask the Holy Spirit to open your minds and hearts to new truth, and then together begin to mine the rich treasure contained in this passage.

(1 Samuel 17:1) Now the Philistines gathered their forces for war and assembled at Socoh in Judah. They pitched camp at Ephes Dammim, between Socoh and Azekah.

(2) Saul and the Israelites assembled and camped in the Valley of Elah and drew up their battle line to meet the Philistines.

(3) The Philistines occupied one hill and the Israelites another, with the valley between them.

(4) A champion named Goliath, who was from Gath, came out of the Philistine camp. He was over nine feet tall.

(5) He had a bronze helmet on his head and wore a coat of scale armor of bronze weighing five thousand shekels;

(6) on his legs he wore bronze greaves, and a bronze javelin was slung on his back.

(7) His spear shaft was like a weaver's rod, and its iron point weighed six hundred shekels. His shield bearer went ahead of him.

Read all of 1 Samuel 17. Jot down notes as the Holy Spirit gives you insights into the ways this story applies to your engagements in spiritual battle. Discuss these in your group and take additional notes as new insights emerge. Discuss the practical applications of the truths you uncover.

_____

_____

_____

_____

_____

_____

_____

_____

_____

_____

_____

_____

_____

_____

_____

_____

(8) Goliath stood and shouted to the ranks of Israel, "Why do you come out and line up for battle? Am I not a Philistine, and are you not the servants of Saul? Choose a man and have him come down to me.

(9) If he is able to fight and kill me, we will become your subjects; but if I overcome him and kill him, you will become our subjects and serve us."

(10) Then the Philistine said, "This day I defy the ranks of Israel! Give me a man and let us fight each other."

(11) On hearing the Philistine's words, Saul and all the Israelites were dismayed and terrified.

(12) Now David was the son of an Ephrathite named Jesse, who was from Bethlehem in Judah. Jesse had eight sons, and in Saul's time he was old and well advanced in years.

(13) Jesse's three oldest sons had followed Saul to the war: The firstborn was Eliab; the second, Abinadab; and the third, Shammah.

(14) David was the youngest. The three oldest followed Saul,

(15) but David went back and forth from Saul to tend his father's sheep at Bethlehem.

(16) For forty days the Philistine came forward every morning and evening and took his stand.

(17) Now Jesse said to his son David, "Take this ephah of roasted grain and these ten loaves of bread for your brothers and hurry to their camp.

(18) Take along these ten cheeses to the commander of their unit. See how your brothers are and bring back some assurance from them.

(19) They are with Saul and all the men of Israel in the Valley of Elah, fighting against the Philistines."

(20) Early in the morning David left the flock with a shepherd, loaded up and set out, as Jesse had directed. He reached the camp as the army was going out to its battle positions, shouting the war cry.

(21) Israel and the Philistines were

drawing up their lines facing each other.

(22) David left his things with the keeper of supplies, ran to the battle lines and greeted his brothers.

(23) As he was talking with them, Goliath, the Philistine champion from Gath, stepped out from his lines and shouted his usual defiance, and David heard it.

(24) When the Israelites saw the man, they all ran from him in great fear.

(25) Now the Israelites had been saying, "Do you see how this man keeps coming out? He comes out to defy Israel. The king will give great wealth to the man who kills him. He will also give him his daughter in marriage and will exempt his father's family from taxes in Israel."

(26) David asked the men standing near him, "What will be done for the man who kills this Philistine and removes this disgrace from Israel? Who is this uncircumcised Philistine that he should defy the armies of the living God?"

(27) They repeated to him what they had been saying and told him, "This is what will be done for the man who kills him."

(28) When Eliab, David's oldest brother, heard him speaking with the men, he burned with anger at him and asked, "Why have you come down here? And with whom did you leave those few sheep in the desert? I know how conceited you are and how wicked your heart is; you came down only to watch the battle."

(29) "Now what have I done?" said David. "Can't I even speak?"

(30) He then turned away to someone else and brought up the same matter, and the men answered him as before.

(31) What David said was overheard and reported to Saul, and Saul sent for him.

(32) David said to Saul, "Let no one lose heart on account of this Philistine; your servant will go and fight him."

(33) Saul replied, "You are not able to go out against this Philistine and fight him; you are only a boy, and he has been a fighting man from his youth."

(34) But David said to Saul, "Your servant has been keeping his father's sheep. When a lion or a bear came and carried off a sheep from the flock,

(35) I went after it, struck it and rescued the sheep from its mouth. When it turned on me, I seized it by its hair, struck it and killed it.

(36) Your servant has killed both the lion and the bear; this uncircumcised Philistine will be like one of them, because he has defied the armies of the living God.

(37) The Lord who delivered me from the paw of the lion and the paw of the bear will deliver me from the hand of this Philistine." Saul said to David, "Go, and the Lord be with you."

(38) Then Saul dressed David in his own tunic. He put a coat of armor on him and a bronze helmet on his head.

(39) David fastened on his sword over the tunic and tried walking around, because he was not used to them. "I cannot go in these," he said to Saul, "because I am not used to them." So he took them off.

(40) Then he took his staff in his hand, chose five smooth stones from the stream, put them in the pouch of his shepherd's bag and, with his sling in his hand, approached the Philistine.

(41) Meanwhile, the Philistine, with his shield bearer in front of him, kept coming closer to David.

(42) He looked David over and saw that he was only a boy, ruddy and handsome, and he despised him.

(43) He said to David, "Am I a dog, that you come at me with sticks?" And the Philistine cursed David by his gods.

(44) "Come here," he said, "and I'll give your flesh to the birds of the air

and the beasts of the field!"

(45) David said to the Philistine, "You come against me with sword and spear and javelin, but I come against you in the name of the Lord Almighty, the God of the armies of Israel, whom you have defied.

(46) This day the Lord will hand you over to me, and I'll strike you down and cut off your head. Today I will give the carcasses of the Philistine army to the birds of the air and the beasts of the earth, and the whole world will know that there is a God in Israel.

(47) All those gathered here will know that it is not by sword or spear that the Lord saves; for the battle is the Lord's, and he will give all of you into our hands."

(48) As the Philistine moved closer to attack him, David ran quickly toward the battle line to meet him.

(49) Reaching into his bag and taking out a stone, he slung it and struck the Philistine on the forehead. The stone sank into his forehead, and he fell facedown on the ground.

(50) So David triumphed over the Philistine with a sling and a stone; without a sword in his hand he struck down the Philistine and killed him.

(51) David ran and stood over him. He took hold of the Philistine's sword and drew it from the scabbard. After he killed him, he cut off his head with the sword. When the Philistines saw that their hero was dead, they turned and ran.

(52) Then the men of Israel and Judah surged forward with a shout and pursued the Philistines to the entrance of Gath and to the gates of Ekron. Their dead were strewn along the Shaaraim road to Gath and Ekron.

(53) When the Israelites returned from chasing the Philistines, they plundered their camp.

(54) David took the Philistine's head and brought it to Jerusalem, and he put the Philistine's weapons in his own tent.

(55) As Saul watched David going out to meet the Philistine, he said to Abner, commander of the army, "Abner, whose son is that young man?" Abner replied, "As surely as you live, O king, I don't know."

(56) The king said, "Find out whose son this young man is."

(57) As soon as David returned from killing the Philistine, Abner took him and brought him before Saul, with David still holding the Philistine's head.

(58) "Whose son are you, young man?" Saul asked him. David said, "I am the son of your servant Jesse of Bethlehem."

_____

_____

_____

_____

_____

_____

_____

_____

_____

_____

Review/Conclusion:

Appearances are deceiving. So often we are confronted with problems that seem overwhelming at first. But as we lay them prayerfully before the Lord, they suddenly shrink down to manageable size. Before God, no giant stands tall. So it is with all the gigantic problems the Enemy can bring before us.

Also, just as David was offered the armor of human solutions, so too sometimes we are tempted to confront spiritual enemies with our frail human resources and the well-meaning advice of friends. We need to remember always that our struggle is not with the seen but with the unseen. The only armor that is fitting and that will fit is God's full armor. The only sword we need is the sword of the Spirit, and the only advice we need is the Word of the Lord. If we ever become "used to" the false armor of the world, we are in deep trouble.

And finally, we go into battle, not in the strength of our own abilities, talents, or positive mental powers. We go in the name of the Lord, armed with the stark simplicity of His wisdom and the universe-sustaining power of His truth. If He gives us five smooth stones and a sling, that's all the weaponry and defense we need. We can go out in confidence and victory against all our foes, no matter how tall they stand.

LESSON 4: *Job*

Scripture for Meditation:

"For my thoughts are not your thoughts, nei-ther are your ways my ways," declares the Lord. "As the heavens are higher than the earth, so are my ways higher than your ways and my thoughts than your thoughts." (Isaiah 55:8–9)

Yet, O Lord, you are our Father. We are the clay, you are the potter; we are all the work of your hand. Do not be angry beyond measure, O Lord; do not remember our sins forever. Oh, look upon us, we pray, for we are all your peo-ple. (Isaiah 64:8–9)

A Beginning Prayer:

Heavenly Father, You are the Sovereign Lord over my life and I willingly place myself com-pletely in Your care. I know that what happens to me in this physical world is temporal and fleeting. My hope is in You and my home is in heaven. Help me to remain faithful and true regardless of the circumstances You allow to come around me. Use me for Your glory, O Lord, whether in life or in death. Amen.

Lesson:

In the early 1980s, a small book was published that rose to the top of the best-seller lists. The book was the author's attempt to explain how God could allow suffering to come upon good people, particularly his loss of a young son. On the final page of the book he writes, "Are you capable of forgiving and loving God even when you have found out that He is not perfect, even when He has let you down and disappointed you by permitting bad luck and sickness and cru-elty in His world, and permitting some of those things to happen to you? Can you learn to love and forgive Him despite His limitations, as Job does?" (Harold S. Kushner, *When Bad Things Happen to Good People* [New York: Schocken, 1981]).

The problem with the premise of this author, which is also the thinking of a great number of people, is that it is infected with a sinful, selfish, thoroughly unbiblical presupposition. It is a view that says life has to be fair because I want it to be fair—and fair on my terms. It is a view that says God has to be good to me all the time because I deserve His goodness. It is a view that says I have a right to be happy all the time if I live a good life as I determine on my own what goodness is. It is a view that is full of the devil's lies.

God is not imperfect, but our understanding of Him is. He is not limited in any way, but our experience of Him is. And Job understood these things much better than the author cited above does.

A persistent and insidious fallacy held both by believers and unbelievers is that if I'm a Christian and if I'm good and if I walk faithfully according to God's Word, my life will be pain-less, void of worry, and free of struggle. This fallacy is written into books, preached in sermons, supported by scriptural "proof texts" quoted out of context, and presented to us with the enthusiasm of spiritual bumper stickers. This "happiness-all-the-time" teaching strips out all references in the Word to pain, suffering, and trial as key elements in shaping the mature Chris-tian life.

In Job's case, if there was any imperfection, it was in his life and the lives of his friends, not in God. Fortunately for Job, he knew God well enough that despite devastating and soul-crushing circumstances that shook his faith, his faith ultimately stood firm and was strength-ened. In fact, the ordeal shook loose the sediment of self-righteousness hidden in Job's life, which needed to be removed.

(Job 1:1) In the land of Uz there lived a man whose name was Job. This man was blameless and upright; he feared God and shunned evil.

(2) He had seven sons and three daughters,

(3) and he owned seven thousand sheep, three thousand camels, five hundred yoke of oxen and five hundred donkeys, and had a large number of servants. He was the greatest man among all the people of the East.

(4) His sons used to take turns holding feasts in their homes, and they would invite their three sisters to eat and drink with them.

(5) When a period of feasting had run its course, Job would send and have them purified. Early in the morning he would sacrifice a burnt offering for each of them, thinking, "Perhaps my children have sinned and cursed God in their hearts." This was Job's regular custom.

What kind of a man was Job?

_____

_____

_____

How careful was Job to observe God's laws?

_____

_____

_____

_____

Was this done from a sense of legalism or out of a real desire to please God?

_____

_____

_____

What "habits of holiness" have you cultivated in your life?

_____

_____

_____

_____

_____

_____

(6) One day the angels came to present themselves before the Lord, and Satan also came with them.

(7) The Lord said to Satan, "Where have you come from?" Satan answered the Lord, "From roaming through the earth and going back and forth in it."

(8) Then the Lord said to Satan, "Have you considered my servant Job? There is no one on earth like him; he is blameless and upright, a man who fears God and shuns evil."

(9) "Does Job fear God for nothing?" Satan replied.

(10) "Have you not put a hedge around him and his household and everything he has? You have blessed the work of his hands, so that his

What insights into the spiritual realm does this passage offer? What do you see now that you didn't realize before?

_____

_____

_____

What is God's own testimony concerning Job?

_____

_____

_____

What do you think Satan meant by his statement, "Does Job fear God for nothing?"

_____

flocks and herds are spread throughout the land.

(11) But stretch out your hand and strike everything he has, and he will surely curse you to your face."

(12) The Lord said to Satan, "Very well, then, everything he has is in your hands, but on the man himself do not lay a finger." Then Satan went out from the presence of the Lord.

(13) One day when Job's sons and daughters were feasting and drinking wine at the oldest brother's house,

(14) a messenger came to Job and said, "The oxen were plowing and the donkeys were grazing nearby,

(15) and the Sabeans attacked and carried them off. They put the servants to the sword, and I am the only one who has escaped to tell you!"

(16) While he was still speaking, another messenger came and said, "The fire of God fell from the sky and burned up the sheep and the servants, and I am the only one who has escaped to tell you!"

(17) While he was still speaking, another messenger came and said, "The Chaldeans formed three raiding parties and swept down on your camels and carried them off. They put the servants to the sword, and I am the only one who has escaped to tell you!"

(18) While he was still speaking, yet another messenger came and said, "Your sons and daughters were feasting and drinking wine at the oldest brother's house,

Are we to fear God because of who He is or because of the good things He does for us?

_____

_____

_____

Satan asked God to strike Job, but what was God's response?

_____

_____

_____

Describe a time in your life when you received one piece of bad news after another, when it seemed as if every day brought a new challenge:

_____

_____

_____

_____

_____

_____

_____

_____

Now describe the emotions that came over you as each new discouragement was encountered:

_____

_____

_____

_____

_____

_____

_____

(19) when suddenly a mighty wind swept in from the desert and struck the four corners of the house. It collapsed on them and they are dead, and I am the only one who has escaped to tell you!"

(20) At this, Job got up and tore his robe and shaved his head. Then he fell to the ground in worship

(21) and said: "Naked I came from my mother's womb, and naked I will depart. The Lord gave and the Lord has taken away; may the name of the Lord be praised."

(22) In all this, Job did not sin by charging God with wrongdoing.

How did you initially and finally respond to these problems and pains? How did your response compare to Job's?

_____

_____

_____

_____

Why do you think Job was able to worship God and avoid all sin during this incredible time of grief?

_____

_____

This was only the beginning of Job's incredible ordeal. Job stood firm in his faith, and Satan turned up the heat. Even Job's wife failed to support him in his faithfulness, telling him, "Curse God and die!" His wife crumbled under the horror of the trials. With his children all dead, his possessions and wealth gone, and his skin covered with disease, the one person he needed the most for support failed him, and failed God.

Read chapter 2 of Job and put yourself in his place. Discuss in your group how you would feel—what kinds of emotions would be washing over your heart and mind in a situation like that. Write some of your observations down:

_____

_____

Now read chapter 3. Given his circumstances, do you think his response is reasonable? Is he blaming God at all? How does his response compare to how you respond to trouble?

_____

_____

Finally, after enduring the misguided musings of his friends, Job begins to reveal his true heart in chapters 26–31. In 27:1, the first hint of Job's flaw is revealed when he states, "As surely as God lives, who has denied me justice." Does God ever deny anyone true justice?

_____

_____

The second glimmer is revealed in verses 3 through 11. Repeatedly Job says "I will" this and "I will" that. Scan through the next chapters, where Job is speaking, and look for more "I" statements as well as "my" and "me" statements. Who is the focus on in these statements, Job or God? What does this expose in Job?

_____

_____

In chapter 31, the "I," "my," and "me" statements flow like a raging torrent of self-righteousness. The sediment at the bottom of Job's heart finally breaks loose and rises to the surface. First John 2:16 in the King James states, "For all that is in the world, the lust of the flesh, and the lust of the eyes, and the pride of life, is not of the Father, but is of the world." The NIV translates "pride of life" as "the boasting of what he has and does." What is the hidden sin now revealed in Job's life? (Look also at Job 32:1.)

_____

_____

Read chapters 39–42. In 40:8, what is God's response to Job's accusations?

_____

_____

In 40:4–5 and finally 42:1–6, how does Job respond to God?

_____

_____

In 42:7–9, ultimately, is God pleased or angry with Job's friends? Why or why not? And what about the fourth counselor, Elihu (32:1–37:24)?

_____

_____

In 42:10–16, ultimately, is God pleased or angry with Job? Why or why not?

_____

_____

Is material wealth always a sign of God's blessing? Is the absence of material wealth always a sign of God's disfavor?

_____

_____

Write down all the reasons you believe God allowed Job to experience these disasters and trials. Who benefited? How and why? Did God receive glory in this? How and why or why not?

_____

_____

What have you learned about spiritual warfare from Job's experience? What practical truths can you apply to your life and situation? Write down your insights and discuss with your group. Take notes on their contributions.

_____

_____

Review/Conclusion:

Job was a good and godly man. If anyone deserved to receive only good things in life, he did. Yet, despite the outward appearance of his goodness and the very real inward goodness he possessed, he harbored a problem of sin that was hidden from his view. Job learned deep truths about himself, about those he loved, about his friends, and most important, about God. No other set of circumstances would have revealed these things to him.

Could Job have lived a long, happy, and productive life without this tragedy? Yes. But he would have missed out on all that God wanted for him. The point of our lives does not lie in our achieving all the happiness we can, but in our becoming the righteousness of God, the spotless bride of Christ. Our earthly lives are only a small blip on the timeline of eternity. To focus all our attention on the here and now of our fleshly existence is shortsighted and self-centered. God desires us to have an eternal perspective and a pure heart. Only then can we walk in sweet intimacy with Him.

Satan will attack us, meaning to do us harm, but that doesn't mean that he will be able to fulfill his ultimate intentions. He can hurt us and destroy much, but only under God's limits. He cannot rob us of our souls and God's love for us. Imagine how tremendously frustrated and disappointed Satan was at the end of Job's ordeal! God took an attack of the devil and turned it into a benefit for Job, for those around him, and for us!

We live in an evil, sinful world. This evil will have an effect upon us and those we love. We will be hurt by life, and in God's purposes may even be tormented by Satan and his demon army. No one is immune.

But that's not so distressing because we know the end of the story. We know who the real King of all creation is. We know who we have believed, and we know He is able to keep us who are committed to Him until the day He returns to take us home. With that view in mind, we need to see life as but a passing experience and heaven as the true reality. We are to just keep on rowing, rowing, rowing toward that golden shore!

LESSON 5: *Jesus*

Scripture for Meditation:

"Anyone who has seen me [Jesus] has seen the Father." (John 14:9)

How great is the love the Father has lavished on us, that we should be called children of God! And that is what we are! The reason the world does not know us is that it did not know him. Dear friends, now we are children of God, and what we will be has not yet been made known. But we know that when he appears, we shall be like him, for we shall see him as he is. Everyone who has this hope in him purifies himself, just as he is pure. (1 John 3:1–3)

A Beginning Prayer:

Heavenly Father, I welcome the Holy Spirit into every area of my life. Move through me, work through me, change me, and mold me more and more into the true, pure image of my Lord and Savior, Jesus Christ. Amen.

Lesson:

A popular item among Christian young people today is a cloth bracelet bearing the embroidered letters *WWJD*. While it looks like the call letters of a radio station, the initials stand for the question, What would Jesus do? It is a reminder to evaluate actions and reactions in all circumstances against the example of Christ's life. For the Christian, there is no greater example to model.

To model Christ's life we must know *about* Him and we must *know* Him. To know about Him we need to read all of God's Word, including the four Gospels: Matthew, Mark, Luke, and

John. To know Him we must walk in relationship with Him.

From the beginning of Christ's earthly life, the devil's fury dogged His steps. Satan tried many approaches. At times he would cower in defeat before the majesty of Christ, but then he would mindlessly hurl himself back into confrontation with Him, foolishly believing in the vain hope of winning the next time. Satan never stopped trying to defeat our Lord, and he never ever stopped losing. It could be no other way. Blinded by his evil, self-centered rage against heaven, Satan refused to see the truth of his defeat.

Throughout Christ's life on earth, He encountered the devil over and over. Each time Satan failed. The first failures came just prior to and just following the birth of Christ. Caesar Augustus was manipulated by Satan with the intent of trying to cause Mary to miscarry by making her travel by donkey to Bethlehem and having her lodge in less than desirable circumstances (Luke 2:1–7). Then Satan tried to kill Jesus through the machinations of King Herod and his decree ordering the execution of innocent children (Matthew 2:1–18; cf. Revelation 12:4).

Read the story of Christ's birth in Matthew 1–2 and Luke 1–2. What other elements of spiritual warfare were present?

_____

_____

Read the lineage of Christ in Matthew 1 and look up some of the names mentioned. How much human failure and "dysfunction" was evident in the line of Christ? Do you think these "sins of the fathers" were aimed at derailing Christ's ministry? Did Christ let these issues distract Him from serving God effectively?

_____

_____

It was through God's sovereignty through the devout faithfulness of His parents and relatives that Jesus' life was protected when He was in the womb and during His youth from the attacks of the Enemy. From this example, what practical steps can you take to protect your children and the children of others from spiritual attack?

_____

_____

The first recorded face-to-face encounter by Christ with Satan took place in the wilderness shortly after Christ began His public ministry. This is one of the most dramatic examples of effective warfare presented in Scripture. Clearly Jesus understood the value of knowing the Word, and this was surely not the first time He had spent an extended time in prayer and fasting.

(Matthew 4:1) Then Jesus was led by the Spirit into the desert to be tempted by the devil.

Read verses 1 and 2 carefully. What was the purpose of Jesus going into the wilderness?

_____

_____

(2) After fasting forty days and forty nights, he was hungry.

Who directed Jesus into the wilderness? Who was Jesus absolutely obedient to throughout His earthly life?

_____

_____

(3) The tempter came to him and said, "If you are the Son of God, tell these stones to become bread."

Did Satan come to Jesus when He was physically strong or weak?

_____

_____

(4) Jesus answered, "It is written: 'Man does not live on bread alone, but on every word that comes from the mouth of God.'"

(5) Then the devil took him to the holy city and had him stand on the highest point of the temple.

Was Jesus attacked spiritually and tempted because He was bad or a sinner?

_____

_____

_____

_____

(6) "If you are the Son of God," he said, "throw yourself down. For it is written: "'He will command his angels concerning you, and they will lift you up in their hands, so that you will not strike your foot against a stone.'"

What three areas or categories of sin did Satan's temptations address?

_____

_____

_____

(7) Jesus answered him, "It is also written: 'Do not put the Lord your God to the test.'"

(8) Again, the devil took him to a very high mountain and showed him all the kingdoms of the world and their splendor.

(9) "All this I will give you," he said, "if you will bow down and worship me."

(10) Jesus said to him, "Away from me, Satan! For it is written: 'Worship the Lord your God, and serve him only.'"

What would be modern-day equivalents of these sins and temptations you might typically face?

_____

_____

_____

_____

_____

_____

(11) Then the devil left him, and angels came and attended him.

What spiritual disciplines did Jesus exhibit in this passage that we need to apply in our lives?

_____
_____
_____
_____
_____
_____

Christ's ministry was marked by repeated encounters with demonic powers. Each encounter was met with confidence, authority, and fearlessness. In a sense, there was nothing particularly extraordinary about these situations—at least from the heavenly minded perspective of Christ. He knew who He was in God, and He understood that His struggle was not against flesh and blood. Jesus recognized the works of Satan and calmly, yet firmly, demonstrated His authority over all of hell's activities. He wants to demonstrate the same authority through us.

With your group, read through the following passages and share insights each offers into spiritual warfare. Look for practical principles you can pull out and apply to your own arsenal of spiritual defense.

(Matthew 4:24) News about him spread all over Syria, and people brought to him all who were ill with various diseases, those suffering severe pain, the demon-possessed, those having seizures, and the paralyzed, and he healed them.

(8:16) When evening came, many who were demon-possessed were brought to him, and he drove out the spirits with a word and healed all the sick.

How do you think demon activity relates to illness?

_____
_____
_____
_____
_____

Other thoughts about these passages?

_____
_____
_____
_____
_____

(Matthew 8:28) (see also Mark 5:1–20) When he arrived at the other side in the region of the Gadarenes, two demon-possessed men coming from the tombs met him. They were so violent that no one could pass that way.

Did these men possess any self-control at all?

_____
_____
_____

(29) "What do you want with us, Son of God?" they shouted. "Have you come here to torture us before the appointed time?"

(30) Some distance from them a large herd of pigs was feeding.

(31) The demons begged Jesus, "If you drive us out, send us into the herd of pigs."

(32) He said to them, "Go!" So they came out and went into the pigs, and the whole herd rushed down the steep bank into the lake and died in the water.

(33) Those tending the pigs ran off, went into the town and reported all this, including what had happened to the demon-possessed men.

(34) Then the whole town went out to meet Jesus. And when they saw him, they pleaded with him to leave their region.

(Matthew 9:32) While they were going out, a man who was demon-possessed and could not talk was brought to Jesus.

(33) And when the demon was driven out, the man who had been mute spoke. The crowd was amazed and said, "Nothing like this has ever been seen in Israel."

(34) But the Pharisees said, "It is by the prince of demons that he drives out demons."

(35) Jesus went through all the towns and villages, teaching in their synagogues, preaching the good news of the kingdom and healing every disease and sickness.

(36) When he saw the crowds, he had compassion on them, because they were harassed and helpless, like sheep without a shepherd.

(37) Then he said to his disciples, "The harvest is plentiful but the workers are few.

What effect did demon-possession have on them?

_____

_____

_____

_____

Why do you think Jesus allowed the demons to enter the pigs? And why did the people ask Jesus to leave?

_____

_____

_____

_____

Any other thoughts about this passage?

_____

_____

_____

_____

In their accusation aimed at Jesus, what were the Pharisees acknowledging? Can you recall any time in Jesus' ministry where it is recorded that people did not believe in the existence of demons? How does that compare to views commonly held today?

_____

_____

_____

_____

Some people believe that demon activity isn't real. If this is the case, why would Jesus bother giving the authority to drive out demons to his disciples?

_____

_____

_____

_____

Who are Jesus' disciples today? Do we have authority to stand against the authority of evil spirits?

_____

(38) Ask the Lord of the harvest, therefore, to send out workers into his harvest field."

(10:1) He called his twelve disciples to him and gave them authority to drive out evil spirits and to heal every disease and sickness.

(7) "As you go, preach this message: 'The kingdom of heaven is near.'

(8) Heal the sick, raise the dead, cleanse those who have leprosy, drive out demons. Freely you have received, freely give."

_____
_____
_____

Did Jesus go looking for demons "behind every shrub"? How did these encounters occur?

_____
_____
_____

Other thoughts about this passage?

_____
_____
_____
_____

(Mark 3:22) (see also Matthew 12:22–37) And the teachers of the law who came down from Jerusalem said, "He is possessed by Beelzebub! By the prince of demons he is driving out demons."

(23) So Jesus called them and spoke to them in parables: "How can Satan drive out Satan?

(24) If a kingdom is divided against itself, that kingdom cannot stand.

(25) If a house is divided against itself, that house cannot stand.

(26) And if Satan opposes himself and is divided, he cannot stand; his end has come.

Satan can and does use all manner of deception. It is perfectly within his character to set up situations that appear to be godly in nature but are counterfeit. What elements of Christ's ministry marked Him clearly as genuine, making the accusations of the "teachers of the law" even more ludicrous?

_____
_____
_____

Can you think of modern-day examples of these kinds of illogical accusations being made against legitimate ministry?

_____
_____
_____

(27) In fact, no one can enter a strong man's house and carry off his possessions unless he first ties up the strong man. Then he can rob his house.

(28) I tell you the truth, all the sins and blasphemies of men will be forgiven them.

Jesus acknowledges that Satan is a "strong man." But what else does He declare by this statement? Who is stronger than the strong man?

_____
_____

(29) But whoever blasphemes against the Holy Spirit will never be forgiven; he is guilty of an eternal sin."	What do you believe is "blasphemy against the Holy Spirit"?
(30) He said this because they were saying, "He has an evil spirit."	_____
	_____
	_____
	_____

Review/Conclusion:

Through the example of Christ we are given a treasure of rich insight into how to successfully engage in spiritual warfare. Just as Jesus was not preoccupied with demons but readily acknowledged their existence and dealt with them almost matter-of-factly, so should we be of the same mind-set. The powers of darkness are real. Satan is out to destroy everyone. These are absolute facts that apply to believers and nonbelievers alike. No one is immune from evil's intent. However, as believers we are immune from the ultimate effects of evil and we even have power over evil through Christ.

Biblical spiritual warfare is not a "quick-fix" solution to all our problems. It's part and parcel of the normal Christian walk. It is not an occasional extraordinary event of demonic encounters with Hollywood-like special effects filling the air. It is our daily struggle against the flesh, the world, and the devil. It is what Christ has called us to face and equipped us to overcome.

When face-to-face encounters with demonic powers do occur, we can stand confidently and firmly on the absolute truth and authority of God's Word and the wonderful name of our Lord Jesus Christ. When we are in an abiding relationship with Jesus, reading and studying God's Word daily, walking always in the Spirit, we will always be ready for the spiritual conflicts of life.

The problem arises when we allow sin or neglect to creep in between us and our Lord. We get caught up in the daily hustle and bustle of life and let our prayer times dwindle. Memorizing and studying the Word take on less and less significance. Then when the devil throws his darts at us—and he will—we are wounded, dazed, and thrown into spiritual disarray and jeopardy.

Following the example of Christ and others in the Bible, we need to maintain a close relationship with God at all times and set aside regular extended times of prayer, fasting, and worshiping Him. In these disciplines God will continue to give us the strength we need to defeat all the fiery attacks of the "strong man," who has already been defeated by the cross of Calvary.

FROM FOOTHOLD TO STRONGHOLD: CURIOSITY TO POSSESSION

Scripture Memory Verses:

He answered: "'Love the Lord your God with all your heart and with all your soul and with all your strength and with all your mind'; and, 'Love your neighbor as yourself.'" "You have answered correctly," Jesus replied. "Do this and you will live." (Luke 10:27–28)

Unit Learning Goal:

To recognize the various levels of the work of the evil one.

Overview of Unit 9:

Lesson 1: Curiosity

Lesson 2: Compulsion

Lesson 3: Obsession

Lesson 4: Occultism

Lesson 5: Possession

SUMMARY STATEMENT

In order to guard against falling prey to the snares of the devil, we need to know what these snares are to avoid falling into them, to help others avoid falling into them, and to avoid becoming falsely entrapped by thinking we've fallen into them.

Unit 9 Thought Focus:

We've all heard the maxim, "A journey of a thousand miles must begin with a single step" (Lao-tzu). The journey into satanic bondage begins with one compromise that is allowed to stand and take root in our lives. Casual curiosity about sinful things is not a safe or innocent preoccupation for a Christian. This kind of curiosity will defile our innocence and rob us of our freedom.

As Christians we are to flee evil in all its forms. Yes, we need to understand what evil is to avoid it. But understanding evil enough to run away from it does not mean we have to experiment or even expose ourselves to any of it. No Christian needs to open a copy of *Playboy* to know what it contains. If a preview of a TV show suggests sensuality or violence, I don't need to watch the show to see how much evil content will actually be broadcast. A little is too much, and I've seen more than I need to in the preview.

Seriously addicted individuals frequently start out using only a small amount of one kind of drug, but over time they find they need more and more of an ever-broadening array of narcotic substances to satisfy the deadly craving that has possessed them. Initially, their goal was just to have a little fun or relax a little bit. It all seemed so innocent and harmless. Uncontrollable, ever-increasing addiction was not the goal of their initial dabbling.

The same is true for those who dabble in sinful behaviors. We deceive ourselves by saying, "It's not so bad. I'm not hurting anyone." We fail to realize that sin is not a thing to play with. It leads toward a bondage to the one who is obsessed with our destruction. Dabbling in sin exposes our souls to appetites capable of putting us into the clutch of Satan and his demons. Their program is to pull us deeper and deeper into bondage and death.

LESSON 1: *Curiosity*

Scripture for Meditation:

The mind of sinful man is death, but the mind controlled by the Spirit is life and peace; the sinful mind is hostile to God. It does not submit to God's law, nor can it do so. Those controlled by the sinful nature cannot please God. (Romans 8:6–8)

A Beginning Prayer:

Dear heavenly Father, cover my mind with the protection of Your holy discernment. Fill my mind with the light and life of Your holy truth. Strengthen my resolve to flee even the knowledge of evil and to pursue Your righteousness, wisdom, and knowledge. Grant to me a longing to better please and serve You. Amen.

Lesson:

INNOCENT YET SHREWD

The world is full of wonderful things that capture our imagination and arouse our natural sense of curiosity. That is how God made us, and it is in part why we strive to achieve and succeed. Curiosity is a good thing.

But there are things in this world we don't need to know about. Just as Adam and Eve were cautioned to avoid the one tree in the Garden of Eden, so we have been instructed to remain naive about things that are evil. In the illicit pleasures of the world we are to remain unknowing and innocent as children.

The apostle Paul warns that there are shameful things that the disobedient do in secret that we are not even to mention. We are to avoid such exposure to evil (see Ephesians 5:11–13).

Jesus cautioned His disciples by saying, "I am sending you out like sheep among wolves. Therefore be as shrewd as snakes and as innocent as doves" (Matthew 10:16). The Greek word for shrewd is *phronimos* and implies the fuller meaning, which includes thoughtful, sagacious, discreet, of a cautious nature, practically wise, and sensible. The word for innocent is *akeraios* and means unmixed, pure, harmless, and simple. It is the same word Paul uses in Romans 16:19: "Everyone has heard about your obedience, so I am full of joy over you; but I want you to be wise about what is good, and innocent about what is evil."

What are other words that mean the same or nearly the same things as shrewd and innocent? List as many as you can think of:

Synonyms for SHREWD: Synonyms for INNOCENT:

_____   _____

_____   _____

_____   _____

_____   _____

_____   _____

What does it mean to be shrewd in this biblical sense? How does one exercise shrewdness in day-to-day living?

_____

_____

What does it mean to be innocent in this biblical sense? How does one exercise innocence in day-to-day living?

_____

_____

CARNAL KNOWLEDGE

Carnal knowledge is knowing about dark things, worldly things, sinful things. Once awareness of something enters our mind the first time, our innocence about that thing is lost forever. There's no going back or "unknowing."

All of us who have been exposed to disturbing images understand how it becomes virtually impossible to erase these things from our minds. They have a way of rising up in our memories at the most unlikely of times, totally unbidden by us. They are there in our minds and float in and out of consciousness. Sinful thoughts and images are the same way, only worse.

If you've ever viewed pornographic material, or read a sensual romance novel, or watched a movie with illicit content, or exposed yourself to any one of the hundreds upon hundreds of opportunities to know about some form of sin, you understand how indelible these exposures become. What initially appears as a harmless curiosity becomes a devouring, recurring accusation in the hands of our enemy. These are the footholds Satan endeavors to use to gain access into our lives.

Circle **T** for True or **F** for False and then discuss your answers:

T   **F**   I can listen to any kind of music without being at all harmed by the lyrics or the sensual rhythms, even if they are ungodly in nature.

T   **F**   There's nothing wrong with watching an occasional R-rated movie.

T   **F**   As a Christian I should be able to read the articles in prurient magazines without being affected by the pictures. There's nothing wrong with the articles.

T   F   Any exposure to impurity brings impurity into my life.

Does the world view curiosity about anything as dangerous, or is learning about everything encouraged?

_____

_____

_____

What kinds of things does the world encourage us to learn more and more about? How many of these are evil in nature?

_____

_____

Does our secular society ever discourage the pursuit of knowledge and understanding about particular areas? Are all things viewed as equally valid to learn about? Where are there differences? What biases are exhibited?

_____

_____

Review/Conclusion:

Our secular society encourages "adults" to be open-minded and accepting of everything, no matter how perverse or offensive we may find it. Anything less is called censorship. Even if it goes against biblical mandates, we are encouraged to embrace a ravenous quest for all kinds of "truth." Yet, at the same time, we are told that the Bible is full of mistakes, myths, made-up stories, and all manner of error. Following the God of the Bible, we are led to believe, is foolish, anti-intellectual, not what truly enlightened and intelligent people would do.

Unrestrained curiosity about the evil around us is a major step toward becoming devoured by Satan. The devil arouses unholy curiosity in us and cloaks evil desires in the guise of learning and understanding. In some instances ignorance truly is bliss and there are areas from which we need to guard our minds and awareness.

LESSON 2: *Compulsion*

Scripture for Meditation:

For the word of God is living and active. Sharper than any double-edged sword, it penetrates even to dividing soul and spirit, joints and marrow; it judges the thoughts and attitudes of the heart. (Hebrews 4:12)

A Beginning Prayer:

Heavenly Father, I seek to bring my life into submission to Your holy will. I lay my will at your feet and choose to take up my cross daily. I acknowledge no other Lord of my life but You and will not yield the members of my body—external or internal—to any other power but Yours. Let Your eternal holiness reign and rule in my heart, mind, soul, and body. Amen.

Lesson:

COMPULSIONS

The definition of compulsion is "being compelled" by an "irresistible impulse to act" without regard for "the rationality of the motivation." Most people are, from time to time, struck by impulses to do something out of the ordinary—something out of character for them. These impulses range from the absurd and outrageous to the indecent and criminal. When struck by such impulses, the mature, mentally healthy individual will cast them off and ignore them. We are not compelled to engage in acting them out. But still, if the impulse or the thought is powerful enough and timed to coincide with other emotional stirrings, they can leave a mark on us.

This is an area where the devil frequently lurks. While our will cannot be yielded without our consent, Satan and his demons are free to shower our minds with impulsive, compelling thoughts. Once we begin to fantasize about these ideas and consider for even a moment acting on them, we are giving up significant ground to the Enemy.

Sometimes, these thoughts can even take on a religious guise. When such thoughts come from the Enemy they come with a strong coercive force that is much different from the gentle constraining of the Holy Spirit's direction. The Holy Spirit may urge us gently and strongly toward an act that is completely consistent with God's Word, but He will never compel us to act. Nor will He drive us toward behavior that is contrary to the teachings of Scripture.

When we are being bombarded with impulsive thoughts and compelling urges, particularly when they are attempting to drive us toward sinful behavior, we know where they are coming from and we are responsible to take authority over the attack.

Read Philippians 4:6–9. If thoughts are creating anxiety in us, where are those thoughts probably coming from? Why or why not?

_____

_____

What would be the consequences of acting out these thoughts? How would you be affected? How would others around you be affected?

_____

_____

If you were to act on these thoughts, would God be glorified through your actions?

_____

_____

Do we have to yield to these anxious thoughts? What's the proper response?

_____

_____

With what can we fill our minds so that impulsive/compulsive thoughts will have no room?

_____

_____

Instead of acting out the impulsive/compulsive thoughts, what kind of behavior can we engage in that will help overcome the attack?

_____

_____

What kinds of impulsive/compulsive thoughts have you experienced? How did you deal with them? Are you still struggling with them?

_____

_____

TRUSTWORTHY FRIENDS

If you are struggling with these kinds of thoughts, you may wish to seek the help of one or more trustworthy believing friend. Satan loves for us to keep our struggles hidden, which isolates us from others and makes us even more vulnerable to his attacks. This is why it's so important for Christians to be actively involved in a believing body, in a church. We need the wisdom, perspective, and support of other believers to keep us from being victimized by irrational thoughts and emotions.

A powerful weapon against these kinds of thoughts is simply to talk about them. Speaking about them to another will help you recognize more clearly how foolish they are, help you see the consequences if you were to act on them, and will let you discover that you're not alone! When we open up to others, they will often open up to us, revealing that they've been experiencing the same kind of attack. Once the lie and trickery of the Enemy is exposed, you can then join together in prayer for one another to combat the attacks, covering each other with intercession.

Circle **T** for True or **F** for False and then discuss your answers:

T F Every impulse I feel I must act upon.

T F Resisting evil will make evil leave.

T F If I experience evil thoughts, I must be an evil person.

T F The Holy Spirit forces me to behave properly.

T F Satan and his demons can read my mind.

T F God empowers me to resist Satan and all manner of evil all the time.

Review/Conclusion:

Curiosity can lead to compulsion. Once the door to darkness is opened the Enemy will come rushing in. If you've yielded to curiosity in the past and have dabbled in any kind of sinful behavior, then you know what it's like to wrestle with compulsive desires and emotions. It's important to understand two key truths:

- You do not have to act on them!
- You aren't generating these thoughts and emotions.

You are responsible for your behavior, and you are responsible for any thinking that you hold onto and mull over. But you are not responsible for these random, irrational thoughts that float into your mind. Like the saying says, you can't stop birds from flying into your hair, but you can keep them from nesting there.

The Enemy will work very hard to make you feel guilty just because you thought the thought or because you felt the emotion. Unless we are careful to ask our Lord Jesus Christ to protect us from all demonic activity while we sleep, Satan may infect our dreams with lewd and scintillating, or angry and prideful images that will linger when we awake. You have no control over what you dream, just as you have no control over the thoughts that the devil throws into your head while you are awake. The momentary thought is not the sin. The emotion is not the sin. The dream is not the sin.

In Christ, we are to take control over our thoughts. Christians do have complete control over what stays in their minds and what they choose to act upon. The more these kinds of thoughts and emotions are resisted and the more you fill your mind with God's Word and your time with prayer, the less these attacks will come. When he realizes you're not giving in, Satan will back off. But don't let down your guard. Be alert for him to come back from a different direction.

If, on the other hand, a Christian yields to impulsive/compulsive thoughts and begins to entertain them and even act on them, Satan's forces will inevitably attempt to build strongholds of control in his life.

LESSON 3: *Obsession*

Scripture for Meditation:
Therefore, holy brothers, who share in the heavenly calling, fix your thoughts on Jesus, the apostle and high priest whom we confess. (Hebrews 3:1)

A Beginning Prayer:
Heavenly Father, the world appears to be in a death grip of evil. All around us the message being proclaimed is to indulge, enjoy, and revel in decadence and dissolution. Lord, give me a deep yearning to see the lost saved, a craving to pursue Your holiness and share Your Gospel, and an overwhelming desire to intercede for those around me who are in need of Your great salvation. Let my mind and heart be fixed on You and Your example. Amen.

Lesson:

OBSESSIONS

Despite Calvin Klein's advertisements, obsession is not healthy, attractive, or sweet-smelling. It's soul-deadly. To be obsessed is defined as being preoccupied with a "fixed idea or unwanted feeling or emotion usually coupled with anxiety." It is related to mania and fetishes. Some of the most grotesque and dangerous human behavior arises out of obsessions.

To be obsessed cuts ties with reality and often becomes a pawn of evil control. Obsession serves compulsion—it is a form of idolatry—worshiping desire rather than desiring to worship. It demands the relentless feeding of whatever want, whatever urge, whatever selfish thing that comes into our minds and hearts without any regard to the consequences to others or ourselves. The pursuit of an obsession will cause a person to use and abuse others. Nothing is allowed to stand between an obsessed person and the thing desired.

The evils of uncontrolled obsession seem to have no bounds. In 1995 in Wheaton, Illinois, Jacqueline Annette Williams became obsessed with having a baby of her own, yet was unable to have a child. So, she enlisted the help of her boyfriend and a cousin to carry out an attack on Debra Evans, who lived in a nearby suburb and who had three young children and a baby due in a few days. First Evans was shot in the head; then her full-term fetus was ripped from her womb. Then Evans's ten-year-old daughter was stabbed and her seven-year-old son Joshua was abducted. His body was later found in an alley ten miles away. This is the ultimate result of obsession.

For a Christian to be obsessed means that a stronghold of evil is being established in his life. The line between obsession and control often is very blurred.

DEFENDING AGAINST OBSESSIONS

Read Deuteronomy 11:16–18; Proverbs 4:23–25; 2 Corinthians 4:18; and Hebrews 3:1; 12:1–3. Where are we to "fix" the following things on:

Eyes: _____

_____

Heart: _____

_____

Mind: _____

_____

Hands: _____

_____

Thoughts: _____

_____

What of ourselves are we to guard, and what things are we to guard against?

_____

_____

How are we to guard our lives against these things?

_____

_____

What are we to throw off? (Make this personal—what are your entanglements?)

_____

_____

How can we guard against becoming sinfully obsessed?

_____

_____

What are some examples of obsessions being expressed in our society? How are they being expressed?

_____

_____

What are the consequences of people acting on these obsessions?

_____

_____

Review/Conclusion:

Every day the news is filled with stories of abuse, rape, murder, kidnappings, stalking, and more—all evidences of individuals who have given themselves over to obsessions and acted them out. The visible results and consequences are devastating for victims, survivors, bystanders, and the one obsessed.

Not only do we need to guard our own lives against obsession, but we need to enter into warfare prayer against this attempt of evil to control us. In the power and authority of Jesus Christ we can effectively pray and resist compulsion and obsession. In the Lord Jesus Christ people can find freedom from this painful pressure. The prayer support of other believers is a vital help toward freedom.

The world is in trouble. The answer is Christ. More than ever we need Christians who will take the responsibility to weep and pray for our lost and dying world. Looking around us at the devastating effects of sin should motivate believers to intense intercession. Effectual, fervent prayer will push back the darkness from the lives of those around us and provide the atmosphere for the Holy Spirit to draw them to our Lord Jesus Christ.

LESSON 4: *Occultism*

Scripture for Meditation:

"'Do not practice divination or sorcery.'" (Leviticus 19:26b)

The images of their gods you are to burn in the fire. Do not covet the silver and gold on them, and do not take it for yourselves, or you will be ensnared by it, for it is detestable to the Lord your God. Do not bring a detestable thing into your house or you, like it, will be set apart for destruction. Utterly abhor and detest it, for it is set apart for destruction. (Deuteronomy 7:25–26)

When you enter the land the Lord your God is giving you, do not learn to imitate the detestable ways of the nations there. Let no one be found among you who sacrifices his son or daughter in the fire, who practices divination or sorcery, interprets omens, engages in witchcraft, or casts spells, or who is a medium or spiritist or who consults the dead. Anyone who *does these things is detestable to the Lord, and because of these detestable practices the Lord your God will drive out those nations before you. You must be blameless before the Lord your God.* (Deuteronomy 18:9–13)

A Beginning Prayer:

Heavenly Father, open my eyes to every form of evil that I have allowed to touch me. Forgive me, Lord Jesus Christ, for those things I've knowingly allowed in my life and those things I've unknowingly allowed to influence me that were linked to the occult. Cut off from me all the power and influence that occult sins have given to the kingdom of darkness. Strengthen my resolve to avoid these things in all their forms and to protect others from being drawn into such evil. Amen.

Lesson:

DIVINATION AND SORCERY

The occult is everywhere around us. It proceeds from tarot cards, Ouija® boards, and daily horoscopes to mediumistic channeling, many forms of witchcraft, and even open Satan worship.

"It's only a phase" is a phrase sometimes heard when parents talk about the weird and bizarre behavior, clothing, music, and markings of their teenage offspring. "It'll pass," they intone hopefully.

With some behaviors this is true. They come and go as fads do from generation to generation. But there is a terrible darkness behind so much that is affecting our youth culture in these troubling times.

In 1998 the news reported that in Ingalls, Indiana, police uncovered a ring of teenage Satanists involved in animal sacrifice. As many as fourteen cats and dogs disappeared over a five-month period. "Police," said the article, "found some nailed to picnic tables in the town park." This is not "innocent childish pranks." This is sinister evil.

In Deuteronomy 18:10–12, we are shown very clearly how God views these practices: "Let no one be found among you who sacrifices his son or daughter in the fire, who practices divination or sorcery, interprets omens, engages in witchcraft, or casts spells, or who is a medium or spiritist or who consults the dead. Anyone who does these things is detestable to the Lord, and because of these detestable practices the Lord your God will drive out those nations before you."

God's Word links rebellion and arrogance together with these "detestable" sins: "For rebellion is like the sin of divination, and arrogance like the evil of idolatry. Because you have rejected the word of the Lord, he has rejected you as king" (1 Samuel 15:23). Like King Saul, teens who are defiantly rebellious against parental (or any other) authority are into sinfulness like witchcraft. No wonder that they are often drawn into music with lyrics related to devil worship, fashions and makeup that evoke evil, and marking their bodies with wicked-looking tattoos. The Enemy has deceived them.

TOLERANCE OF EVIL

Read Psalm 106:34–39. A common theme being promoted in churches, schools, and society in general today in regard to what are unbiblical and sinful behaviors is "tolerance." We are told that the way to peace and brotherhood is through an acceptance that embraces philosophies and practices that Scripture clearly calls evil. How does this relate to these verses from Psalms? What evidences of "mingling" are taking place in our culture, and where do you think this is leading us?

_____

_____

Is it possible to read horoscopes or have our palms read merely as entertainment without violating scriptural commands? Why or why not?

_____

_____

If we are offended, even outraged, by the portrayal of homosexual lifestyles, adulterous situations, sacrilegious behavior, and the like in books, movies, and other media, why are we not equally concerned about portrayals of even subtle occult activity? Why or why not?

_____

_____

By watching movies or television shows that present occult activities (witches, magic, etc.) in amusing, cute, and seemingly harmless situations, are we conditioning ourselves to a light attitude about the demonic? Why or why not?

_____

_____

What evidences of the occult, from the very subtle to the very extreme, are you aware of in your community?

_____

_____

How are you protecting your family against these things? What stand are you taking against these things? How are you combating these things?

_____

_____

Are you allowing your children to use symbols, emblems, or other markings on their bodies, clothes, books, or other possessions that represent death, evil, or the occult? Would you even recognize these things if they were present?

_____

_____

(A longer discussion of this subject can be found in the readings from *Raising Lambs Among Wolves,* pages 97–101, found in Appendix A: Supplemental Readings.)

Review/Conclusion:

We need to distance ourselves from recognized evil in all its forms. When it comes to the occult, there is no such thing as indulging "just a little bit" or "just for the fun of it" that will not leave us vulnerable and open to serious spiritual harm. We are to flee this evil. There is no exception. (See Ephesians 5:8–17.)

We need to raise a caution. The world is full of evil, but not everything that looks evil is really evil. For example, a few years ago someone impulsively decided that a decades-old Procter and Gamble logo, which includes a man in the moon symbol surrounded by some stars, was connected to the occult. Important research has proven that *it is not.* Yet, without investigation, an elaborate rumor developed which has persisted despite Procter and Gamble's expending a steady stream of dollars and man-hours to combat this stupid lie. Worse, the company has received thousands of calls and letters from ill-informed Christians expressing their outrage over Procter and Gable's alleged ties to the occult. Such mindless, undiscerning behavior on the part of believers brings shame and ridicule to the Christian cause. It is critical that we recognize evil and take action against it. Yet we need to do so intelligently, ensuring that the things we are attacking are really evil. To chase after spiritual windmills is to be maneuvered away from the real battle by the very one we're supposed to be battling against.

LESSON 5: *Possession*

Scripture for Meditation:

Do you not know that your body is a temple of the Holy Spirit, who is in you, whom you have received from God? You are not your own; you were bought at a price. Therefore honor God with your body. (1 Corinthians 6:19–20)

For he who was a slave when he was called by the Lord is the Lord's freedman; similarly, he who was a free man when he was called is Christ's slave. You were bought at a price; do not become slaves of men. (1 Corinthians 7:22–23)

A Beginning Prayer:

Lord Jesus Christ, I thank You that You loved me so much that You gave Yourself up that I might have eternal life in You. I thank You that I am Your possession, that my body is the temple of Your Holy Spirit, that I am possessed by no other spirit but Your Spirit. I thank You that I have full assurance of salvation based on the truth of Your Word and that my destiny rests securely in Your hands and care. Amen.

Lesson:

To *take possession* of something means to own it, hold it, occupy it, exercise full control over it, and dominate it. No, a Christian cannot be demon-possessed. Yes, a Christian who grows cold in his faith and allows sin to establish a foothold in his life *can render limited control,* but it is not possession.

Have you ever been troubled by these questions? Why do you think that is? Do you know someone else who is troubled over these issues? How would you counsel them?

_____

_____

As Christians our concern should not be focused on whether or to what degree we can be demonized. Believers who are truly walking in intimate fellowship with our heavenly Father, opening their lives to the fullness of the Holy Spirit, abiding in the finished work of Jesus Christ on the cross, and feeding daily on the Word need have no concern about being demonized. We cannot be owned by two opposing masters. We cannot be bought by the blood of Christ and yet be owned by darkness. It is not possible. Our lives are "hidden with Christ in God" (Colossians 3:3).

However, we do need to be concerned about those around us who may be controlled by darkness to any degree. We need to be concerned because they are souls that need to be freed from their torments. God has placed us here to minister help and freedom to those suffering from the control of darkness (Isaiah 61:1–3).

Read Acts 19:13–16. Why were these men attacked? What does this episode teach us about dealing with the demon-possessed?

_____

_____

Read Matthew 9:32–33; 12:22; 15:22–28; and Mark 1:23–27; 5:1–20. What do these events have in common?

_____

_____

What differences exist among these events?

_____

_____

What principles can be drawn from these events for dealing with demonically troubled individuals?

_____

_____

Why do you think demons possess people or take up residence in objects or animals? What's the purpose? (Keep in mind the character of Satan, who is bent on robbing, destroying, and killing and who is the father of lies and deceit.)

_____

_____

How do you think we can know if someone is demonically tormented?

_____

_____

What can we do to help free someone who is suffering from demonic control?

_____

_____

Review/Conclusion:

What would Jesus do? This is our focus when we are encountered by those who are demonized. How did Jesus prepare for these encounters? In His humanity, His daily prayer life and His taking in of the Word were part of His preparation to deal with whatever the Enemy might do. Encountering demonic powers was not a "special event" for Him. How did He deal with demons? From the basis of His authority and position in the Father. How did He discern demon activity? Through the enlightenment of the Holy Spirit. What do we have at our disposal as Christians to use to deal with demons? We have the Word, the Holy Spirit, and prayer, and we have the Lord Jesus Christ to shepherd us to walk in His freedom.

PROTECTING THE FAMILY IN A WICKED DAY

Scripture Memory Verses:

The Lord saw how great man's wickedness on the earth had become, and that every inclination of the thoughts of his heart was only evil all the time. (Genesis 6:5)

The wrath of God is being revealed from heaven against all the godlessness and wickedness of men who suppress the truth by their wickedness, since what may be known about God is plain to them, because God has made it plain to them. (Romans 1:18–19)

Unit Learning Goal:

To begin applying the principles learned so far; rebuilding the walls of protection.

Overview of Unit 10:

Lesson 1: Protecting Your Marriage

Lesson 2: Protecting Your Children

Lesson 3: Protecting the Body of Christ

Lesson 4: Overcoming in a Demonized Culture

Lesson 5: Looking Toward Revival

SUMMARY STATEMENT

We live in a wicked and perverse culture—a culture that extends globally and is not limited to any one region or country. Satan knows that his time for wreaking havoc is nearing an end. As we are warned in the Scriptures, he seems to be redoubling his efforts to fulfill his intent to steal, kill, and destroy as much as possible (Revelation 12:12). He will stop at nothing to bring down individuals, marriages, families, churches, and anything else that represents biblical morality and truth. As we've learned so far, we may be targets, but we are far from helpless or defenseless. We have ample weapons at our disposal that are more than effective in resisting and rebuffing all of Satan's attacks. Now we must deploy them and establish the boundaries that will curtail Satan's ability to maneuver and destroy.

Unit 10 Thought Focus:

Reading the writings of the prophet Hosea is like reading the morning newspaper. Look at this example: "Hear the word of the Lord, you Israelites, because the Lord has a charge to bring against you who live in the land: 'There is no faithfulness, no love, no acknowledgment of God in the land. There is only cursing, lying and murder, stealing and adultery; they break all bounds, and bloodshed follows bloodshed. Because of this the land mourns, and all who live in it waste away; the beasts of the field and the birds of the air and the fish of the sea are dying'" (Hosea 4:1–3).

Doesn't this describe our situation today? All around us we can give witness to wide-spread corruption, cursing, disloyalty, alienation of affections, and everything else Hosea describes. Trust has broken down. Children and adults are regularly abused and abandoned. Cursing flows from television sitcoms and music lyrics. Lying is a way of life for business executives and politicians. Murder and theft increase daily. Adultery is accepted as normal, even life-affirming. And bloodshed follows bloodshed in millions of abortions, ethnic clashes, rapes, spousal murder, child abuse, and endless warfare. All bounds have been broken. With increasing pollution, the land is mourning and whole species are dying.

Is there no hope? Yes, there *is* hope. For the Christian, hopelessness is never an option. Psalm 33:18–22 triumphantly declares: "But the eyes of the Lord are on those who fear him, on those whose hope is in his unfailing love, to deliver them from death and keep them alive in famine. We wait in hope for the Lord; he is our help and our shield. In him our hearts rejoice, for we trust in his holy name. May your unfailing love rest upon us, O Lord, even as we put our hope in you."

But note that last line. We must by an act of our wills *put our hope in God.* Only as we actively and persistently apply the principles of warfare will we reap the benefits of hope, safety, and peace. Each day we must take up our cross and move into the battle wearing the full armor of God and effectively wielding the sword of the Spirit. Spiritual protection is not passively obtained. It is to be taken hold of through prayer, faith, and practice, and then applied to our lives, our marriages and relationships, our children, our churches, and our communities.

In this time of fragmentation and disarray, Christians need to join together and faithfully intercede for themselves and all those around them. Satan's plans are always defeated by a church full of agreeing, praying, believing Christians standing in unity against the forces of darkness and proclaiming the Gospel message of hope to a dying world. Jesus promised that the gates of hell cannot prevail against a church such as this. We will invade Satan's kingdom and rob his house of those in bondage to him.

LESSON 1: *Protecting Your Marriage*

Scripture for Meditation:

"For this reason a man will leave his father and mother and be united to his wife, and the two will become one flesh." This is a profound mystery—but I am talking about Christ and the church. However, each one of you also must love his wife as he loves himself, and the wife must respect her husband.
(Ephesians 5:31–33)

A Beginning Prayer:

Loving heavenly Father, I thank You for the wonderful family you have given me. Thank You for the opportunity to shepherd my family members in Your ways and teachings. Thank You for enabling me to stand in Your authority against the darkness and extend Your protection and holy covering to all in my family. Enable us to please You, and keep us in Your divine care. Make us be Your beacons of love and hope in the midst of this ever-darkening world. Amen.

Lesson:

EROSION OF THE BIBLICAL MODEL

In our modern culture, lifelong commitment in a relationship is becoming almost nonexistent. Today couples prepare for divorce before they are even married, assuming that it's virtually inevitable. All it takes in most states is for one spouse to decide that he or she no longer wants to be married. With no-fault divorce, the remaining spouse has little or no recourse, as the divorce can be granted with or without his or her consent. In fact, it can be called a dissolution and be done through the mail.

The biblical and traditional God-given model for marriage and family has eroded in our culture. Today, any living arrangement among two or more people can constitute a "family," with marriage being optional. Single women living alone can arrange artificial insemination and have fatherless children. Homosexual couples are increasingly winning the right to receive "married couple" health benefits and to jointly adopt children. It seems only a matter of time before the law will allow them to be legally married, receiving the full legal rights and privileges of historic marriages.

FAMILY AND MARRIAGE IN THE BIBLE

Read Genesis 1:27–2:25; Ephesians 5:21–33; and Colossians 3:16–21. What is the biblical structure of a family? What constitutes a marriage?

_____

_____

Circle **T** for True or **F** for False and then discuss your answers:

T **F** God honors same-sex marriages.

T **F** A family is any group of people of any age or sex living together as a unit in one household.

T **F** Marriage is just a piece of paper; living together is OK.

How are husbands supposed to treat their wives?

_____

_____

How are wives supposed to treat their husbands?

_____

_____

How are parents supposed to treat their children?

_____

_____

Circle **T** for True or **F** for False and then discuss your answers:

T **F** It's OK to "let our hair down" with our families and be ourselves.

T **F** Children are to be controlled by parents.

T **F** Respect always has to be earned (Romans 13:7).

A DEFENSE AGAINST SATAN

A strong, committed, God-centered marriage full of love, faithfulness, and respect is one of the strongest defenses against the ravaging ways of darkness. In this type of setting, evil encroachments are resisted. A biblical family is a strong defense against the Enemy's attempt to destroy those in the home.

That this is true should be obvious to anyone, even nonbelievers. Just look at the evidence. Strong marriages grounded in God are lasting, rewarding, and productive. They are productive in that both the husband and the wife find support to grow, mature, and pursue their full potential as individuals, spouses, and parents. The children of these marriages are reared in a climate that encourages self-esteem, growth of intelligence, and development of the gifts of grace.

THE IMPACT OF DIVORCE

What about loveless, broken, or nontraditional situations? Divorce has created complex "blended" families that are rife with unusual challenges. Children are deprived of mothers or fathers or both. Children of divorce rarely learn how to cope effectively with life. Often they are undisciplined and fall into behavior problems. The debris of shattered homes and shattered lives is scattered across the landscape of our troubled society.

Divorce impacts many, inside and outside the family. Below, check the statements you believe are true and then discuss your responses:

❑ 1. Younger children are more devastated by divorce than older children.

❑ 2. It's easy for divorced spouses to remain friends.

❑ 3. Non-Christians aren't negatively affected when Christians divorce.

❑ 4. Everyone involved, both adults and children, eventually gets over the effects of a divorce.

❑ 5. If a child isn't showing obvious signs of distress, he or she probably is not bothered by the parents' strife.

❑ 6. Relatives and friends of divorcing couples are usually not impacted seriously by the divorce and can just shrug it off.

THE NEED FOR KINDNESS AND FORGIVENESS

Now, as has been mentioned, some nontraditional and broken family situations are created by only one parent breaking the marriage covenant and choosing another alternative. The death of a spouse can also contribute to broken family life. And, often, blended families result from two abandoned or bereaved spouses coming together to form a new family. Single-parent families or subsequent blended families that result from these events deserve and need the support and prayers of a loving church body.

God forgives, heals, and builds up the wounded. The challenges in these kinds of situations are especially arduous and complex. These parents and new families need to experience God's grace, love, and healing through the expressions of kindness, acceptance, and practical support of their fellow believers. We must not add painful insult on top of already devastating injury.

In fact, it is the very lack of these elements—forgiveness, acceptance, expressions of kindness, grace, and love—that causes marriages to crumble. Husbands and wives who truly love the Lord and truly love each other must be especially forgiving toward each other. Forgiveness in every marriage and all other relationships is a critical factor for success.

Read Matthew 6:12–15; 18:21–35. If there is no forgiveness, what exists in its place?

_____

_____

If a person receives condemnation, tacitly or otherwise, instead of forgiveness, what tensions and emotions will be generated between both individuals? Over time, what will happen to the relationship if forgiveness never occurs?

_____

_____

Does the Bible instruct us to forgive only when we feel like forgiving, or to forgive even when we don't feel like it?

_____

_____

Does forgiving mean to forget the offense or to let go of the pain of the offense?

_____

_____

What is true forgiveness? Has God forgiven you of your sins?

_____

_____

If you fail to forgive another, what is the consequence in your life? How will this affect your children or others around you? How does it affect God?

_____

_____

If you claim to be a Christian, yet fail to forgive your spouse and others, what message does this send to your children, your family, unbelievers, and other friends?

_____

_____

Freedom from fear and quiet security instilled in children when their parents deeply love and respect each other sets up a rock-solid foundation for the family. Freedom from fear and quiet security instilled in spouses when they know that forgiveness and acceptance flow freely will engender increased love and deeper intimacy for both. Expressing unconditional love toward one another, forgiving each other just as each would want to be forgiven, and each laying down his or her own rights for the sake of the partner—these actions bring healing and strength to stressed marriages and families. And they speak volumes about the truth of God's ways to the society around us.

It isn't easy. Every marriage suffers painful stresses from time to time. People living together will occasionally clash. The fast pace of our lives, the demands of our work, and living in the midst of a declining culture bring multiplied pressures to bear on the best of marriages. It is only through God's grace and steadfast mutual commitment that couples will be enabled to maintain love, security, and stability in their marriages and in their homes.

(For further insights on this subject, see readings from *Raising Lambs Among Wolves*, pages 62–64, found in Appendix A: Supplemental Readings.)

For each of the following categories, discuss and list specific actions that can be taken by couples and families that will clearly demonstrate the principles of God's Word and the reality of faith present in their families:

Sex: _____
_____

Money: _____
_____

Prayer: _____
_____

Bible study/devotions: _____
_____

School/grades: _____
_____

Work: _____
_____

Socializing/dating: _____
_____

Volunteering/extracurricular activities: _____
_____

Memberships/church participation: _____
_____

Communication: _____
_____

Review/Conclusion:

Growing love in a marriage requires the application of the following ten spiritual necessities:

1. Pray together every day for God's blessing on your marriage.
2. Work and pray toward the practice of biblical principles regarding money.
3. Keep the lines of honest, loving communication wide open at all times.
4. Recognize the high spiritual value of sexual fulfillment within marriage as God ordained it and created us to enjoy.
5. Together, stand on your spiritual authority in Christ against barriers, walls, and relationships being established by the powers of darkness.
6. Verbalize your love and appreciation to your spouse daily.
7. Engage in nonsexual touching with your spouse several times daily.
8. Never hesitate to ask for forgiveness when you know you need it.
9. Never hesitate to give forgiveness freely whenever it's sought.
10. Schedule regular times for doing something you know your spouse enjoys, whether you enjoy it or not.

Putting these ten spiritual necessities into practice will communicate to your spouse that you truly love, are completely devoted, and are seriously committed to him (or her). What a powerful message to send to your spouse and to your children! Not to mention what a clear message it sends to the world of darkness that the boundary line of protection has been firmly set around your family.

LESSON 2: *Protecting Your Children*

Scripture for Meditation:

Sons are a heritage from the Lord, children a reward from him. (Psalm 127:3)

He who fears the Lord has a secure fortress, and for his children it will be a refuge. (Proverbs 14:26)

The righteous man leads a blameless life; blessed are his children after him. (Proverbs 20:7)

A Beginning Prayer:

Heavenly Father, all children—red or yellow, black or white—are precious in Your sight. Lord Jesus Christ, You do love all the children of the world. Extend even now Your hand over every small, precious life, Lord. Cover the children—our children and the children of others—with Your protecting care. Place a strong hedge of protection around each precious life. Place guardian angels about each child to defend that child against the insidious wiles of our enemy. Into Your loving arms, dear Lord Jesus Christ, we give our children to care for them and to place Your hands of blessing upon them and use them for Your glory. Amen.

Lesson:

THE SPIRITUAL PROTECTION OF CHILDREN

Children are God's heritage of blessing to us. They are precious when they are born and completely dependent upon their parents for everything. As parents, we are more than happy to provide all things for them, even in the middle of the night. When our child cries out, we don't hesitate to rouse ourselves from sleep and take care of him. We'll change his diaper, put dry pajamas on him, warm his bottle, rock him, and sing him to sleep. Then we'll gently place him in his crib and bundle him up warmly with soft, clean blankets, quietly turn out the light and leave the room, knowing he is "safe and sound" and in need of nothing.

Or did we forget something?

Even as our children grow, start school, take up sports and musical instruments, and all the rest, we are quick to provide them with all the physical things they need (Matthew 7:11). They always have nice clothes and plenty to eat, and we get them to the doctor at the first sign of a problem.

But are we still forgetting something? What about their spiritual protection and well-being? Are we providing the spiritual nourishment and protection that's vital to their growing up in the Lord?

Read Matthew 11:25; 18:1–7; 19:13–15; Mark 9:36–37; 10:13–16; and Luke 10:21; 18:15–17. How did Jesus view children?

How important and valuable are children in the kingdom of God?

_____

_____

What characteristics of children are important to our spiritual life?

_____

_____

How does God view a person who brings harm to children?

_____

_____

If we fail to pray for our children and train them in the things of God, are we harming them or helping them?

_____

_____

CHILDREN AND SPIRITUAL ASSAULT

Our children seem sweet, innocent, and precious to us, but they are not immune from spiritual assault. Indeed, they are often prime targets of supernatural evil. Satan is a cruel and merciless enemy. He does not spare our children when he attacks our families. He attacks children—and they are especially vulnerable when God's ordained protectors are giving ground through some sinful behavior.

Spiritually strong parents are meant to be a child's earthly defense against the schemes of darkness. The Enemy will try to get at them any way he can if we are not ever-vigilant over their lives. It's important to understand how easily children can come under the influence of the Enemy, for that influence is being expressed everywhere in our modern culture.

(Here would be a good place to _review_ pages 135–39 of _Raising Lambs Among Wolves_ and to _read_ pages 141–43 of _Raising Lambs Among Wolves_. Both sections are given in Appendix A: Supplemental Readings. Pages 135–39 are found in the readings for Unit 7; pages 141–43 are found in the readings for Unit 10.)

Below are some suggested avenues for Satan's influence to reach your children. Give more specific examples beside each, and then list practical ways you as a parent can guard your children against these things. Discuss these matters in your group and share ideas among the other parents:

Television: _____

_____

Role-playing games: _____

_____

Video games: _____

_____

Board games: _____

_____

Dolls and toys: _____

_____

Books: _____

_____

Relationships: _____

_____

Bad dreams: _____

_____

Normal childhood fears (like being afraid of the dark): _____

_____

List other areas of special concern to you and ways to protect against these:

_____

_____

UNCONDITIONAL LOVE

Children deserve and need lots of unconditional love. In fact, regularly expressing genuine love and encouragement to your children is one of the best ways to guard their hearts against demonic intrusion. A heart filled with security and love has no room for or need of anything evil.

There are many ways to help protect our children against spiritual attack. Of those listed below, circle all that you believe are true, then discuss your answers with the group:

A. Never reward them when they have accomplished something positive.
B. Embarrass and make fun of them in front of others.
C. Tell them you love them at least once every day.
D. Discipline them promptly and appropriately after each offense.
E. Take them to Sunday school and drop them off while you run errands.
F. Pray with them and for them every morning and every evening.
G. Never let them catch you arguing or disagreeing with your spouse.
H. Hold them accountable to rigid, strict rules of behavior.
 I. Be aware of what they watch on television, what they're reading, and who they spend time with away from home.
 J. Blame them for things without first gathering the facts or hearing their side of the story.
K. Always treat them and respond to them just like you would an adult.
L. When they talk to you, stop what you're doing and listen intently.
M. Let them see you and your spouse being affectionate with each other.
N. Play with them, doing things they like to do. Have fun together.
O. Make them your ally against your spouse, with whom you are angry.
P. Never show weakness by apologizing, even if you're wrong.
Q. Exhibit frequent affection, with loving hugs and kisses.
R. Encourage and help them to pursue the things that interest them.
S. Share with them stories about your family and your life.
T. Never take them seriously if they express fears or concerns.

One of the easiest doors for the Enemy to step through is the door of the wounded spirit. Apologizing to your child when you have wounded him communicates caring love. Loving our children at all times, treating them with respect and dignity, providing a secure environment for them, keeping in mind that they are impressionable children, and praying for them continually will virtually seal the protective power of the Holy Spirit around them. Prayer that is not coupled with good parenting reaps little reward. It takes both to be effective.

Review/Conclusion:

Children are precious. As Jesus warned, woe to the one who causes a little one to stumble. This is double woe for parents. We have an awesome responsibility as parents, but also a wonderful privilege. There are few things that bring greater joy than receiving the love of a child and watching the child grow "in wisdom and stature, and in favor with God and men." Parenting is a tough job with high risk and even greater rewards. If we are faithful to Him, God is faithful to provide us with all the stamina, wisdom, and discernment we will need to be effective parents.

If our children are being attacked by the Enemy, how can we know? Observing and carefully listening to your child are vital. If you notice a sudden or drastic change in your child's behavior or attitude, you know something is wrong. If physical ailments or reasonable emotional distress have been ruled out, then this could be spiritual assault. Even with emotional or physical ailments present, we need to remain alert. Further, if your child ever mentions seeing or hearing things no one else sees or hears, pay attention and take your child seriously.

If you suspect the demonic, don't panic! Begin to exert your authority in Christ through protective prayer over the life of your child. It is both your spiritual right and a commandment of God to care for every aspect of your child's well-being.

- Pray with and over your child in your God-given parental authority, and in the name of the Lord Jesus Christ command the Enemy to cease his work and leave your child and go where Jesus sends him.

- Daily pray a hedge of protection around your home and family. Ask God to bind the strong man and rebuke the Enemy. In the authority and name of the Lord Jesus Christ pray for the protection of holy angels and the Savior's blood over your family and your home. Using the biblical prayers of Scripture, such as Psalm 91:9–13, is powerfully effective.

- If your child is being frightened at night, before he goes to bed prayerfully walk through your home and his room asking the Lord to cleanse your home from any evil work and welcoming the Holy Spirit. As you put the child to bed, read verses such as Psalm 3:5 and 4:8 and other encouraging passages out loud with him. Explain to your child that God is always watching over him and protecting him. Pray with him, asking God to send His guardian angels to stand watch over him to restrain any fearful dreams or activity from touching him.

- With your spouse, regularly dedicate your family, home, and property to the Lord, asking that these will stand as an example of hope to the neighborhood. Ask God to permeate your home with an atmosphere of holiness and blessing.

(Pages 213–23 of *Raising Lambs Among Wolves* give examples of specific doctrinal prayers of protection of children. [This series of prayers is not given in the appendix.] For specific signs of possible demonic attack against your child, see pages 169–79 of *Raising Lambs Among Wolves,* given in Appendix A: Supplemental Readings.)

LESSON 3: *Protecting the Body of Christ*

Scripture for Meditation:

If one part suffers, every part suffers with it; if one part is honored, every part rejoices with it. Now you are the body of Christ, and each one of you is a part of it. (1 Corinthians 12:26–27)

A Beginning Prayer:

Dear heavenly Father, protect me from contributing any damage to my church by guarding me from allowing sin in my life. Help me not to become an agent of the Enemy by yielding parts of my life to him. Strengthen each person in my church, and draw us together in unity, love, and the mutual caring that is Your will and plan for us. Help us to recognize those who are hurting and those who are wounded from sin. Grant to us the wisdom to come around those persons quickly to minister Your protection, healing, and restoration. Amen.

Lesson:

THE DESTRUCTIVE POWER OF SIN

Marriages are under attack. Children are under attack. And churches are under attack. Many church bodies struggle financially, fail to grow, or are filled with strife and dissension because darkness has been given a foothold within the body through the fleshly sinful acts of its members. Let's take another look at Ephesians 4:25, but include a little context with it:

> Therefore each of you must put off falsehood and speak truthfully to his neighbor, for *we are all members of one body.* "In your anger do not sin": Do not let the sun go down while you are still angry, and do not give the devil a foothold. (Ephesians 4:25–27, italics added)

Not only can your sin bring trouble into your life, the life of your spouse, and the lives of your children, but it can also bring trouble to your church body and extend out to the whole body of believers.

Several years ago prominent televangelists were caught up in scandals of notoriety that effectively destroyed their ministries. Their marriages fell apart, their families were scattered, and hundreds of supporters were hurt financially, spiritually, and emotionally. But that's not all. The denominations with which they were affiliated were disgraced, all television ministries were called into question, and the entire body of Christ was injured. The repercussions kept rippling out farther and farther to bring harm to many.

A WORST-CASE SCENARIO

You may think that the extent of the damage was so great because these were public ministries. Let's try to understand the personal implications with the following case study. Read it through carefully. Then discuss and answer the questions at the end.

You live in a small town of thirty thousand or so near a major metropolitan area. You have a good job at a midsized corporation that employs over five thousand people. You're married with two children. You are faithful to your church of five hundred members, where you teach Sunday school and are involved in a variety of ministries. You are also active in a national parachurch group called The Hands of Jesus that serves homeless and other needy people, and you are an officer in a local community organization. People at work and in the community know who you are and your spiritual reputation.

One week your spouse is away at a seminar and your children are attending band and choir camps. You're home alone. Toward the end of the week, you're tired after a lot of activity at work and completing chores around the house. You're lonely, missing your family, when unexpectedly a person you know casually from church, Pat, calls and asks for your help with a problem in an area in which he's been told you have expertise. In order to help, you will have to go to Pat's home, where he lives alone. Pat is single, of the opposite sex, and someone you've noticed. You've noticed because Pat is very attractive and charming.

You're caught a bit off guard by the invitation to help and don't want to appear rude by declining. You're also flattered by the referral and that Pat called you. Having been in Pat's situation before, you understand his distress and want to be helpful. You agree to come over to his house within the hour. You shower, change, and head over.

When you arrive, you're startled yet somewhat pleased to find Pat casually and comfortably clothed, looking very handsome and lovely. Pat is also engaging, sweet, and even a bit flirtatious.

On the one hand, you're a bit wary and sense that maybe this wasn't such a good idea. But on the other hand, you're here now and to leave would be viewed as insulting and rude. You don't want to be thought of that way, and besides, you know you're a strong person. You're confident you can handle this situation even though the appearance of your being there alone with Pat could be misconstrued.

You go in and begin tackling Pat's problem. This requires the two of you to be in close proximity to each other, as you need Pat's help and active involvement. As you're working, you're also chitchatting and becoming more and more comfortable with each other. The hours pass and your guard drops as you become caught up in the work. This is something you happen to be good at and really enjoy. Pat's quite pleased and very complimentary. In fact, Pat has been complimentary about your appearance, your manner, and more.

As you're leaving, Pat is genuinely appreciative and embraces you warmly in a grateful hug. The hug lingers. It feels good. Too good. Suddenly you become acutely aware that if you want this situation to go further, Pat would allow it and welcome your affection. You also realize that it would be pleasurable, at least for the moment.

Your head is swimming with emotion and tiredness. You hug Pat back and share a very brief kiss. Then you come to your senses and step back. You apologize profusely for what you've done. Pat seems embarrassed, too, and also apologizes. You forgive each other and part company quickly.

The next day you're attending a breakfast meeting of one of the community organizations of which you are an officer. One of the members approaches you. "You know, I'm confused about something," he says. "You're married, aren't you?"

Confused, you state, "Why, yes. As a matter of fact the whole family is coming home tonight. They've been gone all week at seminars. Why do you ask?"

"Oh, the family was away? I live near Pat. I saw you go in and then come out much later, and it looked like you two kissed as you were leaving. I know you're a Christian and involved with The Hands of Jesus. I just can't believe you're having an affair with Pat!" You try to explain.

When you get home, there's a message on your answering machine. It's your pastor. He's calling to tell you that he's gotten a phone call from Pat, who was very upset. It seems Pat went to the pastor and claimed that you made a pass. Your head is spinning and you sit down. You can't believe this is happening to you.

Your family comes home that night and you say nothing about the situation. The next day at church, the pastor pulls you aside and says Pat has told at least three other people about the affair. You look over and see your spouse's face fill with shock as someone whispers something into your spouse's ear. At that moment, your world begins to unravel.

Sin is often excused as "not being that big of a deal." In this case study, how many people potentially will be harmed?

_____

_____

Other than the obvious sexual attractions, what other behaviors or attitudes contributed to this situation? Ego? Arrogance? Others? What behaviors or attitudes were missing?

Present: _____

_____

Missing: _____

_____

Given a worst-case scenario, what could happen to all: the spouse, the children, the other people involved or that become aware of the situation, the church, and the organizations you are a part of?

_____

Could this bring harm to The Hands of Jesus nationally? If so, how?

_____

_____

How will your church be viewed by the community now?

_____

_____

Who was at fault?

_____

_____

How will this incident reflect on the church body?

_____

_____

Even if the situation between you, Pat, the pastor, and your family is resolved and forgiven, what might be the ongoing consequences to the local church body?

_____

_____

What do you think were Pat's motives in making false claims? Which of your enemies would be behind this kind of behavior and the resulting consequences?

_____

_____

Is it likely that someone could point to this situation and use it to justify his own sinful behavior? Why or why not?

_____

_____

What other repercussions can you think of that will result from this situation?

_____

_____

What steps need to be taken to save your marriage, restore peace and security to your family, and maintain unity and healing in the local church body?

_____

_____

What decisions can you make to insure that an incident of this type will never occur again?

_____

_____

What new insights have you gained from working through this exercise?

_____

_____

What other avenues or means might Satan use to gain a foothold within the body? What kinds of deception and behavior must we guard against?

_____

_____

Review/Conclusion:

Sin can offer Satan a foothold within a body of believers through any number of means. This entry can come through our own fleshly sins we choose to pursue or through the sins of others we unwittingly support. It can come through scandal, rumor, arguments, gossip, false doctrine, miscommunication, and more (see 2 Peter 2).

We need to walk in the Spirit and remain on guard all the time to avoid being the conduit Satan uses to attack our churches. Again, the key is to abide in intimate relationship with Jesus Christ and to fill our lives with His Word. Only as we are grounded on the Rock of truth will we be able to stand up against the devices of Satan. He is more than capable of setting us up by arranging circumstances against us that will expose our weaknesses to temptation.

That is why the Lord Jesus Christ prayed for unity and health in the body of Christ in His high priestly prayer in John 17. The unity and spiritual health of His body are vital to the work He has for His church. We need each other. We need each other's wisdom, insight, love, discipline, forgiveness, encouragement, and support. When one part suffers, even if it's self-inflicted, we need to come around that person and help to build him back up in the faith. Then, when he has been restored, we need to come around him and rejoice together over his restoration and thank God that he'll be there when *we* need to be picked up.

The consequence of sin in the body of Christ is far-reaching and profound. The kingdom of darkness works hard to see churches split. But the love and healing power of Christ is more profound and reaches even farther than the worst sin. If we focus on Him and maintain unity in love, then evil's darkness will be quenched and the gates of hell will not prevent or hinder the Lord building up His church.

LESSON 4: *Overcoming in a Demonized Culture*

Scripture for Meditation:

We know that we are children of God, and that the whole world is under the control of the evil one. (1 John 5:19)

First of all, you must understand that in the last days scoffers will come, scoffing and following their own evil desires. (2 Peter 3:3)

For where you have envy and selfish ambition, there you find disorder and every evil practice. (James 3:16)

A Beginning Prayer:

Dear Lord Jesus Christ, embolden me to take Your Word to heart and refuse to give any particle of ground to Satan. Strengthen me in the battle that I might not faint or falter. Let me pursue the vision of the victory You have already won. Fill me with compassion and mercy for my fellow believers who are wounded, and show me how to minister healing to them. Establish Your kingdom firmly in my heart and teach me how to promote the establishing of Your kingdom firmly in my world. Amen.

Lesson:

CHRIST IN A FALLEN WORLD

Have you ever been traveling on a cloudy day in unfamiliar territory? Even with a map, if you assume you're traveling north and you're really headed south, and you refuse to reorient yourself, you'll experience a great deal of frustration and waste a lot of time and gas getting nowhere fast. Your premise—or worldview—is wrong. Until you recognize this, no amount of effort or positive thinking will get you headed in the right direction.

If you fail to understand that we live in a fallen, evil world, you are setting yourself up for grave disappointment, endless confusion, and serious spiritual defeat. Despite the random acts of kindness that occur and the startling beauty of nature, the hard reality is that spiritually this is an ugly, dark, and dying world. It is being consumed by evil, and that evil touches our lives and destroys millions of souls every day.

No amount of positive thinking or believing the best about people will change this spiritual reality. Our perception of things may be sunny, sweet, and positive, but as in all things, perception is not reality. We are born sinful into a sinful world. If at no point in our lives do we recognize our need for a Savior and receive Him into our lives, we will be lost, and all our doing and striving will be done through the deceptions of evil. No philosophy, teaching, political agenda, or amount of good deeds can counter this reality. There is one and *only* one way out of sin—through the precious blood of Christ (John 14:6).

If you have not acknowledged your sin and your need of a Savior, confessed your sinfulness, and asked and accepted Jesus Christ into your heart, then your life remains under the control of darkness. So it is with anyone—without exception—who rejects salvation in Christ as it is clearly taught in God's Word (Ephesians 2:1–3).

STIRRED INTO ACTION AND ALERT

Circle **T** for True or **F** for False and then discuss your answers:

T   **F**   All roads marked "Faith" lead to the same destination.

T   **F**   As long as I believe in God as I understand Him to be, I'll make it to heaven.

T   **F**   Jesus was a teacher just like Muhammad, Buddha, and other men who were very spiritual and wise.

T   **F**   People earn points with God by being good and kind to each other.

T   F   Animals, trees, fish, and all living things have souls and are as valuable and important as human beings.

T   F   Biblical Christianity is all-inclusive, welcoming, and embracing all people with love and acceptance, regardless of their lifestyles, worldly orientation, or moral perversion.

All of the above statements are false. Yet the world screams that they are true, *insists* that we accept them as true, and marks us as narrow-minded, heartless bigots if we insist that they are false. Living is this fallen, dark world is not an easy thing for any Christian. But this should not dissuade us from the hope we have in Christ or invalidate the infinite goodness of God we enjoy as His children. It should, however, elicit two responses in us.

First, we should be grieved over the loss of Christless souls to the jaws of hell. We need to know that it is our Lord's will for us to be stirred to action to support every worthy missionary effort we encounter. We must be emboldened to share the Gospel of Jesus' love at every opportunity without hesitation. We need to follow God's Spirit and go out into the highways and byways of society to gather in the lost and reveal to them the wonderful light of God's forgiving and cleansing love.

God is love, and He loves all and desires that none should perish. He is a jealous God who has provided all we need to live holy lives, obey His Word, and be separated from the ways of the world. God does not accept or embrace any behavior, lifestyle, intellectual viewpoint, political agenda, or other philosophy that runs counter to His holiness and divine plan. Those who reject Him and choose their own way are condemned to hell by their own actions.

Second, we need to be on the alert at all times, prayerfully watching over our own lives and the lives of our families, always on the lookout for any attempt at incursion into our lives by the Enemy. We are responsible to speak out regarding the evil that surrounds us, alerting all who will listen to the tragedy of ignoring or embracing sin. We must be quick to respond to our wounded brothers and sisters with love, prayer, and hands-on help, snatching them back from the hands of the Enemy, who is always clawing at their lives.

Overcoming in a demonized culture requires bold, aggressive, determined devotion to God and resistance of evil. We should follow the example of David, who, when Goliath "moved closer to attack him, . . . ran quickly toward the battle line to meet him" (1 Samuel 17:48). We have nothing to fear as we move into warfare "in the name of the Lord Almighty, the God of the armies of Israel, whom [evil has] defied" (v. 45).

With the help of your group, list all the evidences you can think of that indicate how our culture is demonized:

_____

_____

For each evidence listed above, what specific action can you take to counteract the evil?

_____

_____

Based on all you've learned so far in this study, what are some other specific, practical, positive actions you can take on the offensive against the powers of darkness as they are expressed through our culture?

_____

_____

Review/Conclusion:

We are told in Deuteronomy 20:4: "The Lord your God is the one who goes with you to fight for you against your enemies to give you victory." We need not circle our wagons in despair over the evil lurking outside our homes and churches. We need not resign ourselves to enduring the wickedness that pursues our children. We need not allow darkness to encroach against our lives.

We are children of the living God, and there is no power in heaven or on earth that can withstand Him. When we stand on God's authority and move out under the banner of His name, Satan in all his unholy terror must defer and retreat. As Jesus Himself said, believers have been made aware of the evil that grips this earth not so that they would become fearful but so that in Christ they "may have peace" (John 16:33). Jesus says: "In this world you will have trouble. But take heart! I have overcome the world" (v. 33). Christ also prayed in John 17 that we would be protected from the world's deception and the "evil one" (vv. 11–19). And we know that the prayers of our Lord Jesus Christ are always answered (11:41–42).

LESSON 5: *Looking Toward Revival*

Scripture for Meditation:

"Repent, then, and turn to God, so that your sins may be wiped out, that times of refreshing may come from the Lord, and that he may send the Christ, who has been appointed for you—even Jesus." (Acts 3:19–20)

A Beginning Prayer:

Lord Jesus Christ, send revival to us, we pray. We confess our sinfulness to You and seek Your cleansing in all areas of our lives. We confess our complacency and seek renewed fervor for Your holiness. We confess our failure to confront sin around us, and we ask for holy boldness. We confess to You our need for deep spiritual renewal. We hunger and thirst for the power of Your Holy Spirit to sweep through our lives. We cry out, O Lord, for revival that Your name may be glorified and proclaimed throughout the land with our voices. Amen.

Lesson:

GLIMMERS OF REVIVAL

Glimmers of a possible spiritual awakening have been cropping up all around the world. Stories of spontaneous revivals that last for months have even made it into the secular press. Widespread calls to prayer are being issued and heeded by many believers. Nations that were once off-limits to evangelism efforts have opened their borders and welcomed the Gospel message. Walls that once divided brother from brother are crumbling. In the midst of worldwide darkness, these bright spots of hope shine all the more brightly. The Spirit of God is at work. But revolutionary revival is not yet here.

THE HOLY SPIRIT IN REVIVAL

We need revival, and our world is ripe for one. Given the breakdown of family and home life, rampant drug and alcohol addiction, economic upheaval, worldwide epidemics of AIDS and other diseases, and the increasing display of satanic imagery and worship, the only answer is a massive movement of the Holy Spirit. Legislation, economic reforms, and other political action or grassroots movements by concerned citizens cannot cope with these issues. Only the power of God can turn the tide.

(At the back of this workbook is an address you can write to receive a booklet, *Prayer Patterns for Revival*. Also, Appendix B: Spiritual Warfare Prayers, gives the text of three prayers:

"Prayer for Spiritual Victory," "Prayer Against Temptation," and "Prayer to Wear the Armor of God," that you may find helpful.)

A demonized culture can be saved and brought back from ruin only by a powerful movement of a Holy Spirit–authored revival. What can we do to help usher into this age this much-needed spiritual renewal?

- We must walk in personal victory over the world, the flesh, and the devil. God honors personal holiness (Romans 12:1–2). It is important to confess our sins openly and quickly as they are brought to our attention by the Holy Spirit.

Discuss with your group and list practical ways to apply this step.

_____

_____

- We must commit to personally pray for revival (Matthew 6:6). We need to set aside regular times of extended prayer and allow the Holy Spirit to help us develop a biblical style of intercessory prayer.

Discuss with your group and list practical ways to apply this step.

_____

_____

- We must join with others in times of corporate prayer and fasting (Acts 1:14). As we pray together, we need to share how the Holy Spirit is speaking to each of our hearts so that we can gain a fuller view of what God is doing and will do through us.

Discuss with your group and list practical ways to apply this step.

_____

_____

- We must persist in prayer for as long as it takes without regard to our personal time-tables and agendas (Isaiah 40:28–31). God will move in His time and His wisdom. Timing is not our concern; faithfulness in prayer is (Psalm 27:13–14).

Discuss with your group and list practical ways to apply this step.

_____

_____

What else can you do to help usher in revival?

_____

_____

THE BENEFITS OF REVIVAL

Revival brings increased fervor for the Lord and renewed focus on holiness. List some of the other benefits of revival. Why are these important to us as believers (individually, to our families, to our churches, to our communities, and to our culture)?

_____

_____

In addition to the benefits above, revival also brings renewed accountability, deeper awareness of sin, and recognition of the need to change behaviors. What would be the impact on your personal lifestyle of true revival? What might it cost you?

_____

_____

In light of these costs and impacts, can you honestly say you really want to see revival? Can reluctance to yield some things of the world hinder the work of the Holy Spirit? If so, how?

_____

_____

Review/Conclusion:

We need revival. We say we want revival. Are we participating in God's plan for revival? What about our lives? Are we changing to prove this desire is real? What are we doing to bring about revival? What do we need to lay aside that we might be more focused on Him? Do we turn off our favorite TV show, decide not to go to the basketball game, or stay home from shopping to spend time in earnest prayer and seeking the Lord? We want to receive much, but are we willing to lay aside anything that may hinder revival?

God waits to respond to our cries for refreshing. But the cries must be more than motions that do not come from hearts that are broken and hungry. God wants us to ask Him for this. God is not mocked. He knows the difference between repentance and shallow pretense.

We've heard these verses dozens of times, but their truth still stands:

"When I shut up the heavens so that there is no rain, or command locusts to devour the land or send a plague among my people, if my people, who are called by my name, will humble themselves and pray and seek my face and turn from their wicked ways, then will I hear from heaven and will forgive their sin and will heal their land. Now my eyes will be open and my ears attentive to the prayers offered in this place" (2 Chronicles 7:13–15).

Revivals are all of God and all of grace, but they bring about human change and move forward through Holy Spirit–empowered lives and churches ignited by the fire of God's plan and will.

SUPPLEMENTAL READINGS

This appendix contains supplemental readings from two books by Mark I. Bubeck: *Overcoming the Adversary: Warfare Praying Against Demon Activity* (Chicago: Moody, 1984) and *Raising Lambs Among Wolves: How to Protect Your Children from Evil* (Chicago: Moody, 1997). These excerpts are listed according to the unit and lesson in the workbook with which they are associated.

FIRST READING FOR UNIT 2: OUR POSITION IN CHRIST

Lesson 4: Battling the Flesh, the World, and the Devil
From *Raising Lambs Among Wolves,* pages 124–25:

RESOURCES FOR BELIEVERS TO DEFEAT SATAN
AND WALK IN FREEDOM FROM SATAN'S RULE

A. God has provided four citadels that make a believer invincible over Satan's kingdom in the doing of God's will (Ephesians 6:10–20).
  1. The believer's union with Jesus Christ in all of His person and work (Ephesians 6:10a). The phrase "Be strong in the Lord" or its equivalent is used more than forty times in Ephesians.
     a. In His name (Acts 9:15; Colossians 3:17; Revelation 3:11–13)
     b. In His incarnation (Colossians 1:22; 2:9–10)
     c. In His cross (Galatians 2:20; Hebrews 2:14–15)
     d. In His resurrection (Ephesians 2:6; John 14:19)
     e. In His ascension (Ephesians 1:20–23; 2:6–7)
     f. In His glorification (Ephesians 2:6; Romans 8:30)
     g. In His return (Colossians 3:4; 1 Thessalonians 4:15–18)
  2. The person and work of the Holy Spirit (Ephesians 6:10b). We must keep the focus of His ministries to believers.
     a. Convicting ministry (John 16:7–11)
     b. Indwelling ministry (Romans 8:9)
     c. Sealing ministry (Ephesians 1:13–14)
     d. Baptizing ministry (1 Corinthians 12:13)
     e. Quickening ministry (Romans 8:9–10)
     f. Interceding ministry (Romans 8:26–27)
     g. Filling ministry (Ephesians 5:17–18)

3. The whole armor of God (Ephesians 6:11–17)
    a. Belt of truth (Ephesians 6:14a)
    b. Breastplate of righteousness (Ephesians 6:14b)
    c. Shoes of peace (Ephesians 6:15)
    d. Shield of faith (Ephesians 6:16)
    e. Helmet of salvation (Ephesians 6:17a)
    f. Sword of the Spirit (Ephesians 6:17b)
4. The allness of prayer (Ephesians 6:18–20)
    a. The Paraclete of prayer ("in the Spirit")
    b. The persistence of prayer ("on all occasions")
    c. The parameters of prayer ("with all kinds of prayer")
    d. The protection of prayer ("be alert")
    e. The panorama of prayer ("for all the saints")
    f. The projection of prayer ("for me"). Paul wanted prepared, penetrating, courageous words to share.
B. To walk in freedom requires the aggressive application of the provided victory and not passive assumption. (Note the frequent imperatives in Ephesians 6.)

[For a greater understanding of the often misunderstood filling of the Holy Spirit, read Lewis Sperry Chafer, *Systematic Theology*, vol. 1, abridged ed. (Grand Rapids: Kregel, 1992), 260–77.]

SECOND READING FOR UNIT 2: OUR POSITION IN CHRIST

Unit Sidebar: "ETEB"
    See the excerpts from *Raising Lambs Among Wolves*, pages 135–39, given in this Appendix under the readings for Unit 7, Lesson 2, II.

FIRST READING FOR UNIT 3: THE ARMOR OF GOD

Lesson 2: Belt, Breastplate, and Boots
From *Overcoming the Adversary*, pages 85–91:
    Romans 5:1 declares, "Therefore, since we have been justified through faith, *we have peace with God* through our Lord Jesus Christ" (italics added). This kind of peace is not subjective, experiential peace; it is objective, legal fact. The only way you gain this peace is to know it in your mind and receive it by faith. Through God's decree of justification, you have peace with God. That means God is not angry with you anymore. The war between God and the believer has ended.
    Peace with God is meant to bring peace to the believer's intellect, his mind. Justification is not an experiential, feeling-based truth. The only way believers know we are justified—declared righteous in God's sight—is because God says so and we believe Him. Inner peace comes when we accept the plain fact of what God has done. As a result, we have peace with God.
    God does not pour His anger upon His own children. He does not punish us in the sense of punitive hurt. The Lord chastens or disciplines His own to correct them, but He does not judge or punish His servants. That was settled at the cross of Christ. Now all believers are justified. As a result, we all have peace with God.
    Knowing and living in the reality of this truth is so important to invincible warfare. The mind needs to lay hold of this great fact. We must walk in the shoes of peace with God. If the

soldier is always ill at ease with the thought that God may be angry with him or that he has to toe the mark to keep God's anger away, he will make a poor soldier.

Philippians 4:6–7 reads, "Do not be anxious about anything, but in everything, by prayer and petition, with thanksgiving, present your requests to God. And *the peace of God,* which transcends all understanding, will guard your hearts and your minds in Christ Jesus" (italics added).

The peace *with* God is an intellectual peace; the peace *of* God is an emotional, experiential peace. We can know all the facts about God's provisions, but if emotions do not support our knowledge, we will not be able to act upon what we know to be true. The peace of God applies a balm of inner serenity to our emotions. If you have the peace of God, you feel at peace in mind and heart—the total inner person.

The bully we face, our enemy Satan, and his kingdom are too great for us to face alone, but when the God of peace is with us, we need have no fear. As Paul closed the book of Romans, he stated, "The *God of peace* will soon crush Satan under your feet" (Romans 16:20, italics added).

How do we maintain a walk in the shoes of peace? Proverbs 16:7 states, "When a man's ways are pleasing to the Lord, he makes even his enemies live at peace with him." That proverb harmonizes with Philippians 4:9. Both texts stress obedience. As a believer seeks to walk in obedience to his Lord, the special protective presence of the God of peace abides with that believer. Disobedience will make us vulnerable to the attacks of Satan.

If you are resisting God's will, you must deal with that resistance. Defeat for you and victory for your enemy will soon result unless the God of peace is put in control.

There is nothing more foundational to successful warfare than having the right shoes on your feet—the shoes of peace. Peace with God, the peace of God, the God of peace, and the Person of peace, the Lord Jesus Christ, are essentials of shoes that enable us to firmly stand.

Satan's attempts to defeat us are seldom more obvious than when he attacks our sense of peace. His strategy is to create chaos within a person. A universal characteristic of those under satanic or demonic attack is the turmoil, the disquiet, the torment, the lack of peace they endure. The demonic man of Gadara described in Mark 5 is a tragic study in the extent of the lack of peace Satan can generate.

SECOND READING FOR UNIT 3

Lesson 2: Belt, Breastplate, and Boots
THE ARMOR OF GOD
From *Overcoming the Adversary,* pages 67–69:
> The Word of God sets forth . . . strongholds of truth that are part of the belt of truth.
> *First, the Lord Jesus Christ is the Person of Truth.*
>
> Jesus answered, I am the way and the *truth* and the life. No one comes to the Father except through me" (John 14:6, italics added).
>
> The Word became flesh and made his dwelling among us. We have seen his glory, the glory of the One and Only, who came from the Father, full of grace and truth (John 1:14, italics added).
>
> Jesus Christ is the very embodiment of absolute truth. He is our ultimate and total protection from takeover by Satan and his kingdom. In warning the Roman believers to avoid the sinful entrapments of the world, the flesh, and the devil, the apostle Paul urged in Romans 13:14, "Rather, clothe yourselves with the Lord Jesus Christ."
>
> Objective truth must be subjectively appropriated. That is why a young man . . . under

fierce attack has to aggressively act with his mind to claim and apply his victory. Victorious warfare requires our action. We cannot be passive, hoping someone else will act for us.

The Word of God is the word of truth. One argument for the inerrancy of Scripture is its own often-repeated claim to be the "word of truth." In 2 Timothy 2:15 we read, "Do your best to present yourself to God as one approved, a workman who does not need to be ashamed and who correctly handles the *word of truth*" (italics added). James reminds us, "He chose to give us birth through *the word of truth*, that we might be a kind of firstfruits of all he created" (James 1:18, italics added). The psalmist prays, "Then I shall answer the one who taunts me, for I trust in your word. Do not snatch the *word of truth* from my mouth, for I have put my hope in your laws" (Psalm 119:42–43, italics added).

The Holy Spirit is the Spirit of truth. The Holy Spirit is the One who illumines and opens the Word of truth to our understanding and profit. This is made clear in 1 Corinthians 2:6–16, which states that natural man left to himself could never understand the Word of truth since he does not have the Spirit of truth to illumine the Word of truth to his spiritual understanding.

FIRST READING FOR UNIT 7: DEALING WITH THE FLESH: SEXUAL AND OTHER BONDAGES

Lesson 1: Original Sin and the Sinful Nature

From *Raising Lambs Among Wolves*, pages 132–33:

Theologians and Bible translators have struggled to find the proper words to describe this basic sin problem. The King James Version uses the word *flesh* to describe an internal struggle Christians face: "Walk in the Spirit, and ye shall not fulfil the lust of the flesh" (Galatians 5:16 KJV). Newer translations, such as the *New International Version*, use different words to convey this internal malady: "So I say, live by the Spirit, and you will not gratify the desires of the sinful nature."

"Lust of the flesh" and "desires of the sinful nature" both describe an internal problem with temptation to sin that all Christians face, including young children and teens. Our children need biblical insight (which parents can provide) to overcome this basic desire to live out a sinful life. We must not blame a Christian's temptation problems all on the devil; that's an incomplete picture. At the core of the problem is an internal, depraved human condition, according to the Bible.

Understanding this basic doctrine is important to a believer's comprehension of the struggle he has with sin. A lifetime of biblical study and the counseling of many believers has convinced me that dealing with the flesh demands priority attention. Most believers don't know how to deal with this most basic human problem for every believer.

Our "fleshly" desires and temptations reflect the internal condition of our very person. We inherited this condition through the fall of Adam. Even after our new birth through saving faith, our fleshly desires remain totally wicked and depraved. These desires can never be reformed or improved because they derive from the sin of the Fall. Only by consistently applying the death and resurrection of Christ to our lives can we believers be free from the control of our fleshly desires.

The Lord Jesus Christ Himself gave the definitive statement about the nature of human defilement. He declared that defilement is an inward heart condition and not removed by outward ritual (such as the Pharisees washing their hands before eating). He told His inquiring disciples: "What comes out of a man is what makes him 'unclean.' For from within, out of men's hearts, come evil thoughts, sexual immorality, theft, murder, adultery, greed, malice, deceit, lewdness, envy, slander, arrogance and folly. All these evils come from inside and make a man 'unclean'" (Mark 7:20–23; cf. Matthew 15:18–20 NIV).

SECOND READING FOR UNIT 7:
DEALING WITH THE FLESH: SEXUAL AND OTHER BONDAGES

Lesson 2: Sins of the Intellect

From *Raising Lambs Among Wolves,* pages 135–39:

STEPS TO OVERCOME THE RULE OF YOUR FLESH

The fleshly desires are part of our lives as believers, but they need not control us. Here, in outline form, is what is required to overcome the rule of our flesh.

I. Know doctrinal truth upon which freedom is based: the three absolutes.
    Colossians 3 is one of the classic New Testament passages that helps believers deal with their flesh. The chapter begins by focusing upon what I call three absolutes of grace. An absolute is a truth that stands alone. It is an indisputable fact because God Himself has made it true. Acting upon these three absolutes will enable us to walk in our freedom from fleshly rule.

    A. Every believer has resurrection life (Colossians 3:1–2).
        This resurrection with Christ occurred even before we put our faith in Him as our personal Lord and Savior. It happened during the historic event itself. Christ's resurrection was your resurrection, according to the apostle Paul. The mighty power that raised the Lord Jesus Christ from the grave dwells in each believer's life. Our conduct is to flow out of understanding this truth. Since resurrection life dwells in us, we are to set our hearts and minds on heavenly things.

    B. Every believer has union with Christ in His death (Colossians 3:3).
        At the cross, every believer died, even before he or she believed. The death of Christ was your death. It's your union with Christ that freed you from the penalty of sin and the power of sin to hold you in bondage. Our union with Christ as believers is so secure and safe: "Your life is now hidden with Christ in God." Understanding this lofty doctrinal truth is crucial to overcoming the desires of your flesh.

    C. Every believer has union with Christ in His second coming (Colossians 3:4).
        This absolute hasn't happened yet, but it is just as certain as the first two that are based on historic events. Every believer will appear with Christ in the glory of His second coming. Absolutes are like that. Since they are based upon God's person, what is yet to happen is just as sure as what has already happened.

II. Know the necessary biblical steps in order to apply your freedom.
    Great doctrinal truth based on the absolutes of God is not meant to be passively accepted. These truths are to be lived in the crucible of daily life. Note how clear this is made in this matter of walking in our freedom from the rule of our fleshly desires and temptations.

    A. Walk in honest admission and confession (Colossians 3:5–10).
        The word therefore in verse 5 ("Put to death, therefore . . . ") points us back to the three absolutes of grace mentioned in the first four verses and the first point of this outline. Believers can walk in freedom from the rule of this long list of sins when we apply these three absolutes.
        According to Galatians 5:19, "the acts of the sinful nature are obvious." To whom are these acts of the flesh obvious? They are obvious to God and to our Lord Jesus Christ. God knows these desires flow to us from our fallen condition, and He wants us to know it, too. Understanding this truth is crucial to freedom. We must not expect more of ourselves than what God has presently provided us. This truth can liberate us from much false guilt.

    B. Walk in the truth of your death with Christ.
        Four key New Testament texts declare the believer's death with Christ or command that

we act as those who are dead to our sinful nature: Romans 6:11; Galatians 5:24; Colossians 3:3; 3:5. Each text speaks to the necessity of recognizing how God has equipped the believer to overcome the desires of the flesh by the cross of Christ.

C. Walk in the control of the Holy Spirit (Galatians 5:16, 18, 22–23, 25).

When the Holy Spirit controls the believer, a much different life is produced than what our fleshly, earthly nature can produce. We need to remember our identity as Christ's followers. According to Colossians 3:12, we are God's chosen people, holy, and dearly loved.

God chose us to be the channels through which His message of love and grace would flow to the world. God calls us holy, even though we may not feel at times we are living in a holy way. Justification has made every believer holy in God's sight. The very righteousness of Jesus Christ has been credited to each believer in his standing before God. And though we may struggle with earthly, fleshly sins (as the Colossae believers were to whom Paul was writing) we are greatly loved. The Lord is on your side. He is not angry and displeased with you because of your failures. He loves you.

According to Colossians 3:12, you are to "clothe yourselves with compassion, kindness, humility, gentleness and patience." Ask yourself: "Who was more compassionate, kind, humble, gentle, and patient?" Jesus! Be like Jesus is the imperative. You can be more like Jesus. As we allow the power that raised Jesus Christ from the dead to control our minds, wills, emotions, and bodies, Christ's likeness will be seen in each of us. This is the Holy Spirit's work. He is the one who brings resurrection life into the experience of each believer.

PRAYERS IN APPLYING THE STEPS

The three steps under point II above are practical and can be applied through prayer and by following Christ. Let's consider each step in practical terms.

First, *honest admission and confession* of temptation clearly requires that we be honest with ourselves and the Lord. When a fleshly temptation or desire first presents itself to our consciousness, we are to be honest in addressing our need to our Lord, praying about it specifically. We should state it to Him in a manner such as this:

Lord Jesus Christ, my old fleshly nature is tempting me to _____ (name the temptation, e.g., lust, anger, gossip) and I know that if it's left to itself, it is wicked enough to cause me to sin against You.

Such honesty is liberating in itself, it helps you recognize your need. You don't need to "save face" by trying to convince yourself that your flesh isn't as bad as God states it to be. Honest admission is a part of recognizing our need to avail ourselves of the absolutes of grace.

Second, acting upon the truth that we have *died with Christ* and so should "count [ourselves] dead to sin but alive to God in Christ Jesus" (Romans 6:11), requires we acknowledge this truth to Christ in prayer. You may want to express your freedom to overcome sin in this way:

Lord Jesus Christ, I affirm that through the work of Your cross I am dead with You to the rule and control of my flesh and its desire to _____ (name of fleshly temptation being experienced at that moment, i.e., anger, lust, etc.).

Being free from sin's control does not mean our Lord promised that we would be free from experiencing the temptations of our flesh. Just the opposite is true. He told us these are the temptations and desires our flesh will present to us as we live our earthly lives. It's only after we go to be with our Lord that the temptations are forever gone. I believe this to be a major reason why the Lord planned that each of us would be left to deal with our fleshly desires: Dealing with them keeps us close to the Cross and the work done for us there.

Third, to *walk in the control of the Holy Spirit,* we must *turn* to the Holy Spirit. The Holy Spirit doesn't force His control upon us. God respects our dignity too much for that. He waits for us to ask the Holy Spirit to do what He is within us to do. In prayer, we should take this third step in this manner:

> *Blessed Holy Spirit, I ask You now to replace this fleshly desire that is tempting me to _____ (state the fleshly appeal; i.e., anger, lust, jealousy, etc.) with the fruit of Your control. Put within my mind, will, emotions, and body Your love, joy, peace, patience, and all the virtues that my Lord Jesus Christ enables me to live out for His glory.*

Of course, as Ephesians 5:18 notes, we are to continue being filled with the Spirit. Each fleshly desire needs this application of truth every time we feel its pressure. All three steps should be applied moment by moment as we walk through each day.

THIRD READING FOR UNIT 7:
DEALING WITH THE FLESH: SEXUAL AND OTHER BONDAGES

Unit Sidebar: The Principle of the Delayed Harvest
From *Raising Lambs Among Wolves,* pages 47–51:

WHAT TRANSFERENCE OF THE FATHER'S SINS MEANS

Believers do well to try to understand how God visits the sins of the fathers upon the children to the third and fourth generation. Several factors need our evaluation and careful thought:

1. *A parent's sinful choices of environment and example do have far-reaching consequences upon his or her children and the children's children.* Many see the basic message of God's warning referring to the influences of the home environment. As children suffer the wounds and negatives of the failing aspects of the home and parental influence, the children carry on those negatives to the next generation.

Most would admit this as part of this sobering warning. Children reared in a climate of cursing, pornography, drug usage, immorality, or drunkenness will be wounded by any of those environmental factors. Dysfunction by parents creates a dysfunctional family. Children reared in an unhealthy climate are often conditioned to carry out the same patterns as they mature. They may hate their past home life but still be caught in its web.

2. *A parent's sinful emotional wounding and physical brutalizing have far-reaching consequences upon the children.* In chapter 1 Linn described the footprints in the carpet by a godly father. When Ted entered his children's rooms after they were asleep to pray over his daughter and son, the benefits would come later. Linn remembers those visits fondly.

Yet, tragically, such nightly visits from fathers or stepfathers are not always noble. I and other counselors hear much too often of quiet visits from a dad who took sexual advantage of his daughter or son during the night. What an abomination! Other fathers in acts of anger have verbally assaulted their children, using cutting words to belittle, ridicule, or even reject their kids. Some have struck their children in fits of rage.

The emotional wounding that comes from sexual or physical abuse can last a lifetime. Healing is long and difficult in a person's life when he or she has been exposed to such abusiveness. But of all the kinds of physical abuse, little has more devastating consequences than sexual abuse. It rips at a child's identity, esteem, security, and trust in an adult. In my judgment, only parent-authored satanic ritual abuse does more damage to the child.

These problems often transfer from one generation to another. A sexually abusive parent usually was sexually abused by some trusted family member when he was a child. Abusers produce abusers. . . .

3. *A parent's sinful physical vices can have negative consequences on the children.* We are living in a time when much is being said by the medical community about the damage that the sins of the parents can bring to their children. Except the medical professionals don't call it sin; they call the activities *vices* or *unhealthy habits.* It doesn't matter. The outcome is the same: damaging and often far-reaching consequences to the children. Little babies are being born addicted to crack, heroin, or some other illegal drug. A pregnant mother drinking alcohol during her pregnancy can mean both mental and physical damage to her baby. The dangers concerning a mother smoking or even being in the environment of tobacco smoke during her pregnancy are being studied carefully. The unborn may suffer detrimental consequences from such exposure.

The dangers of such unhealthy behaviors can last years. (Experts say "crack babies" remain unstable, aggressive, and hostile for as long as two years as the parent's drug affects the nervous system.) The consequences may even last a lifetime. (Ask the adult child of an alcoholic who struggles as he finds himself seeking the bottle, even though he despises his alcoholic parent for doing so.) . . .

HOW TO LIMIT TRANSFERENCE

Negative generational transference can be overcome with consistent prayers and godly examples. Similarly, the lack of consistent prayers and godly living by our forbears makes our children (and us) more vulnerable to transference.

That our fathers can give a positive legacy should encourage us in seeing that sins need not be passed down. Great spiritual benefits do flow forth to children and grandchildren from the prayers and godly watchfulness of ancestors. Timothy wasn't the only son and grandson to be blessed by the faith that first lived in a mother or godly grandmother (2 Timothy 1:5).

Sadly, many people must face life with all of its complexities and temptations without the supportive prayers of godly forbears. This puts them at a terrible disadvantage. As one who has so benefited, I can only praise God for such a heritage. Only the love and grace of God can overrule the terrible lack of such heritage blessings.

READING FOR UNIT 9:
FROM FOOTHOLD TO STRONGHOLD: CURIOSITY TO POSSESSION

Lesson 4: Occultism
From *Raising Lambs Among Wolves,* pages 97–101:
SPIRITISTIC AND OCCULT INFLUENCES

Today, the influences of spiritism, far from subsiding, have exploded. Many shades of spiritism overshadow "New Age" thinking in books and movies; they invade textbooks and curriculum, even children's toys. Spiritistic influences are in music and most media; indeed, almost everywhere you look. Christian parents must communicate about the dangers of these things. We dare not leave our children in ignorance. Too much is at stake.

What is a proper approach to such issues? How does a concerned parent communicate adequate warning?

The Bible contains the best answer to meet this need. Let the Word of God express its own warning. Plan a time when you can talk separately with each child. Inform him and her of the presence of spiritistic messages. Explain how the seeming innocence and even playfulness of such things as ghosts, witches, and the supernatural actually mask the true dangers of these phenomena. This will provide opportunity for good dialogue as well as learning important information. At that point, you may want to look at Scripture with your child. A great learning text would be Deuteronomy 18:9–12 (NKJV).

> When you come into the land which the Lord your God is giving you, you shall not learn to follow the abominations of those nations. There shall not be found among you anyone who makes his son or his daughter pass through the fire, or one who practices witchcraft, or a soothsayer, or one who interprets omens, or a sorcerer, or one who conjures spells, or a medium, or a spiritist, or one who calls up the dead. For all who do these things are an abomination to the Lord, and because of these abominations the Lord your God drives them out from before you.

This passage is direct and has sufficient strength to remove any doubt that such things are dangerously wrong. You may want to look up the various words in a dictionary, such as *sorcerer* or *abominations,* to give your child the modern interpretation, while a Bible dictionary will give biblical insight. The broad, inclusive warning of Deuteronomy 18 should remove most questions about the modern-day dabblings being done by so many.

New Testament insight should be added by using a text like Ephesians 5:6–13:

> Because of such things God's wrath comes on those who are disobedient. Therefore do not be partners with them. For you were once darkness, but now you are light in the Lord. Live as children of light. . . . Have nothing to do with the fruitless deeds of darkness, but rather expose them. For it is shameful even to mention what the disobedient do in secret. But everything exposed by the light becomes visible. (Ephesians 5:6b–8, 11–13)

A child gains the advantage when he knows why he avoids the spiritism of the day. If he knows a text like the Deuteronomy passage, all he needs to do is read it to those pressuring him. It's very difficult to dispute with such a direct word from God. A study about the dark spiritism of Artemis of the Ephesians would help to shed light on where such spiritism always leads.

MEDIA INFLUENCES

By definition, the media are channels that communicate information. As such, they are tools that can be used for good, conveying information, entertainment, and building a sense of community. However, that does not mean they are neutral or always used for good. What information to include and how to present (interpret) it is determined by those who control the media, whether producers, advertisers, editors, or writers. Their perspectives color the information we receive. Thus as parents we need to both monitor and discuss content with our children.

The pressures of Congress and the public have convinced the television broadcasting industry to allow the so-called V-chip to be added to TV sets to protect what our children see. This computer chip will help parents to limit the broadcast of shows with high levels of violence and sex. The need for such a chip and the TV industry's willingness to develop criteria demonstrate how even secular agencies recognize the influence of TV programming among the young.

As parents, we must communicate our love by telling our children about these media influences and helping them to discern the wolves that threaten to devour their innocence as children growing into adults. Here are two areas to talk about.

Music Influences. Our purpose here is not to debate or rehash the arguments concerning the various styles and beats of music. Much good information is available. The issue here is communication. There is sufficient evil present in the lyrics, the performers' lifestyles, and the general seductive influences in the "rock" music world to open doors for bondage to many kinds of sin. Again, the public and the recording industry have recognized the danger with a rating system that discloses the nature of the lyrics. But that does not exempt parents from their duties to help children evaluate the music they hear.

Parents must start while their children are young enough to influence, to communicate with good supportive information concerning their position. We dare not wait until our children are locked into listening to some harmful music to hold their views and change their habits. Music can be an inspiring friend or a very dark enemy in the lives of children and youth. Parents must lead the way in making it an uplifting, inspiring friend that honors God.

[Two resources that can facilitate communication with your children on the music issue are the following: (1) Frank Garlock, *Music in the Balance* (Greenville, S.C.: Majesty Music, 1993). (Garlock also has six videotapes discussing music theory and its application to biblical principles. Write him at Majesty Music Co., P.O. Box 654, Greenville, SC.). (2) Al Menconi and Dave Hart, *Today's Music: A Window to Your Child's Soul* (Colorado Springs, Cook: 1990).]

Movies, Television, and Cartoons. When it comes to television programs, all children need parental, protective communication and supervision. Though there is some good fare on PBS and occasionally on other TV networks, most children's programs feature slapstick violence, graphic realism, and even semi-adult plots. Monsters, witches, ghosts, aliens, and other occult figures fly across the landscape. Saturday morning cartoons are no longer the innocent domain of Bugs Bunny, Mighty Mouse, or Muppet Babies. The more indulgent our culture becomes, the more parents must exercise protective oversight. Fear is to Satan's kingdom what faith is to God. It activates evil and spiritual harm.

Again, the movie industry has adopted a rating code, yet parents sometimes ignore them; even G and PG movies can contain references to New Age thinking (the *Star Wars* trilogy) or make parents look like fools and kids wise and independent (the *Home Alone* series). And if you have a videocassette recorder or cable TV, your child has an ever greater access to movies. However will you monitor them?

Here are several guidelines to help you and your children consider the shows they may watch:

- Does the fare offered promote fear, bad language, or disrespect for authority?
- Are there supernatural themes and actions displayed that are unbiblical and fanciful?
- Does the fare tend to desensitize concerning death, bloodshed, and respect for life?
- Does the viewing present an unbiblical view of sexuality, respect for parents, and spiritual values?
- Are occultism, magic, séances, sorcery, witchcraft, and other spiritistic themes presented favorably?
- Is the Christian faith held in respectful esteem by the fare presented?
- Will what's presented promote love, joy, peace, patience, gentleness, meekness, faithfulness, and self-control as desirable virtues?

PUBLIC SCHOOL CURRICULUM

In a pluralistic society that has become afraid to teach values and tells children to decide for themselves, value-free education has only recently come under attack, as the public has begun to call for the teaching of moral values in our schools. Meanwhile, certain public school systems have introduced New Age and spiritistic approaches to relaxation and learning techniques. Reading textbooks have added stories featuring witches and the occult. In my grandson's classroom in Iowa a curriculum called "Talented and Gifted" has led elementary-school-aged children into meditation in which children are told to "totally empty your mind of all distractions" and to "watch now for someone who is coming to help you. Let him lead you."

What can Christian parents do with such reality beginning to invade the secular, public school system? A Christian school or home-schooling may be an answer. That does not work for everyone, however. Finances, abilities, and time limitations may necessitate public school for many Christian parents.

Here are four guidelines worthy of consideration:

- Communicate and keep in touch by carefully listening to your children's reports on school life.

- Keep a good flow of communication with your child, asking about and responding to ideas presented in the classroom. That way you will be able to maintain the major teaching role in your child's life.

- Teach your children to recognize the errors being promoted by the public school on evolution, moral permissiveness, prayer opposition, and humanism.

- Be an active parent in every appropriate way to influence public school decisions. That includes telling school officials and teachers about practices you deem detrimental to your children.

FIRST READING FOR UNIT 10: PROTECTING THE FAMILY IN A WICKED DAY

Lesson 1: Protecting Your Marriage
From *Raising Lambs Among Wolves,* pages 62–64:
LOVE VERSUS FEAR
Children suffer deeply when the parents they love resort to abusive words and actions toward each other. Feelings of fear and guilt usually plague a child exposed to nasty, shouting exchanges between angry parents. In his confused immaturity, a child often feels he is responsible for his parents' anger. Because he loves each of them, he is unable to assign responsibility to them. The child's security, derived from his parents' love of each other, is lost. Panic takes over. Relative to the child's sensitivity level, terror and torment often replace the sense of loving security every child needs.

The inspired words of the apostle John should speak deeply to Christian parents:

There is no fear in love. But perfect love drives out fear, because fear has to do with punishment. The one who fears is not made perfect in love. We love because he first loved us. (1 John 4:18–19)

Failure to understand the deep damage that parents' angry shouting matches place upon their children's live is dangerous. In contrast, the inverse of that is liberating. The freedom from fear and quiet security instilled in children when their parents deeply love and respect each other sets up solid rock foundations for the family. God desires that Christian parents provide that level of security to each of their children.

It may surprise you, but the first way to love our lambs, those children whom God has given us, is to love our spouses. In doing this, we establish a foundation that steadies our children against the attack of wolves. We will look at the importance of such love shortly. But first consider John's warning later in chapter 4. Though he was writing to all believers in his first epistle, his sobering words have a special application in a Christian marriage:

If anyone says, "I love God," yet hates his brother, he is a liar. For anyone who does not love his brother, whom he has seen, cannot love God, whom he has not seen. And he has given us this command: Whoever loves God must also love his brother. (1 John 4:20–21)

Loving your "brother" applies to husband/wife relationships. The capacity to control anger and speak with love and respect to one's spouse is part of Christian grace. It goes with faith's "turf." The victory of our Christian walk meets its greatest test in the home. When it works there, the benefits are rich and ongoing. Everyone benefits from the security—your spouse, your children, and, of course, you. Neighbors often notice. Spiritual freedom means that we are daily learning to live out our faith, especially in the intimacy of marriage and parenting.

SECOND READING FOR UNIT 10: PROTECTING THE FAMILY IN A WICKED DAY

Lesson 2: Protecting Our Children
From *Raising Lambs Among Wolves,* pages 141–143:

TEACHING OUR CHILDREN THE BIBLICAL PRINCIPLES

. . . . How much better when we prepare our children while young to deal with their first-line enemy. Instead, well-meaning Christian parents often fall into a dangerous trap of trying to help their children reform or improve their fleshly desires. By discipline and shame tactics, we try to force our children to live out better behavior. Even after our children come to know the Lord Jesus Christ as personal Lord and Savior, we use these tactics.

Anger, jealousy, quarreling, and factions are common fleshly sins all children experience. If they know the Lord Jesus, we should be teaching them about their spiritual resources. Yes, discipline does have its place. Children need to learn that these sins are unacceptable and wrong. They are not only wrong because they create miserable family living, but they are wrong in God's sight. However, discipline doesn't change and free a child from sinful behavior. Shame fails even more tragically. Shame creates guilt feelings and a loss of self-worth. "I'm no good" thoughts and feelings begin to rule a child who is shamed and put down for his bad behavior.

Wise parents, however, will *begin to train children in the biblical principles of defeating sinful nature temptations.* You can introduce your children to these principles at a very young age. It will require patience, persistence, and repeated times of loving instruction, but the rewards will be phenomenal. . . .

GUIDELINES FOR TEACHING VICTORY OVER THE FLESH TO CHILDREN

Teaching your child the biblical principles of this chapter are vital. If your child knows Jesus as his or her Savior, it is not too early to start. Here are several guidelines to remember as you work with your child to teach the three steps to freedom from fleshly rule.

1. Be sure that you as a Christian parent understand and practice your own freedom from fleshly rule.
2. Make sure that your child has made a personal decision of asking the Lord Jesus Christ into his/her life as Lord and Savior.
3. Watch for the major "besetting" sin evident in each child's life. (Anger, lying, greed, and jealousy are common to children.) Arrange a quiet talk time about the problem and teach the three steps of freedom on the child's level of understanding.
4. Pray for the Lord to help the child apply application of this truth as the child grows and other fleshly nature sins appear.
5. When you note the successful use of the steps to overcome the flesh, commend the child and let him/her know that you noticed.

6. Carefully avoid dependence on shame and discipline to transform the fleshly nature. Depend on the application of spiritual truth to effect change.
7. Watch for evidence that might indicate demonic attempts to rule your child. Consistently practice aggressive spiritual warfare protection of your children.

[For further information on this subject, and a review, see pages 135–39 of *Raising Lambs Among Wolves*, given in the readings for Unit 7, Lesson 2.]

THIRD READING FOR UNIT 10: PROTECTING THE FAMILY IN A WICKED DAY
Lesson 2: Protecting Your Children
Reading from *Raising Lambs Among Wolves*, pages 169–79:
EVIDENCES OF SPIRITISTIC ACTIVITY IN OUR CHILDREN
. . . . If one or more of the signs [listed below] appear in your child, do not automatically conclude that spirit powers are trying to rule and destroy your son or daughter. The appearance in your child of several of these *may* mean your child is under attack. A combination of evidences should cause us to pray more directly and authoritatively to watch over our children and victoriously "wrestle" in their behalf.

Abnormal fears and phobias . . .

Out-of-control anger and "fits of rage" behavior patterns . . .

Seeing apparitions in the room or hearing voices . . .

Cruel treatment of animals or playmates . . .

A controlling conduct of hate . . .

Trancelike states of sleep . . .

Compulsive behavior patterns . . .

Physical symptoms that defy medical diagnosis or treatment and may change or vary in kind and degree . . .

A preoccupation with blood, death, feces, fire, or violence . . .

Clairvoyant and ESP "gifts" that emerge in a child's life . . .

Cutting or hurting of self and certain instances of accident proneness . . .

Withdrawal from family and friends and a loner mentality . . .

Inability to concentrate and learn even when average and above average abilities are evident . . .

Overt interest in ghosts, magic, occultism, fortune-telling, and other similar fare . . .

Perverted sexual interests or activity even before puberty . . .

Inability to give or accept gestures of kindness and love . . .

Destructive acts . . .

Extreme depression and expressed thoughts about suicide . . .

Sleep problems . . .

A hateful, rebellious response toward corrective discipline . . .

Inability to enjoy play, laughter, and fun games . . .

The appearance of occult and satanic symbols on a child's books, clothing, possessions, or body . . .

As a parent you may observe one or more of these evidences of possible spiritistic influence mentioned above. If that happens, what do you do? Here are five suggestions for dealing with possible demonic activity in your child's life:

1. Be calm and do not fear. Fear is a chief tool of Satan to rule and destroy. He will relentlessly try to upset you and thus your child. Don't panic and display frantic concern. Remember, the Lord Jesus Christ has given each born-again believer all the power and authority needed to overcome darkness and protect our children.

2. Keep a biblical balance . . . Don't seek out a "faith healer" or "expert in spiritual warfare" to cast our demons from your child. That sensational approach, as noted earlier, can be very harmful to a child. Furthermore, it typically is looking for a quick fix. Instead, seek a biblically balanced approach as you apply spiritual truth and parental protection to your child.

3. Express your concerns to your pastor if he has spiritual insights and a growing understanding of biblical spiritual warfare. Describe the battle and enlist his prayer support. Careful counsel from him may provide important insights.

4. Use biblical warfare praying on a daily basis. The prayers appearing in the final chapter [of *Raising Lambs*] offer helpful guidance and insights on how to use your authority to resist the Enemy.

5. Make your own private list of suspicious evidences of spiritistic activity against your child. This is helpful for your times of prayerful intercession. It can also assist in addressing directly your parental authority against powers of darkness.

Before you use this final suggestion to confront the power of darkness through prayer, prepare yourself spiritually. Prepare your own heart with a day of fasting and prayer for the Lord to grant you the wisdom and courage to use your authority in Christ to free your child from the harassment of the powers of darkness.

SPIRITUAL WARFARE PRAYERS

PRAYER FOR SPIRITUAL VICTORY

Dear heavenly Father, I praise You that I am united with the Lord Jesus Christ in all of His life and work. By faith I desire to enter into the victory of the incarnation of my Lord today. I invite Him to live His victory in me. Thank You, Lord Jesus Christ, that You experienced all temptation that I experience and yet never sinned.

I enter by faith into the mighty work of the crucifixion of my Lord. Thank You, dear Father, that through Jesus' blood there is moment-by-moment cleansing from sin, permitting me to fellowship with You. Thank You that the work of the Cross brings Satan's work to nothing.

I enter by faith into the full power and authority of my Lord's resurrection. I desire to walk in the newness of life that is mine through my Lord's resurrection. Lead me into a deeper understanding of the power of the Resurrection. By faith I enter into my union with the Lord Jesus Christ in His ascension. I rejoice that my Lord displayed openly His victory over all powers as He ascended into glory through the very realm of the prince of the power of the air.

I enter into my victory aggressively and claim my place as more than a conqueror through Him who loves me. I offer up this prayer in the name of the Lord Jesus with thanksgiving. Amen.

PRAYER AGAINST TEMPTATION

The fleshly desires are part of our lives as believers, but they need not control us. Through prayer, we can apply three biblical steps to freedom from fleshly desires. First, honest admission and confession of temptation (Colossians 3:5–10):

Lord Jesus Christ, my old fleshly nature is tempting me to _____ (name the temptation; e.g., lust, anger, gossip), and I know that if it's left to itself, it is wicked enough to cause me to sin against You.

Second, the realization that we have died with Christ (Romans 6:11; Galatians 5:24). We should "count [ourselves] dead to sin but alive to God in Christ Jesus." Acknowledge this truth to Christ in prayer:

Lord Jesus Christ, I affirm that through the work of Your cross I am dead with You to the rule and control of my flesh and its desire toward _____ (name of fleshly temptation being experienced at that moment; e.g., anger, lust).

Third, living in the control of the Holy Spirit (Galatians 5:16–25). This requires that we turn to the Holy Spirit:

Blessed Holy Spirit, I ask You now to replace this fleshly desire that is tempting me toward _____ (state the fleshly appeal; e.g., jealousy, lust) with the fruit of Your control. Put within my mind, will, and emotions Your love, joy, peace, patience, and all the virtues that my Lord Jesus Christ enables me to live out for His glory. Amen.

PRAYER TO WEAR THE ARMOR OF GOD

Heavenly Father, I put on the armor of God with gratitude and praise. You have provided all I need to stand in victory against Satan and his kingdom.

I confidently take the belt of truth. Thank You that Satan cannot stand against the bold use of truth.

Thank You for the breastplate of righteousness. I embrace that righteousness which is mine by faith in Jesus Christ. I know that Satan must retreat before the righteousness of God.

You have provided the solid rock of peace. I claim the peace with God that is mine through justification. I desire the peace of God that touches my emotions and feelings through prayer and sanctification (Philippians 4:6–7).

Eagerly, Lord, I lift up the shield of faith against all the blazing missiles that Satan fires at me. I know that You are my shield.

I recognize that my mind is a particular target of Satan's deceiving ways. I cover my mind with the powerful helmet of salvation.

With joy I lift the sword of the Spirit, which is the Word of God. I choose to live in its truth and power. Enable me to use Your Word to defend myself from Satan, and also to wield the sword well, to push Satan back, to defeat him.

Thank You, dear Lord, for prayer. Help me to keep this armor well oiled with prayer. All these petitions I offer to You through the mighty name of our Lord Jesus Christ. Amen.

"Prayer Patterns for Revival" are available in pocket booklet form from the International Center for Biblical Counseling in Sioux City, Iowa (712-277-4760).

Moody Press, a ministry of Moody Bible Institute,
is designed for education, evangelization, and edification.
If we may assist you in knowing more about Christ
and the Christian life, please write us without obligation:
Moody Press, c/o MLM, Chicago, Illinois 60610.